Digital Filter
Designer's Handbook

Other McGraw-Hill Books of Interest

Handbooks

BAKER · *C Mathematical Function Handbook*
BENSON · *Audio Engineering Handbook*
BENSON · *Television Engineering Handbook*
CHEN · *Computer Engineering Handbook*
COOMBS · *Printed Circuits Handbook*
DI GIACOMO · *Digital Bus Handbook*
DI GIACOMO · *VLSI Handbook*
FINK AND CHRISTIANSEN · *Electronics Engineers' Handbook*
HARPER · *Electronic Packaging and Interconnection Handbook*
HICKS · *Standard Handbook of Engineering Calculations*
INGLIS · *Electronic Communications Handbook*
JURAN AND GRYNA · *Juran's Quality Control Handbook*
KAUFMAN AND SEIDMAN · *Handbook of Electronics Calculations*
TUMA · *Engineering Mathematics Handbook*
WILLIAMS AND TAYLOR · *Electronic Filter Design Handbook*

Other

ANTOGNETTI · *Power Integrated Circuits*
ANTOGNETTI AND MASSOBRIO · *Semiconductor Device Modeling with SPICE*
BUCHANAN · *CMOS/TTL Digital Systems Design*
BUCHANAN · *BiCMOS/CMOS Systems Design*
BYERS · *Printed Circuit Board Design with Microcomputers*
EDWARDS · *Automatic Logic Synthesis Techniques for Digital Systems*
ELLIOTT · *Integrated Circuits Fabrication Technology*
FORSYTHE AND GOODALL · *Digital Control*
HECHT · *The Laser Guidebook*
MUN · *GaAs Integrated Circuits*
PERRY · *VHDL*
RORABAUGH · *Circuit Design and Analysis*
RORABAUGH · *Communications Formulas and Algorithms*
SILICONIX · *Designing with Field-Effect Transistors*
SZE · *VLSI Technology*
WATERS · *Active Filter Design*
WOBSCHALL · *Circuit Design for Electronic Instrumentation*
WYATT · *Electro-Optical System Design*

To order or receive additional information on these or any other McGraw-Hill titles in the United States, please call 1-800-822-8158. In other countries, contact your local McGraw-Hill representative.   MH92

Digital Filter Designer's Handbook

Featuring C Routines

C. Britton Rorabaugh

McGraw-Hill, Inc.

New York St. Louis San Francisco Auckland Bogotá
Caracas Lisbon London Madrid Mexico Milan
Montreal New Delhi Paris San Juan São Paulo
Singapore Sydney Tokyo Toronto

Library of Congress Cataloging-in-Publication Data

Rorabaugh, Britt.
    Digital filter designer's handbook : featuring C routines / C.
  Britton Rorabaugh.
        p.   cm.
    Includes index.
    ISBN 0-07-911166-1 :
    1. Electric filters, Digital—Design and construction—Data
  processing.   2. Electric circuit design—Data processing.
  I. Title.
  TK7872.F5R68   1993
  621.3815'324—dc20

                                        92-28846
                                        CIP

1 2 3 4 5 6 7 8 9 0 DOC/DOC 9 8 7 6 5 4 3 2

P/N 053654-6
PART OF
ISBN 0-07-911166-1

*The sponsoring editor for this book was Daniel A. Gonneau, the editing
supervisor was Marci Nugent, and the production supervisor was Donald
F. Schmidt. It was set in Century Schoolbook by Datapage.*

Printed and bound by R. R. Donnelley & Sons Company.

To Joyce, Geoff, and Amber

Contents

List of Programs

Preface

If you're going to own only one book on digital filters, this is the one to have. If you already own several, you need this book anyway—it contains quite a lot of useful information not available in any other book. I wrote this book for individuals faced with the need to design working digital filters—it is not intended as an academic text. All the necessary theoretical background is provided in the early chapters, and practical digital filter design techniques are provided in the later chapters. These design techniques are supported by numerous computer routines written in the C programming language. The techniques and programs presented in this book will prove to be very useful to engineers, students, and hobbyists engaged in the design of digital filters.

All of the programs in this book were written and tested using Think C for the Apple Macintosh computer. I made a conscientious effort to limit the programs to the ANSI standard subset of Think C and to avoid any machine dependencies. Potential efficiencies were sacrificed for the sake of portability and tutorial clarity. However, a few specific items need to be pointed out:

1. Constants used by several different functions are collected into a single "include" file called **globDefs.h** (a listing of this file is provided in App. A). The "new" style of ANSI prototyping was used throughout all of the software generated for this book. All the pertinent prototypes are collected in a file called **protos.h**, which is provided in App. B.

2. Nice long file names such as **computeRemezAmplitude.c** are allowed on the Macintosh, but on MS-DOS machines file names are limited to eight characters plus a three-character extension. Except for the two header files mentioned above, all the files on the accompanying disk have names that are keyed to the chapter number in which the listing appears.

3. I found it convenient to define a new type **real** that is the same as **double.** For use on machines with limited memory, **real** could be redefined as **float** to save memory, but accuracy could suffer. Being a long-time Fortran user, I also found it convenient to create a **logical** type. The lack of intrinsic complex types in C was overcome via a **complex** structure definition, and a set of complex arithmetic functions is detailed in App. C.

Britt Rorabaugh

Mathematical Review

Electronic signals are complicated phenomena, and their exact behavior is impossible to describe completely. However, simple mathematical models can describe the signals well enough to yield some very useful results that can be applied in a variety of practical situations. Furthermore, linear systems and digital filters are inherently mathematical beasts. This chapter is devoted to a concise review of the mathematical techniques that are used throughout the rest of the book.

1.1 Exponentials and Logarithms

Exponentials

There is an irrational number, usually denoted as e, that is of great importance in virtually all fields of science and engineering. This number is defined by

$$e \triangleq \lim_{x \to +\infty} \left(1 + \frac{1}{x}\right)^x \simeq 2.71828 \cdots \tag{1.1}$$

Unfortunately, this constant remains unnamed, and writers are forced to settle for calling it "the number e" or perhaps "the base of natural logarithms." The letter e was first used to denote the irrational in (1.1) by Leonhard Euler (1707–1783), so it would seem reasonable to refer to the number under discussion as "Euler's constant." Such is not the case, however, as the term *Euler's constant* is attached to the constant γ defined by

$$\gamma = \lim_{N \to \infty} \left(\sum_{n=1}^{N} \frac{1}{n} - \log_e N\right) \simeq 0.577215664 \cdots \tag{1.2}$$

The number e is most often encountered in situations where it raised to some real or complex power. The notation $\exp(x)$ is often used in place of e^x, since the former can be written more clearly and typeset more easily than the latter—especially in cases where the exponent is a complicated expression rather just a single variable. The value for e raised to a complex power z can be expanded in an infinite series as

$$\exp(z) = \sum_{n=0}^{\infty} \frac{z^n}{n!} \tag{1.3}$$

The series in (1.3) converges for all complex z having finite magnitude.

Logarithms

The *common logarithm*, or *base-10 logarithm*, of a number x is equal to the power to which 10 must be raised in order to equal x:

$$y = \log_{10} x \iff x = 10^y \tag{1.4}$$

The *natural logarithm*, or *base-e logarithm*, of a number x is equal to the power to which e must be raised in order to equal x:

$$y = \log_e x \iff x = \exp(y) \equiv e^y \tag{1.5}$$

Natural logarithms are also called *napierian logarithms* in honor of John Napier (1550–1617), a Scottish amateur mathematician who in 1614 published the first account of logarithms in *Mirifici logarithmorum canonis descripto* ("A Description of the Marvelous Rule of Logarithms") (see Boyer 1968). The concept of logarithms can be extended to any positive base b, with the base-b logarithm of a number x equaling the power to which the base must be raised in order to equal x:

$$y = \log_b x \iff x = b^y \tag{1.6}$$

The notation log without a base explicitly indicated usually denotes a common logarithm, although sometimes this notation is used to denote natural logarithms (especially in some of the older literature). More often, the notation ln is used to denote a natural logarithm. Logarithms exhibit a number of properties that are listed in Table 1.1. Entry 1 is sometimes offered as the definition of natural logarithms. The multiplication property in entry 3 is the theoretical basis upon which the design of the slide rule is based.

Decibels

Consider a system that has an output power of P_{out} and an output voltage of V_{out} given an input power of P_{in} and an input voltage of V_{in}. The gain G, in decibels (dB), of the system is given by

$$G_{dB} = 10 \log_{10}\left(\frac{P_{out}}{P_{in}}\right) = 10 \log_{10}\left(\frac{V_{out}^2/Z_{out}}{V_{in}^2/Z_{in}}\right) \tag{1.7}$$

TABLE 1.1   Properties of Logarithms

1. $\ln x = \int_1^x \frac{1}{y}\, dy \qquad x > 0$

2. $\frac{d}{dx}(\ln x) = \frac{1}{x} \qquad x > 0$

3. $\log_b(xy) = \log_b x + \log_b y$

4. $\log_b\left(\frac{1}{x}\right) = -\log_b x$

5. $\log_b(y^x) = x \log_b y$

6. $\log_c x = (\log_b x)(\log_c b) = \dfrac{\log_b x}{\log_b c}$

7. $\ln(1 + z) = \sum\limits_{n=1}^{\infty} (-1)^{n-1} \dfrac{z^n}{n} \qquad |z| < 1$

If the input and output impedances are equal, (1.7) reduces to

$$G_{\text{dB}} = 10 \log_{10}\left(\frac{V_{\text{out}}^2}{V_{\text{in}}^2}\right) = 20 \log_{10}\left(\frac{V_{\text{out}}}{V_{\text{in}}}\right) \tag{1.8}$$

Example 1.1   An amplifier has a gain of 17.0 dB. For a 3-mW input, what will the output power be? Substituting the given data into (1.7) yields

$$17.0\ \text{dB} = 10 \log_{10}\left(\frac{P_{\text{out}}}{3 \times 10^{-3}}\right)$$

Solving for P_{out} then produces

$$P_{\text{out}} = (3 \times 10^{-3})10^{(17/10)} = 1.5 \times 10^{-1} = 150\ \text{mW}$$

Example 1.2   What is the range in decibels of the values that can be represented by an 8-bit unsigned integer?

solution   The smallest value is 1, and the largest value is $2^8 - 1 = 255$. Thus

$$20 \log_{10}\left(\frac{255}{1}\right) = 48.13\ \text{dB}$$

The abbreviation dBm is used to designate power levels relative to 1 milliwatt (mW). For example:

$$30\ \text{dBm} = 10 \log_{10}\left(\frac{P}{10^{-3}}\right)$$

$$P = (10^{-3})(10^3) = 10^0 = 1.0\ \text{W}$$

1.2 Complex Numbers

A complex number z has the form $a + bj$, where a and b are real and $j = \sqrt{-1}$. The *real part* of z is a, and the *imaginary part* of z is b. Mathematicians use i to denote $\sqrt{-1}$, but electrical engineers use j to avoid confusion with the traditional use of i for denoting current. For convenience, $a + bj$ is sometimes represented by the ordered pair (a, b). The *modulus*, or *absolute value*, of z is denoted as $|z|$ and is defined by

$$|z| = |a + bj| = \sqrt{a^2 + b^2} \tag{1.9}$$

The *complex conjugate* of z is denoted as z^* and is defined by

$$(z = a + bj) \Leftrightarrow (z^* = a - bj) \tag{1.10}$$

Conjugation distributes over addition, multiplication, and division:

$$(z_1 + z_2)^* = z_1^* + z_2^* \tag{1.11}$$

$$(z_1 z_2)^* = z_1^* z_2^* \tag{1.12}$$

$$\left(\frac{z_1}{z_2}\right)^* = \frac{z_1^*}{z_2^*} \tag{1.13}$$

Operations on complex numbers in rectangular form

Consider two complex numbers:

$$z_1 = a + bj \qquad z_2 = c + dj$$

The four basic arithmetic operations are then defined as

$$z_1 + z_2 = (a + c) + j(b + d) \tag{1.14}$$

$$z_1 - z_2 = (a - c) + j(b - d) \tag{1.15}$$

$$z_1 z_2 = (ac - bd) + j(ad + bc) \tag{1.16}$$

$$\frac{z_1}{z_2} = \frac{ac + bd}{c^2 + d^2} + j\frac{bc - ad}{c^2 + d^2} \tag{1.17}$$

Polar form of complex numbers

A complex number of the form $a + bj$ can be represented by a point in a coordinate plane as shown in Fig. 1.1. Such a representation is called an *Argand diagram* (Spiegel 1965) in honor of Jean Robert Argand (1768–1822), who published a description of this graphical representation of complex num-

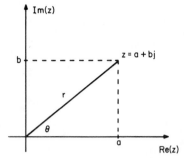

Figure 1.1 Argand diagram representation of a complex number.

bers in 1806 (Boyer 1968). The point representing $a + bj$ can also be located using an angle θ and radius r as shown. From the definitions of sine and cosine given in (1.25) and (1.26) of Sec. 1.3, it follows that

$$a = r \cos \theta \qquad b = r \sin \theta$$

Therefore,
$$z = r \cos \theta + jr \sin \theta = r(\cos \theta + j \sin \theta) \qquad (1.18)$$

The quantity $(\cos \theta + j \sin \theta)$ is sometimes denoted as cis θ. Making use of (1.58) from Sec. 1.3, we can rewrite (1.18) as

$$z = r \text{ cis } \theta = r \exp(j\theta) \qquad (1.19)$$

The form in (1.19) is called the *polar form* of the complex number z.

Operations on complex numbers in polar form

Consider three complex numbers:

$$z = r(\cos \theta + j \sin \theta) = r \exp(j\theta)$$

$$z_1 = r_1(\cos \theta_1 + j \sin \theta_1) = r_1 \exp(j\theta_1)$$

$$z_2 = r_2(\cos \theta_2 + j \sin \theta_2) = r_2 \exp(j\theta_2)$$

Several operations can be conveniently performed directly upon complex numbers that are in polar form, as follows.

Multiplication

$$z_1 z_2 = r_1 r_2 [\cos(\theta_1 + \theta_2) + j \sin(\theta_1 + \theta_2)]$$

$$= r_1 r_2 \exp[j(\theta_1 + \theta_2)] \qquad (1.20)$$

Division

$$\frac{z_1}{z_2} = \frac{r_1}{r_2}\left[\cos(\theta_1 - \theta_2) + j\,\sin(\theta_1 - \theta_2)\right]$$

$$= \frac{r_1}{r_2}\exp[\,j(\theta_1 - \theta_2)] \tag{1.21}$$

Powers

$$z^n = r^n[\cos(n\theta) + j\,\sin(n\theta)]$$

$$= r^n \exp(\,jn\theta) \tag{1.22}$$

Roots

$$\sqrt[n]{z} = z^{1/n} = r^{1/n}\left[\cos\left(\frac{\theta + 2k\pi}{n}\right) + j\,\sin\left(\frac{\theta + 2k\pi}{n}\right)\right]$$

$$= r^{1/n}\exp\left[\frac{j(\theta + 2k\pi)}{n}\right] \qquad k = 0, 1, 2, \ldots \tag{1.23}$$

Equation (1.22) is known as *De Moivre's theorem*. In 1730, an equation similar to (1.23) was published by Abraham De Moivre (1667–1754) in his *Miscellanea analytica* (Boyer 1968). In Eq. (1.23), for a fixed n as k increases, the sinusoidal functions will take on only n distinct values. Thus there are n different nth roots of any complex number.

Logarithms of complex numbers

For the complex number $z = r\,\exp(\,j\theta)$, the natural logarithm of z is given by

$$\ln z = \ln[r\,\exp(\,j\theta)]$$

$$= \ln\{r\,\exp[j(\theta + 2k\pi)]\}$$

$$= (\ln r) + j(\theta + 2k\pi) \qquad k = 0, 1, 2, \ldots \tag{1.24}$$

The *principal value* is obtained when $k = 0$.

1.3   Trigonometry

For x, y, r, and θ as shown in Fig. 1.2, the six trigonometric functions of the angle θ are defined as

$$\text{Sine:} \qquad \sin\theta = \frac{y}{r} \tag{1.25}$$

$$\text{Cosine:} \qquad \cos\theta = \frac{x}{r} \tag{1.26}$$

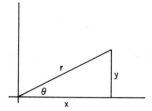

Figure 1.2 An angle in the cartesian plane.

$$\text{Tangent:} \quad \tan\theta = \frac{y}{x} \tag{1.27}$$

$$\text{Cosecant:} \quad \csc\theta = \frac{r}{y} \tag{1.28}$$

$$\text{Secant:} \quad \sec\theta = \frac{r}{x} \tag{1.29}$$

$$\text{Cotangent:} \quad \cot\theta = \frac{x}{y} \tag{1.30}$$

Phase shifting of sinusoids

A number of useful equivalences can be obtained by adding particular phase angles to the arguments of sine and cosine functions:

$$\cos(\omega t) = \sin\left(\omega t + \frac{\pi}{2}\right) \tag{1.31}$$

$$\cos(\omega t) = \cos(\omega t + 2n\pi) \quad n = \text{any integer} \tag{1.32}$$

$$\sin(\omega t) = \sin(\omega t + 2n\pi) \quad n = \text{any integer} \tag{1.33}$$

$$\sin(\omega t) = \cos\left(\omega t - \frac{\pi}{2}\right) \tag{1.34}$$

$$\cos(\omega t) = \cos[\omega t + (2n+1)\pi] \quad n = \text{any integer} \tag{1.35}$$

$$\sin(\omega t) = -\sin[\omega t + (2n+1)\pi] \quad n = \text{any integer} \tag{1.36}$$

Trigonometric identities

The following trigonometric identities often prove useful in the design and analysis of signal processing systems.

$$\tan x = \frac{\sin x}{\cos x} \tag{1.37}$$

$$\sin(-x) = -\sin x \tag{1.38}$$

$$\cos(-x) = \cos x \tag{1.39}$$

$$\tan(-x) = -\tan x \tag{1.40}$$

$$\cos^2 x + \sin^2 x = 1 \tag{1.41}$$

$$\cos^2 x = \tfrac{1}{2}[1 + \cos(2x)] \tag{1.42}$$

$$\sin(x \pm y) = \sin x)(\cos y) \pm (\cos y)(\sin y) \tag{1.43}$$

$$\cos(x \pm y) = (\cos x)(\cos y) \mp (\sin x)(\sin y) \tag{1.44}$$

$$\tan(x + y) = \frac{(\tan x) + (\tan y)}{1 - (\tan x)(\tan y)} \tag{1.45}$$

$$\sin(2x) = 2(\sin x)(\cos x) \tag{1.46}$$

$$\cos(2x) = \cos^2 x - \sin^2 x \tag{1.47}$$

$$\tan(2x) = \frac{2(\tan x)}{1 - \tan^2 x} \tag{1.48}$$

$$(\sin x)(\sin y) = \tfrac{1}{2}[-\cos(x + y) + \cos(x - y)] \tag{1.49}$$

$$(\cos x)(\cos y) = \tfrac{1}{2}[\cos(x + y) + \cos(x - y)] \tag{1.50}$$

$$(\sin x)(\cos y) = \tfrac{1}{2}[\sin(x + y) + \sin(x - y)] \tag{1.51}$$

$$(\sin x) + (\sin y) = 2 \sin \frac{x + y}{2} \cos \frac{x - y}{2} \tag{1.52}$$

$$(\sin x) - (\sin y) = 2 \sin \frac{x - y}{2} \cos \frac{x + y}{2} \tag{1.53}$$

$$(\cos x) + (\cos y) = 2 \cos \frac{x + y}{2} \cos \frac{x - y}{2} \tag{1.54}$$

$$(\cos x) - (\cos y) = -2 \sin \frac{x + y}{2} \sin \frac{x - y}{2} \tag{1.55}$$

$$A \cos(\omega t + \psi) + B \cos(\omega t + \phi) = C \cos(\omega t + \theta) \tag{1.56}$$

where $C = [A^2 + B^2 - 2AB \cos(\phi - \psi)]^{1/2}$

$$\theta = \tan^{-1}\left(\frac{A \sin \psi + B \sin \phi}{A \cos \psi + B \cos \phi}\right)$$

$$A \cos(\omega t + \psi) + B \sin(\omega t + \phi) = C \cos(\omega t + \theta) \tag{1.57}$$

where $C = [A^2 + B^2 - 2AB \sin(\phi - \psi)]^{1/2}$

$$\theta = \tan^{-1}\left(\frac{A \sin \psi - B \cos \phi}{A \cos \psi + B \sin \phi}\right)$$

Euler's identities

The following four equations, called *Euler's identities*, relate sinusoids and complex exponentials.

$$e^{jx} = \cos x + j \sin x \qquad (1.58)$$

$$e^{-jx} = \cos x - j \sin x \qquad (1.59)$$

$$\cos x = \frac{e^{jx} + e^{-jx}}{2} \qquad (1.60)$$

$$\sin x = \frac{e^{jx} - e^{-jx}}{2j} \qquad (1.61)$$

Series and product expansions

Listed below are infinite series expansions for the various trigonometric functions (Abramowitz and Stegun 1966).

$$\sin x = \sum_{n=0}^{\infty} \frac{(-1)^n x^{2n+1}}{(2n+1)!} \qquad (1.62)$$

$$\cos x = \sum_{n=0}^{\infty} \frac{(-1)^n x^{2n}}{(2n)!} \qquad (1.63)$$

$$\tan x = \sum_{n=1}^{\infty} \frac{(-1)^{n-1} 2^{2n}(2^{2n}-1)B_{2n} x^{2n-1}}{(2n)!} \qquad |x| < \frac{\pi}{2} \qquad (1.64)$$

$$\cot x = \sum_{n=0}^{\infty} \frac{(-1)^n 2^{2n} B_{2n} x^{2n-1}}{(2n)!} \qquad |x| < \pi \qquad (1.65)$$

$$\sec x = \sum_{n=0}^{\infty} \frac{(-1)^n E_{2n} x^{2n}}{(2n)!} \qquad |x| < \frac{\pi}{2} \qquad (1.66)$$

$$\csc x = \sum_{n=0}^{\infty} \frac{(-1)^{n-1} 2(2^{2n-1}-1)B_{2n} x^{2n-1}}{(2n)!} \qquad |x| < \pi \qquad (1.67)$$

Values for the Bernoulli number B_n and Euler number E_n are listed in Tables 1.2 and 1.3, respectively. In some instances, the infinite product expansions for sine and cosine may be more convenient than the series expansions.

$$\sin x = x \prod_{n=1}^{\infty} \left(1 - \frac{x^2}{n^2 \pi^2} \right) \qquad (1.68)$$

$$\cos x = \prod_{n=1}^{\infty} \left[1 - \frac{4x^2}{(2n-1)^2 \pi^2} \right] \qquad (1.69)$$

TABLE 1.2   Bernoulli Numbers
$B_n = N/D$ $B_n = 0$ for $n = 3, 5, 7, \ldots$

n	N	D
0	1	1
1	-1	2
2	1	6
4	-1	30
6	1	42
8	-1	30
10	5	66
12	-691	2730
14	7	6
16	-3617	510
18	43867	798
20	-174611	330

TABLE 1.3   Euler Numbers
$E_n = 0$ for $n = 1, 3, 5, 7, \ldots$

n	E_n
0	1
2	-1
4	5
6	-61
8	1385
10	-50521
12	2,702,765
14	$-199,360,981$
16	19,391,512,145
18	$-2,404,879,675,441$
20	370,371,188,237,525

Orthonormality of sine and cosine

Two functions $\phi_1(t)$ and $\phi_2(t)$ are said to form an *orthogonal* set over the interval $[0, T]$ if

$$\int_0^T \phi_1(t)\, \phi_2(t)\, dt = 0 \tag{1.70}$$

The functions $\phi_1(t)$ and $\phi_2(t)$ are said to form an *orthonormal* set over the interval $[0, T]$ if in addition to satisfying (1.70) each function has unit energy over the interval

$$\int_0^T [\phi_1(t)]^2\, dt = \int_0^T [\phi_2(t)]^2\, dt = 1 \tag{1.71}$$

Consider the two signals given by

$$\phi_1(t) = A\, \sin(\omega_0 t) \tag{1.72}$$

$$\phi_2(t) = A\, \cos(\omega_0 t) \tag{1.73}$$

The signals ϕ_1 and ϕ_2 will form an orthogonal set over the interval $[0, T]$ if $\omega_0 T$ is an integer multiple of π. The set will be orthonormal as well as orthogonal if $A^2 = 2/T$. The signals ϕ_1 and ϕ_2 will form an approximately orthonormal set over the interval $[0, T]$ if $\omega_0 T \gg 1$ and $A^2 = 2/T$. The orthonormality of sine and cosine can be derived as follows.

Substitution of (1.72) and (1.73) into (1.70) yields

$$\int_0^T \phi_1(t)\, \phi_2(t)\, dt = A^2 \int_0^T \sin \omega_0 t \cos \omega_0 t\, dt$$

$$= \frac{A^2}{2} \int_0^T [\sin(\omega_0 t + \omega_0 t) + \sin(\omega_0 t - \omega_0 t)]\, dt$$

$$= \frac{A^2}{2} \int_0^T \sin 2\omega_0 t\, dt = \frac{A^2}{2} \left(\frac{\cos 2\omega_0 t}{2\omega_0} \right) \Big|_{t=0}^T$$

$$= \frac{A^2}{4\omega_0 T} (1 - \cos 2\omega_0 T) \tag{1.74}$$

Thus if $\omega_0 T$ is an integer multiple of π, then $\cos(2\omega_0 T) = 1$ and ϕ_1 and ϕ_2 will be orthogonal. If $\omega_0 T \gg 1$, then (1.74) will be very small and reasonably approximated by zero; thus ϕ_1 and ϕ_2 can be considered as approximately orthogonal. The energy of $\phi_1(t)$ on the interval $[0, T]$ is given by

$$E_1 = \int_0^T [\phi_1(t)]^2\, dt = A^2 \int_0^T \sin^2 \omega_0 t\, dt$$

$$= A^2 \left(\frac{t}{2} - \frac{\sin 2\omega_0 t}{4\omega_0} \right) \Big|_{t=0}^T$$

$$= A^2 \left(\frac{T}{2} - \frac{\sin 2\omega_0 T}{4\omega_0} \right) \tag{1.75}$$

For ϕ_1 to have unit energy, A^2 must satisfy

$$A^2 = \left(\frac{T}{2} - \frac{\sin 2\omega_0 T}{4\omega_0} \right)^{-1} \tag{1.76}$$

When $\omega_0 T = n\pi$, then $\sin 2\omega_0 T = 0$. Thus (1.76) reduces to

$$A = \sqrt{\frac{2}{T}} \tag{1.77}$$

Substituting (1.77) into (1.75) yields

$$E_1 = 1 - \frac{\sin 2\omega_0 T}{2\omega_0 T} \tag{1.78}$$

When $\omega_0 T \gg 1$, the second term of (1.78) will be very small and reasonably approximated by zero, thus indicating that ϕ_1 and ϕ_2 are approximately orthonormal. In a similar manner, the energy of $\phi_2(t)$ can be found to be

$$E_2 = A^2 \int_0^T \cos^2 \omega_0 t\, dt$$

$$= A^2 \left(\frac{T}{2} + \frac{\sin 2\omega_0 T}{4\omega_0} \right) \tag{1.79}$$

Thus
$$E_2 = 1 \quad \text{if } A = \sqrt{\frac{2}{T}} \quad \text{and} \quad \omega_0 T = n\pi$$

$$E_2 \doteq 1 \quad \text{if } A = \sqrt{\frac{2}{T}} \quad \text{and} \quad \omega_0 T \gg 1$$

1.4   Derivatives

Listed below are some derivative forms that often prove useful in theoretical analysis of communication systems.

$$\frac{d}{dx} \sin u = \cos u \, \frac{du}{dx} \tag{1.80}$$

$$\frac{d}{dx} \cos u = -\sin u \, \frac{du}{dx} \tag{1.81}$$

$$\frac{d}{dx} \tan u = \sec^2 u \, \frac{du}{dx} = \frac{1}{\cos^2 u} \frac{du}{dx} \tag{1.82}$$

$$\frac{d}{dx} \cot u = \csc^2 u \, \frac{du}{dx} = \frac{1}{\sin^2 u} \frac{du}{dx} \tag{1.83}$$

$$\frac{d}{dx} \sec u = \sec u \, \tan u \, \frac{du}{dx} = \frac{\sin u}{\cos^2 u} \frac{du}{dx} \tag{1.84}$$

$$\frac{d}{dx} \csc u = -\csc u \, \cot u \, \frac{du}{dx} = \frac{-\cos u}{\sin^2 u} \frac{du}{dx} \tag{1.85}$$

$$\frac{d}{dx} e^u = e^u \, \frac{du}{dx} \tag{1.86}$$

$$\frac{d}{dx} \ln u = \frac{1}{u} \frac{du}{dx} \tag{1.87}$$

$$\frac{d}{dx} \log u = \frac{\log e}{u} \frac{du}{dx} \tag{1.88}$$

$$\frac{d}{dx} \left(\frac{u}{v} \right) = \frac{1}{v^2} \left(v \, \frac{du}{dx} - u \, \frac{dv}{dx} \right) \tag{1.89}$$

Derivatives of polynomial ratios

Consider a ratio of polynomials given by

$$C(s) = \frac{A(s)}{B(s)} \qquad B(s) \neq 0 \tag{1.90}$$

The derivative of $C(s)$ can be obtained using Eq. (1.89) to obtain

$$\frac{d}{ds} C(s) = [B(s)]^{-1} \frac{d}{ds} A(s) - A(s)[B(s)]^{-2} \frac{d}{ds} B(s) \qquad (1.91)$$

Equation (1.91) will be very useful in the application of the Heaviside expansion, which is discussed in Sec. 2.6.

1.5 Integration

Large integral tables fill entire volumes and contain thousands of entries. However, a relatively small number of integral forms appear over and over again in the study of communications, and these are listed below.

$$\int \frac{1}{x} dx = \ln x \qquad (1.92)$$

$$\int e^{ax} dx = \frac{1}{a} e^{ax} \qquad (1.93)$$

$$\int x e^{ax} dx = \frac{ax - 1}{a^2} e^{ax} \qquad (1.94)$$

$$\int \sin(ax) dx = -\frac{1}{a} \cos(ax) \qquad (1.95)$$

$$\int \cos(ax) dx = \frac{1}{a} \sin(ax) \qquad (1.96)$$

$$\int \sin(ax + b) dx = -\frac{1}{a} \cos(ax + b) \qquad (1.97)$$

$$\int \cos(ax + b) dx = \frac{1}{a} \sin(ax + b) \qquad (1.98)$$

$$\int x \sin(ax) dx = -\frac{x}{a} \cos(ax) + \frac{1}{a^2} \sin(ax) \qquad (1.99)$$

$$\int x \cos(ax) dx = \frac{x}{a} \sin(ax) + \frac{1}{a^2} \cos(ax) \qquad (1.100)$$

$$\int \sin^2 ax \, dx = \frac{x}{2} - \frac{\sin 2ax}{4a} \qquad (1.101)$$

$$\int \cos^2 ax \, dx = \frac{x}{2} + \frac{\sin 2ax}{4a} \qquad (1.102)$$

$$\int x^2 \sin ax \, dx = \frac{1}{a^3} (2ax \sin ax + 2 \cos ax - a^2 x^2 \cos ax) \qquad (1.103)$$

$$\int x^2 \cos ax \, dx = \frac{1}{a^3}(2ax \cos ax - 2 \sin ax + a^2 x^2 \sin ax) \qquad (1.104)$$

$$\int \sin^3 x \, dx = -\tfrac{1}{3} \cos x(\sin^2 x + 2) \qquad (1.105)$$

$$\int \cos^3 x \, dx = \tfrac{1}{3} \sin x(\cos^2 x + 2) \qquad (1.106)$$

$$\int \sin x \cos x \, dx = \tfrac{1}{2} \sin^2 x \qquad (1.107)$$

$$\int \sin(mx) \cos(nx) \, dx = \frac{-\cos(m-n)x}{2(m-n)} - \frac{\cos(m+n)x}{2(m+n)} \qquad (m^2 \ne n^2)$$

$$(1.108)$$

$$\int \sin^2 x \cos^2 x \, dx = \tfrac{1}{8}[x - \tfrac{1}{4} \sin(4x)] \qquad (1.109)$$

$$\int \sin x \cos^m x \, dx = \frac{-\cos^{m+1} x}{m+1} \qquad (1.110)$$

$$\int \sin^m x \cos x \, dx = \frac{\sin^{m+1} x}{m+1} \qquad (1.111)$$

$$\int \cos^m x \sin^n x \, dx = \frac{\cos^{m-1} x \sin^{n+1} x}{m+n} + \frac{m-1}{m+n} \int \cos^{m-2} x \sin^n x \, dx \qquad (m \ne -n)$$

$$(1.112)$$

$$\int \cos^m x \sin^n x \, dx = \frac{-\cos^{m+1} x \sin^{n-1} x}{m+n} + \frac{n-1}{m+n} \int \cos^m x \sin^{n-2} x \, dx \qquad (m \ne -n)$$

$$(1.113)$$

$$\int u \, dv = uv - \int v \, du \qquad (1.114)$$

1.6   Dirac Delta Function

In all of electrical engineering, there is perhaps nothing that is responsible for more hand-waving than is the so-called *delta function*, or *impulse function*, which is denoted $\delta(t)$ and which is usually depicted as a vertical arrow at the origin as shown in Fig. 1.3. This function is often called the *Dirac delta function* in honor of Paul Dirac (1902–1984), an English physicist who used delta functions extensively in his work on quantum mechanics. A number of nonrigorous approaches for defining the impulse function can be found throughout the literature. A *unit impulse* is often loosely described as having a zero width and an infinite amplitude at the origin such that the total area

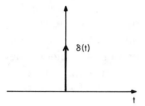

Figure 1.3 Graphical representation of the Dirac delta function.

under the impulse is equal to unity. How is it possible to claim that zero times infinity equals 1? The trick involves defining a sequence of functions $f_n(t)$ such that

$$\int_{-\infty}^{\infty} f_n(t)\, dt = 1 \tag{1.115}$$

and

$$\lim_{n \to \infty} f_n(t) = 0 \qquad \text{for } t \neq 0 \tag{1.116}$$

The delta function is then defined as

$$\delta(t) = \lim_{n \to \infty} f_n(t) \tag{1.117}$$

Example 1.3 Let a sequence of pulse functions $f_n(t)$ be defined as

$$f_n(t) = \begin{cases} \dfrac{n}{2} & |t| \leqslant \dfrac{1}{n} \\ 0 & \text{otherwise} \end{cases} \tag{1.118}$$

Equation (1.115) is satisfied since the area of pulse is equal to $(2n) \cdot (n/2) = 1$ for all n. The pulse width decreases and the pulse amplitude increases as n approaches infinity. Therefore, we intuitively sense that this sequence must also satisfy (1.116). Thus the impulse function can be defined as the limit of (1.118) as n approaches infinity. Using similar arguments, it can be shown that the impulse can also be defined as the limit of a sequence of sinc functions or gaussian pulse functions.

A second approach entails simply defining $\delta(t)$ to be that function which satisfies

$$\int_{-\infty}^{\infty} \delta(t)\, dt = 1 \qquad \text{and} \qquad \delta(t) = 0 \qquad \text{for } t \neq 0 \tag{1.119}$$

In a third approach, $\delta(t)$ is defined as that function which exhibits the property

$$\int_{-\infty}^{\infty} \delta(t)\, f(t)\, dt = f(0) \tag{1.120}$$

While any of these three approaches is adequate to introduce the delta function into an engineer's repertoire of analytical tools, none of the three is sufficiently rigorous to satisfy mathematicians or discerning theoreticians. In particular, notice that none of the approaches presented deals with the thorny issue of just what the value of $\delta(t)$ is for $t = 0$. The rigorous definition of $\delta(t)$ introduced in 1950 by Laurent Schwartz (Schwartz (1950) rejects the notion that the impulse is an ordinary function and instead defines it as a *distribution*.

Distributions

Let S be the set of functions $f(x)$ for which the nth derivative $f^{[n]}(x)$ exists for any n and all x. Furthermore, each $f(x)$ decreases sufficiently fast at infinity such that

$$\lim_{x \to \infty} x^n f(x) = 0 \qquad \text{for all } n \qquad (1.121)$$

A *distribution*, often denoted $\phi(x)$, is defined as a continuous linear mapping from the set S to the set of complex numbers. Notationally, this mapping is represented as an inner product

$$\int_{-\infty}^{\infty} \phi(x)\, f(x)\, dx = z \qquad (1.122)$$

or alternatively

$$\langle \phi(x), f(x) \rangle = z \qquad (1.123)$$

Notice that no claim is made that ϕ is a function capable of mapping values of x into corresponding values $\phi(x)$. In some texts (such as Papoulis 1962), $\phi(x)$ is referred to as a *functional* or as a *generalized function*. The distribution ϕ is defined only through the impact that it has upon other functions. The impulse function is a distribution defined by the following:

$$\int_{-\infty}^{\infty} \delta(t)\, f(t)\, dt = f(0) \qquad (1.124)$$

The equation (1.124) looks exactly like (1.120), but defining $\delta(t)$ as a distribution eliminates the need to tap dance around the issue of assigning a value to $\delta(0)$. Furthermore, the impulse function is elevated to a more substantial foundation from which several useful properties may be rigorously derived. For a more in-depth discussion of distributions other than $\delta(t)$, the interested reader is referred to Chap. 4 of Weaver (1989).

Properties of the delta distribution

It has been shown (Weaver 1989; Brigham 1974; Papoulis 1962; Schwartz and Friedland 1965) that the delta distribution exhibits the following properties:

$$\int_{-\infty}^{\infty} \delta(t)\, dt = 1 \qquad (1.125)$$

$$\frac{d}{dt}\delta(t) = \lim_{\tau \to 0} \frac{\delta(t) - \delta(t - \tau)}{\tau} \qquad (1.126)$$

$$\int_{-\infty}^{\infty} \delta(t - t_0)\, f(t)\, dt = f(t_0) \qquad (1.127)$$

$$\delta(at) = \frac{1}{|a|}\delta(t) \qquad (1.128)$$

$$\delta(t_0)f(t) = f(t_0)\delta(t_0) \qquad (1.129)$$

$$\delta_1(t - t_1) * \delta_2(t - t_2) = \delta[t - (t_1 + t_2)] \qquad (1.130)$$

In Eq. (1.129), $f(t)$ is an ordinary function that is continuous at $t = t_0$, and in Eq. (1.130) the asterisk denotes convolution.

1.7 Mathematical Modeling of Signals

The distinction between a signal and its mathematical representation is not always rigidly observed in the signal processing literature. Mathematical functions that only *model* signals are commonly referred to as "signals," and properties of these models are often taken as properties of the signals themselves.

Mathematical models of signals are generally categorized as either *steady-state* or *transient models*. The typical voltage output from an oscillator is sketched in Fig. 1.4. This signal exhibits three different parts—a *turn-on transient* at the beginning, an interval of *steady-state operation* in the middle, and a *turn-off transient* at the end. It is possible to formulate a single mathematical expression that describes all three parts, but for most uses, such an expression would be unnecessarily complicated. In cases where the primary concern is steady-state behavior, simplified mathematical expres-

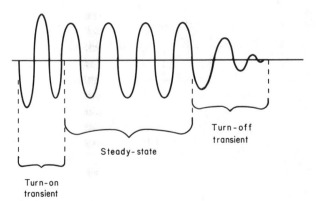

Figure 1.4 Typical output of an audio oscillator.

sions that ignore the transients will often be adequate. The steady-state portion of the oscillator output can be modeled as a sinusoid that theoretically exists for all time. This seems to be a contradiction to the obvious fact that the oscillator output exists for some limited time interval between turn-on and turn-off. However, this is not really a problem; over the interval of steady-state operation that we are interested in, the mathematical sine function accurately describes the behavior of the oscillator's output voltage. Allowing the mathematical model to assume that the steady-state signal exists over all time greatly simplifies matters since the transients' behavior can be excluded from the model. In situations where the transients are important, they can be modeled as exponentially saturating and decaying sinusoids as shown in Figs. 1.5 and 1.6. In Fig. 1.5, the saturating exponential envelope continues to increase, but it never quite reaches the steady-state value. Likewise the decaying exponential envelope of Fig. 1.6 continues to decrease, but it never quite reaches zero. In this context, the steady-state value is sometimes called an *assymptote*, or the envelope can be said to *assymptotically* approach the steady-state value. Steady-state and transient models of signal behavior inherently contradict each other, and neither constitutes a "true" description of a particular signal. The formulation of the appropriate model requires an understanding of the signal to be modeled and of the implications that a particular choice of model will have for the intended application.

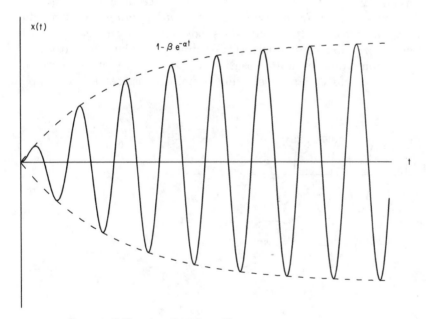

Figure 1.5 Exponentially saturating sinusoid.

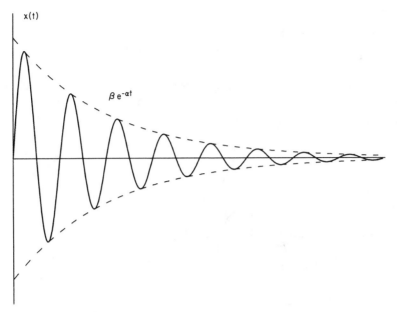

Figure 1.6 Exponentially decaying sinusoid.

Steady-state signal models

Generally, steady-state signals are limited to just sinusoids or sums of sinusoids. This will include virtually any periodic signals of practical interest since such signals can be resolved into sums of weighted and shifted sinusoids using the Fourier analysis techniques presented in Sec. 1.8.

Periodicity. Sines, cosines, and square waves are all periodic functions. The characteristic that makes them periodic is the way in which each of the complete waveforms can be formed by repeating a particular cycle of the waveform over and over at a regular interval as shown in Fig. 1.7.

> **Definition.** A function $x(t)$ is periodic with a period of T if and only if $x(t + nT) = x(t)$ for all integer values of n.

Functions that are not periodic are called *aperiodic*, and functions that are "almost" periodic are called *quasi-periodic*.

Symmetry. A function can exhibit a certain symmetry regarding its position relative to the origin.

> **Definition.** A function $x(t)$ is said to be *even*, or to exhibit *even symmetry*, if for all t, $x(t) = x(-t)$.

> **Definition.** A function $x(t)$ is said to be *odd*, or to exhibit *odd symmetry*, if for all t, $x(t) = -x(-t)$.

An even function is shown in Fig. 1.8, and an odd function is shown in Fig. 1.9.

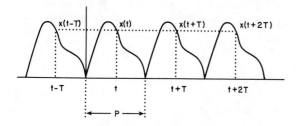

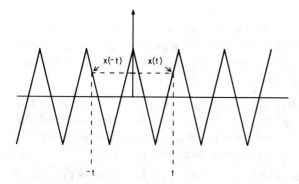

Figure 1.7   Periodic functions.

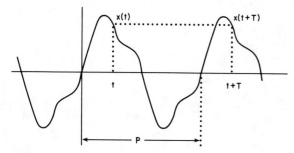

Figure 1.8   Even-symmetric function.

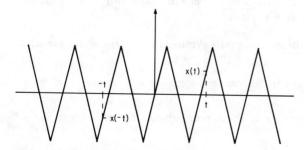

Figure 1.9   Odd-symmetric function.

Symmetry may appear at first to be something that is only "nice to know" and not particularly useful in practical applications where the definition of time zero is often somewhat arbitrary. This is far from the case, however, because symmetry considerations play an important role in Fourier analysis—especially the discrete Fourier analysis that will be discussed in Chap. 7. Some functions are neither odd nor even, but any *periodic* function can be resolved into a sum of an even function and an odd function as given by

$$x(t) = x_{\text{even}}(t) + x_{\text{odd}}(t)$$

where $x_{\text{even}}(t) = \frac{1}{2}[x(t) + x(-t)]$

$x_{\text{odd}}(t) = \frac{1}{2}[x(t) - x(-t)]$

Addition and multiplication of symmetric functions will obey the following rules:

Even + even = even

Odd + odd = odd

Odd × odd = even

Even × even = even

Odd × even = odd

Energy signals versus power signals

It is a common practice to deal with mathematical functions representing abstract signals as though they are either voltages across a 1-Ω resistor or currents through a 1-Ω resistor. Since, in either case, the resistance has an assumed value of unity, the voltage and current for any particular signal will be numerically equal—thus obviating the need to select one viewpoint over the other. Thus for a signal $x(t)$, the instantaneous power $p(t)$ dissipated in the 1-Ω resistor is simply the squared amplitude of the signal

$$p(t) = |x(t)|^2 \tag{1.131}$$

regardless of whether $x(t)$ represents a voltage or a current. To emphasize the fact that the power given by (1.131) is based upon unity resistance, it is often referred to as the *normalized power*. The total energy of the signal $x(t)$ is then obtained by integrating the right-hand side of (1.131) over all time:

$$E = \int_{-\infty}^{\infty} |x(t)|^2 \, dt \tag{1.132}$$

and the average power is given by

$$P = \lim_{T \to \infty} \frac{1}{T} \int_{-T/2}^{T/2} |x(t)|^2 \, dt \tag{1.133}$$

A few texts (for example, Haykin 1983) equivalently define the average power as

$$P = \lim_{T \to \infty} \frac{1}{2T} \int_{-T}^{T} |x(t)|^2 \, dt \tag{1.134}$$

If the total energy is finite and nonzero, $x(t)$ is referred to as an *energy signal*. If the average power is finite and nonzero, $x(t)$ is referred to as a *power signal*. Note that a power signal has infinite energy, and an energy signal has zero average power; thus the two categories are mutually exclusive. Periodic signals and most random signals are power signals, while most deterministic aperiodic signals are energy signals.

1.8 Fourier Series

Trigonometric forms

Periodic signals can be resolved into linear combinations of phase-shifted sinusoids using the *Fourier series*, which is given by

$$x(t) = \frac{a_0}{2} + \sum_{n=1}^{\infty} [a_n \cos(n\omega_0 t) + b_n \sin(n\omega_0 t)] \tag{1.135}$$

where $a_0 = \dfrac{2}{T} \displaystyle\int_{-T/2}^{T/2} x(t) \, dt$ \hfill (1.136)

$$a_n = \frac{2}{T} \int_{-T/2}^{T/2} x(t) \cos(n\omega_0 t) \, dt \tag{1.137}$$

$$b_n = \frac{2}{T} \int_{-T/2}^{T/2} x(t) \sin(n\omega_0 t) \, dt \tag{1.138}$$

$T = $ period of $x(t)$

$\omega_0 = \dfrac{2\pi}{T} = 2\pi f_0 = $ fundamental radian frequency of $x(t)$

Upon application of the appropriate trigonometric identities, Eq. (1.135) can be put into the following alternative form:

$$x(t) = c_0 + \sum_{n=1}^{\infty} c_n \cos(n\omega_0 t - \theta_n) \tag{1.139}$$

where the c_n and θ_n are obtained from a_n and b_n using

$$c_0 = \frac{a_0}{2} \tag{1.140}$$

$$c_n = \sqrt{a_n^2 + b_n^2} \tag{1.141}$$

$$\theta_n = \tan^{-1}\left(\frac{b_n}{a_n}\right) \tag{1.142}$$

Examination of (1.135) and (1.136) reveals that a periodic signal contains only a dc component plus sinusoids whose frequencies are integer multiples of the original signal's *fundamental frequency*. (For a fundamental frequency of f_0, $2f_0$ is the *second harmonic*, $3f_0$ is the *third harmonic*, and so on.) Theoretically, periodic signals will generally contain an infinite number of harmonically related sinusoidal components. In the real world, however, periodic signals will contain only a finite number of measurable harmonics. Consequently, pure mathematical functions are only approximately equal to the practical signals which they model.

Exponential form

The trigonometric form of the Fourier series given by (1.135) makes it easy to visualize periodic signals as summations of sine and cosine waves, but mathematical manipulations are often more convenient when the series is in the exponential form given by

$$x(t) = \sum_{n=-\infty}^{\infty} c_n \, e^{j2\pi nf_0 t} \tag{1.143}$$

where $c_n = \dfrac{1}{T} \displaystyle\int_T x(t) \, e^{-j2\pi nf_0 t} \, dt$ \hfill (1.144)

The integral notation used in (1.144) indicates that the integral is to be evaluated over one period of $x(t)$. In general, the values of c_n are complex; and they are often presented in the form of a magnitude spectrum and phase spectrum as shown in Fig. 1.10. The magnitude and phase values plotted in such spectra are obtained from c_n using

$$|c_n| = \sqrt{[\mathrm{Re}(c_n)]^2 + [\mathrm{Im}(c_n)]^2} \tag{1.145}$$

$$\theta_n = \tan^{-1}\left[\frac{\mathrm{Im}(c_n)}{\mathrm{Re}(c_n)}\right] \tag{1.146}$$

The complex c_n of (1.144) can be obtained from the a_n and b_n of (1.137) and

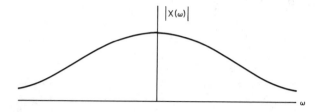

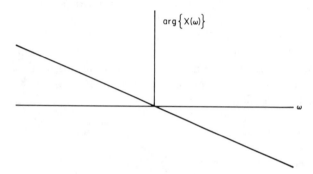

Figure 1.10 Magnitude and phase spectra.

(1.138) using

$$
c_n = \begin{cases} \dfrac{a_n + jb_n}{2} & n < 0 \\[2mm] a_0 & n = 0 \\[2mm] \dfrac{a_n - jb_n}{2} & n > 0 \end{cases} \qquad\qquad (1.147)
$$

Conditions of applicability

The Fourier series can be applied to almost all periodic signals of *practical* interest. However, there are some functions for which the series will not converge. The Fourier series coefficients are guaranteed to exist and the series will converge uniformly if $x(t)$ satisfies the following conditions:

1. The function $x(t)$ is a single-valued function.
2. The function $x(t)$ has at most a finite number of discontinuities within each period.
3. The function $x(t)$ has at most a finite number of extrema (that is, maxima and minima) within each period.

4. The function $x(t)$ is absolutely integrable over a period:

$$\int_T |x(t)|\, dt < \infty \qquad (1.148)$$

These conditions are often called the *Dirichlet conditions* in honor of Peter Gustav Lejeune Dirichlet (1805–1859) who first published them in the 1828 issue of *Journal für die reine und angewandte Mathematik* (commonly known as *Crelle's Journal*). In applications where it is sufficient for the Fourier series coefficients to be convergent in the mean, rather than uniformly convergent, it suffices for $x(t)$ to be integrable square over a period:

$$\int_T |x(t)|^2\, dt < \infty \qquad (1.149)$$

For most engineering purposes, the Fourier series is usually assumed to be identical to $x(t)$ if conditions 1 through 3 plus either (1.148) or (1.149) are satisfied.

Properties of the Fourier series

A number of useful Fourier series properties are listed in Table 1.4. For ease of notation, the coefficients c_n corresponding to $x(t)$ are denoted as $X(n)$, and the c_n corresponding to $y(t)$ are denoted as $Y(n)$. In other words, the Fourier series representations of $x(t)$ and $y(t)$ are given by

$$x(t) = \sum_{n=-\infty}^{\infty} X(n) \exp\left(\frac{j2\pi nt}{T}\right) \qquad (1.150)$$

$$y(t) = \sum_{n=-\infty}^{\infty} Y(n) \exp\left(\frac{j2\pi nt}{T}\right) \qquad (1.151)$$

TABLE 1.4 Properties of the Fourier Series
[*Note*: $x(t)$, $y(t)$, $X(n)$, and $Y(n)$ are as given in Eqs. (1.150) and (1.151).]

Property	Time function	Transform
1. Homogeneity	$ax(t)$	$aX(n)$
2. Additivity	$x(t) + y(t)$	$X(n) + Y(n)$
3. Linearity	$ax(t) + by(t)$	$aX(n) + bY(n)$
4. Multiplication	$x(t)y(t)$	$\sum_{m=-\infty}^{\infty} X(n-m)Y(m)$
5. Convolution	$\frac{1}{T}\int_0^T x(t-\tau)y(\tau)\, d\tau$	$X(n)Y(n)$
6. Time shifting	$x(t-\tau)$	$\exp\left(\frac{-j2\pi n\tau}{T}\right)X(n)$
7. Frequency shifting	$\exp\left(\frac{j2\pi mt}{T}\right)x(t)$	$X(n-m)$

where T is the period of both $x(t)$ and $y(t)$. In addition to the properties listed in Table 1.4, the Fourier series coefficients exhibit certain symmetries. If (and only if) $x(t)$ is real, the corresponding FS coefficients will exhibit even symmetry in their real part and odd symmetry in their imaginary part:

$$Im[x(t)] = 0 \Leftrightarrow Re[X(-n)] = Re[X(n)]$$
$$Im[X(-n)] = -Im[X(n)] \qquad (1.152)$$

Equation (1.152) can be rewritten in a more compact form as

$$Im[x(t)] = 0 \Leftrightarrow X(-n) = X^*(n) \qquad (1.153)$$

where the superscript asterisk indicates complex conjugation. Likewise for purely imaginary $x(t)$, the corresponding FS coefficients will exhibit odd symmetry in their real part and even symmetry in their imaginary part:

$$Re[x(t)] = 0 \Leftrightarrow X(-n) = -[X^*(n)] \qquad (1.154)$$

If and only if $x(t)$ is (in general) complex with even symmetry in the real part and odd symmetry in the imaginary part, then the corresponding FS coefficients will be purely real:

$$x(-t) = x^*(t) \Leftrightarrow Im[X(n)] = 0 \qquad (1.155)$$

If and only if $x(t)$ is (in general) complex with odd symmetry in the real part and even symmetry in the imaginary part, then the corresponding FS coefficients will be purely imaginary:

$$x(-t) = -[x^*(t) \Leftrightarrow Re[X(n)] = 0 \qquad (1.156)$$

In terms of the amplitude and phase spectra, Eq. (1.153) means that for real signals, the amplitude spectrum will have even symmetry and the phase spectrum will have odd symmetry. If $x(t)$ is both real and even, then both (1.153) and (1.155) apply. In this special case, the FS coefficients will be both real and even symmetric. At first glance, it may appear that real even-symmetric coefficients are in contradiction to the expected odd-symmetric phase spectrum; but in fact there is no contradiction. For all the positive real coefficients, the corresponding phase is of course zero. For each of the negative real coefficients, we can choose a phase value of either plus or minus 180°. By appropriate selection of positive and negative values, odd symmetry in the phase spectrum can be maintained.

Fourier series of a square wave

Consider the square wave shown in Fig. 1.11. The Fourier series representation of this signal is given by

$$x(t) = \sum_{n=-\infty}^{\infty} c_n \exp\left(\frac{j2\pi nt}{T}\right) \qquad (1.157)$$

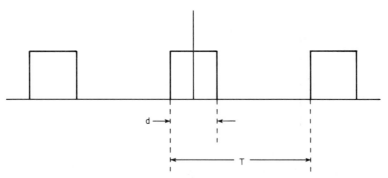

Figure 1.11 Square wave.

where $c_n = \dfrac{\tau A}{T}\,\text{sinc}\!\left(\dfrac{n\tau}{T}\right)$ (1.158)

Since the signal is both real and even symmetric, the FS coefficients are real and even symmetric as shown in Fig. 1.12. The corresponding magnitude spectrum will be even, as shown in Fig. 1.13a. Appropriate selection of $\pm 180°$ values for the phase of negative coefficients will allow an odd-symmetric phase spectrum to be plotted as in Fig. 1.13b.

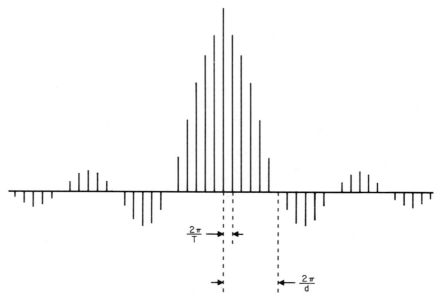

Figure 1.12 Fourier series for a square wave.

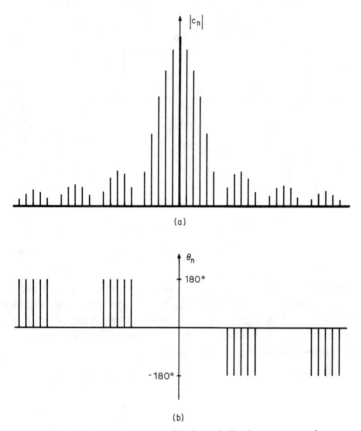

(a)

(b)

Figure 1.13 Fourier series (a) amplitude and (b) phase spectra for a square wave.

Parseval's theorem

The average power (normalized for $1\,\Omega$) of a real-valued periodic function of time can be obtained directly from the Fourier series coefficients by using Parseval's theorem:

$$P = \frac{1}{T}\int_{T} |x(t)|^2\, dt$$

$$= \sum_{n=-\infty}^{\infty} |c_n|^2 = c_0^2 + \sum_{n=1}^{\infty} \tfrac{1}{2}|2c_n|^2 \qquad (1.159)$$

1.9   Fourier Transform

The *Fourier transform* is defined as

$$X(f) = \int_{-\infty}^{\infty} x(t)\, e^{-j2\pi ft}\, dt \qquad (1.160)$$

or in terms of the radian frequency $\omega = 2\pi f$:

$$X(\omega) = \int_{-\infty}^{\infty} x(t)\, e^{-j\omega t}\, dt \tag{1.161}$$

The *inverse transform* is defined as

$$x(t) = \int_{-\infty}^{\infty} X(f)\, e^{j2\pi ft}\, df \tag{1.162a}$$

$$= \frac{1}{2\pi} \int_{-\infty}^{\infty} X(\omega)\, e^{j\omega t}\, d\omega \tag{1.162b}$$

There are a number of different shorthand notations for indicating that $x(t)$ and $X(f)$ are related via the Fourier transform. Some of the more common notations include:

$$X(f) = \mathscr{F}[x(t)] \tag{1.163}$$

$$x(t) = \mathscr{F}^{-1}[X(f)] \tag{1.164}$$

$$x(t) \overset{\text{FT}}{\longleftrightarrow} X(f) \tag{1.165}$$

$$x(t) \underset{\text{IFT}}{\overset{\text{FT}}{\rightleftharpoons}} X(f) \tag{1.166}$$

$$x(t) \lozenge X(f) \tag{1.167}$$

The notation used in (1.163) and (1.164) is easiest to typeset, while the notation of (1.167) is probably the most difficult. However, the notation of (1.167) is used in the classic work on fast Fourier transforms described by Brigham (1974). The notations of (1.165) and (1.166), while more difficult to typeset, offer the flexibility of changing the letters FT to FS, DFT, or DTFT to indicate, respectively, "Fourier series," "discrete Fourier transform," or "discrete-time Fourier transform" as is done in Roberts and Mullis (1987). (The latter two transforms will be discussed in Chap. 6.) The form used in (1.166) is perhaps best saved for tutorial situations (such as Rorabaugh 1986) where the distinction between the transform and inverse transform needs to be emphasized. Strictly speaking, the equality shown in (1.164) is incorrect, since the inverse transform of $X(f)$ is only guaranteed to approach $x(t)$ in the sense of convergence in the mean. Nevertheless, the notation of Eq. (1.164) appears often throughout the engineering literature. Often the frequency domain function is written as $X(j\omega)$ rather than $X(\omega)$ in order to facilitate comparison with the Laplace transform. We can write

$$X(j\omega) = \int_{-\infty}^{\infty} x(t)\, e^{-j\omega t}\, dt \tag{1.168}$$

and realize that this is identical to the two-sided Laplace transform defined by Eq. (2.21) with $j\omega$ substituted for s. A number of useful Fourier transform properties are listed in Table 1.5.

TABLE 1.5 Properties of the Fourier Transform

Property	Time function $x(t)$	Transform $X(f)$
1. Homogeneity	$ax(t)$	$aX(f)$
2. Additivity	$x(t) + y(t)$	$X(f) + Y(f)$
3. Linearity	$ax(t) + by(t)$	$aX(f) + bY(f)$
4. Differentiation	$\dfrac{d^n}{dt^n} x(t)$	$(j2\pi f)^n X(f)$
5. Integration	$\displaystyle\int_{-\infty}^{t} x(\tau)\, d\tau$	$\dfrac{X(f)}{j2\pi f} + \dfrac{1}{2} X(0)\, \delta(f)$
6. Frequency shifting	$e^{-j2\pi f_0 t} x(t)$	$X(f + f_0)$
7. Sine modulation	$x(t) \sin(2\pi f_0 t)$	$\frac{1}{2}[X(f - f_0) + X(f + f_0)]$
8. Cosine modulation	$x(t) \cos(2\pi f_0 t)$	$\frac{1}{2}[X(f - f_0) - X(f + f_0)]$
9. Time shifting	$x(t - \tau)$	$e^{-j\omega\tau} X(f)$
10. Time convolution	$\displaystyle\int_{-\infty}^{\infty} h(t - \tau)\, x(\tau)\, d\tau$	$H(f)X(f)$
11. Multiplication	$x(t)y(t)$	$\displaystyle\int_{-\infty}^{\infty} X(\lambda) Y(f - \lambda)\, d\lambda$
12. Time and frequency scaling	$x\left(\dfrac{t}{a}\right) \quad a > 0$	$aX(af)$
13. Duality	$X(t)$	$x(-f)$
14. Conjugation	$x^*(t)$	$X^*(-f)$
15. Real part	$\mathrm{Re}[x(t)]$	$\frac{1}{2}[X(f) + X^*(-f)]$
16. Imaginary part	$\mathrm{Im}[x(t)]$	$\dfrac{1}{2j}[X(f) - X^*(-f)]$

Fourier transforms of periodic signals

Often there is a requirement to analyze systems that include both periodic power signals and aperiodic energy signals. The mixing of Fourier transform results and Fourier series results implied by such an analysis may be quite cumbersome. For the sake of convenience, the spectra of most periodic signals can be obtained as Fourier transforms that involve the Dirac delta function. When the spectrum of a periodic signal is determined via the Fourier series, the spectrum will consist of lines located at the fundamental frequency and its harmonics. When the spectrum of this same signal is obtained as a Fourier transform, the spectrum will consist of Dirac delta functions located at the fundamental frequency and its harmonics. Obviously, these two different mathematical representations must be equivalent in their physical significance. Specifically, consider a periodic signal $x_p(t)$ having a period of T. The Fourier series representation of $x_p(t)$ is obtained from Eq. (1.143) as

$$x_p(t) = \sum_{n=-\infty}^{\infty} c_n \exp\left(\frac{j2\pi nt}{T}\right) \tag{1.169}$$

We can then define a *generating function* $x(t)$ that is equal to a single period of $x_p(t)$:

$$x(t) = \begin{cases} x_p(t) & |t| \le \dfrac{T}{2} \\ 0 & \text{elsewhere} \end{cases} \tag{1.170}$$

The periodic signal $x_p(t)$ can be expressed as an infinite summation of time-shifted copies of $x(t)$:

$$x_p(t) = \sum_{n=-\infty}^{\infty} x(t - nT) \tag{1.171}$$

The Fourier series coefficients c_n appearing in (1.169) can be obtained as

$$c_n = \frac{1}{T} X\left(\frac{n}{T}\right) \tag{1.172}$$

where $X(f)$ is the Fourier transform of $x(t)$. Thus, the Fourier transform of $x_p(t)$ can be obtained as

$$\mathscr{F}[x_p(t)] = \frac{1}{T} \sum_{n=-\infty}^{\infty} X\left(\frac{n}{T}\right) \delta\left(f - \frac{n}{T}\right) \tag{1.173}$$

Common Fourier transform pairs

A number of frequently encountered Fourier transform pairs are listed in Table 1.6. Several of these pairs are actually obtained as Fourier transforms-in-the-limit.

1.10   Spectral Density

Energy spectral density

The *energy spectral density* of an energy signal is defined as the squared magnitude of the signal's Fourier transform:

$$S_e(f) = |X(f)|^2 \tag{1.174}$$

Analogous to the way in which Parseval's theorem relates the Fourier series coefficients to the average power of a power signal, *Rayleigh's energy theorem*

TABLE 1.6 Some Common Fourier Transform Pairs

Pair No.	$x(t)$	$X(\omega)$	$X(f)$
1	1	$2\pi\,\delta(\omega)$	$\delta(f)$
2	$u_1(t)$	$\dfrac{1}{j\omega} + \pi\,\delta(\omega)$	$\dfrac{1}{2\pi f} + \dfrac{1}{2}\delta(f)$
3	$\delta(t)$	1	1
4	t^n	$2\pi j^n\,\delta^{(n)}(\omega)$	$\left(\dfrac{j}{2\pi}\right)^n \delta^{(n)}(f)$
5	$\sin\omega_0 t$	$j\pi[\delta(\omega+\omega_0) - \delta(\omega-\omega_0)]$	$\dfrac{j}{2}[\delta(f+f_0) - \delta(f-f_0)]$
6	$\cos\omega_0 t$	$\pi[\delta(\omega+\omega_0) + \delta(\omega-\omega_0)]$	$\tfrac{1}{2}[\delta(f+f_0) + \delta(f-f_0)]$
7	$e^{-at}u_1(t)$	$\dfrac{1}{j\omega + a}$	$\dfrac{1}{j2\pi f + a}$
8	$u_1(t)\,e^{-at}\sin\omega_0 t$	$\dfrac{\omega_0}{(a+j\omega)^2 + \omega_0^2}$	$\dfrac{2\pi f_0}{(a+j2\pi f)^2 + (2\pi f_0)^2}$
9	$u_1(t)\,e^{-at}\cos\omega_0 t$	$\dfrac{a+j\omega}{(a+j\omega)^2 + \omega_0^2}$	$\dfrac{a+j2\pi f}{(a+j2\pi f)^2 + (2\pi f_0)^2}$
10	$\begin{cases}1 & |t|\le \tfrac{1}{2}\\ 0 & \text{elsewhere}\end{cases}$	$\mathrm{sinc}\!\left(\dfrac{\omega}{2\pi}\right)$	$\mathrm{sinc}\,f$
11	$\mathrm{sinc}\,t \triangleq \dfrac{\sin\pi t}{\pi t}$	$\begin{cases}1 & |\omega|\le \pi\\ 0 & \text{elsewhere}\end{cases}$	$\begin{cases}1 & |f|\le \tfrac{1}{2}\\ 0 & \text{elsewhere}\end{cases}$
12	$\begin{cases}at\exp(-at) & t>0\\ 0 & \text{elsewhere}\end{cases}$	$\dfrac{a}{(a+j\omega)^2}$	$\dfrac{a}{(a+j2\pi f)^2}$
13	$\exp(-a|t|)$	$\dfrac{2a}{a^2 + \omega^2}$	$\dfrac{2a}{a^2 + 4\pi^2 f^2}$
14	$\mathrm{signum}\,t \triangleq \begin{cases}1 & t>0\\ 0 & t=0\\ -1 & t<0\end{cases}$	$\dfrac{2}{j\omega}$	$\dfrac{1}{j\pi f}$

relates the Fourier transform to the total energy of an energy signal as follows:

$$E = \int_{-\infty}^{\infty} |x(t)|^2\,dt = \int_{-\infty}^{\infty} S_e(f)\,df = \int_{-\infty}^{\infty} |X(f)|^2\,df \qquad (1.175)$$

In many texts where $x(t)$ is assumed to be real valued, the absolute-value signs are omitted from the first integrand in (1.175). In some texts (such as Kanefsky 1985), Eq. (1.175) is loosely referred to as "Parseval's theorem."

Power spectral density of a periodic signal

The *power spectral density* (PSD) of a periodic signal is defined as the squared magnitude of the signal's line spectrum obtained via either a Fourier series or a Fourier transform with impulses. Using the Dirac delta notational conventions of the latter, the PSD is defined as

$$S_p(f) = \frac{1}{T^2} \sum_{n=-\infty}^{\infty} \delta\left(f - \frac{n}{T}\right) \left| X\left(\frac{n}{T}\right) \right|^2 \tag{1.176}$$

where T is the period of the signal $x(t)$. Parseval's theorem as given by Eq. (1.159) of Sec. 1.8 can be restated in the notation of Fourier transform spectra as

$$P = \frac{1}{T^2} \sum_{n=-\infty}^{\infty} \left| X\left(\frac{n}{T}\right) \right|^2 \tag{1.177}$$

2

Filter Fundamentals

Digital filters are often based upon common analog filter functions. There-fore, a certain amount of background material concerning analog filters is a necessary foundation for the study of digital filters. This chapter reviews the essentials of analog system theory and filter characterization. Some common analog filter types—Butterworth, Chebyshev, elliptical, and Bessel—are given more detailed treatment in subsequent chapters.

1.2 Systems

Within the context of signal processing, a *system* is something that accepts one or more input signals and operates upon them to produce one or more output signals. Filters, amplifiers, and digitizers are some of the systems used in various signal processing applications. When signals are represented as mathematical functions, it is convenient to represent systems as *operators* that operate upon input functions to produce output functions. Two alterna-tive notations for representing a system H with input x and output y are given in Eqs. (2.1) and (2.2). Note that x and y can each be scalar valued or vector valued.

$$y = H[x] \tag{2.1}$$

$$y = H\,x \tag{2.2}$$

This book uses the notation of Eq. (2.1) as this is less likely to be confused with multiplication of x by a value H.

A system H can be represented pictorially in a flow diagram as shown in Fig. 2.1. For vector-valued x and y, the individual components are sometimes explicitly shown as in Fig. 2.2a or lumped together as shown in Fig. 2.2b. Sometimes, in order to emphasize their vector nature, the input and output are drawn as in Fig. 2.2c.

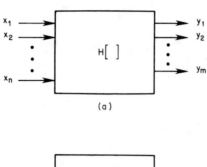

(a)

(b)

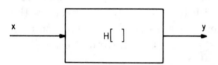

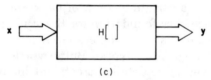

(c)

Figure 2.1 Pictorial representation of a system.

Figure 2.2 Pictorial representation of a system with multiple inputs and outputs.

In different presentations of system theory, the notational schemes used exhibit some variation. The more precise treatments (such as Chen 1984) use x or $x(\cdot)$ to denote a function of time defined over the interval $(-\infty, \infty)$. A function defined over a more restricted interval such as $[t_0, t_1)$ would be denoted as $x_{(t_0, t_1)}$. The notation $x(t)$ is reserved for denoting the value of x at time t. Less precise treatments (such as Schwartz and Friedland 1965) use $x(t)$ to denote both functions of time defined over $(-\infty, \infty)$ and the value of x at time t. When not evident from context, words of explanation must be included to indicate which particular meaning is intended. Using the less precise notational scheme, (2.1) could be rewritten as

$$y(t) = H[x(t)] \tag{2.3}$$

While it appears that the precise notation should be the more desirable, the relaxed conventions exemplified by (2.3) are widespread in the literature.

Linearity

If the relaxed system H is *homogeneous*, multiplying the input by a constant gain is equivalent to multiplying the output by the same constant gain, and

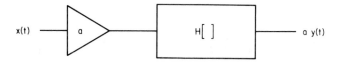

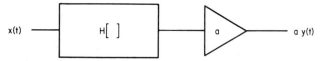

Figure 2.3 Homogeneous system.

the two configurations shown in Fig. 2.3 are equivalent. Mathematically stated, the relaxed system H is homogeneous if, for constant a,

$$H[ax] = a\,H[x] \tag{2.4}$$

If the relaxed system H is additive, the output produced for the sum of two input signals is equal to the sum of the outputs produced for each input individually, and the two configurations shown in Fig. 2.4 are equivalent. Mathematically stated, the relaxed system H is additive if

$$H[x_1 + x_2] = H[x_1] + H[x_2] \tag{2.5}$$

A system that is both homogeneous and additive is said to "exhibit *superposition*" or to "satisfy the principle of superposition." A system that exhibits superposition is called a *linear system*. Under certain restrictions, additivity implies homogeneity. Specifically, the fact that a system H is additive implies that

$$H[\alpha x] = \alpha\,H[x] \tag{2.6}$$

for any rational α. Any real number can be approximated with arbitrary precision by a rational number; therefore, additivity implies homogeneity for real a provided that

$$\lim_{\alpha \to a} H[\alpha x] = H[ax] \tag{2.7}$$

Time invariance

The characteristics of a *time-invariant system* do not change over time. A system is said to be *relaxed* if it is not still responding to any previously

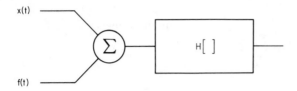

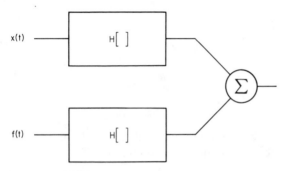

Figure 2.4 Additive system.

applied input. Given a relaxed system H such that

$$y(t) = H[x(t)] \tag{2.8}$$

then H is time invariant if and only if

$$y(t - \tau) = H[x(t - \tau)] \tag{2.9}$$

for any τ and any $x(t)$. A time-invariant system is also called a *fixed system* or *stationary system*. A system that is not time invariant is called a *time-varying system*, *variable system*, or *nonstationary system*.

Causality

In a *causal system*, the output at time t can depend only upon the input at times t and prior. Mathematically stated, a system H is causal if and only if

$$H[x_1(t)] = H[x_2(t)] \qquad \text{for } t \le t_0 \tag{2.10}$$

given that

$$x_1(t) = x_2(t) \qquad \text{for } t \le t_0$$

A *noncausal* or *anticipatory system* is one in which the present output depends upon future values of the input. Noncausal systems occur in theory, but they cannot exist in the real world. This is unfortunate, since we will often discover that some especially desirable frequency responses can be obtained only from noncausal systems. However, causal realizations can be created for noncausal systems in which the present output depends at most upon past, present, and a finite extent of future inputs. In such cases, a causal realization is obtained by simply delaying the output of the system for a finite interval until all the required inputs have entered the system and are available for determination of the output.

2.2 Characterization of Linear Systems

A linear system can be characterized by a differential equation, step response, impulse response, complex-frequency-domain system function, or a transfer function. The relationships among these various characterizations are given in Table 2.1.

Impulse response

The *impulse response* of a system is the output response produced when a unit impulse $\delta(t)$ is applied to the input of a previously relaxed system. This is an especially convenient characterization of a linear system, since the response

TABLE 2.1 Relationships among Characterizations of Linear Systems

Starting with	Perform	To obtain
Time domain differential equation relating $x(t)$ and $y(t)$	Laplace transform	Complex-frequency-domain system function
	Compute $y(t)$ for $x(t) =$ unit impulse	Impulse response $h(t)$
	Compute $y(t)$ for $x(t) =$ unit step	Step response $a(t)$
Step response $a(t)$	Differentiate with respect to time	Impulse response $h(t)$
Impulse response $h(t)$	Integrate with respect to time	Step response $a(t)$
	Laplace transform	Transfer function $H(s)$
Complex-frequency-domain system function	Solve for $$H(s) = \frac{Y(s)}{X(s)}$$	Transfer function $H(s)$
Transfer function $H(s)$	Inverse Laplace transform	Impulse response $h(t)$

$y(t)$ to any continuous-time input signal $x(t)$ is given by

$$y(t) = \int_{-\infty}^{\infty} x(\tau)\, h(t, \tau)\, d\tau \qquad (2.11)$$

where $h(t, \tau)$ denotes the system's response at time t to an impulse applied at time τ. The integral in (2.11) is sometimes referred to as the *superposition integral*. The particular notation used indicates that, in general, the system is time varying. For a time-invariant system, the impulse response at time t depends only upon the time delay from τ to t; and we can redefine the impulse response to be a function of a single variable and denote it as $h(t - \tau)$. Equation (2.11) then becomes

$$y(t) = \int_{-\infty}^{\infty} x(\tau)\, h(t - \tau)\, d\tau \qquad (2.12)$$

Via the simple change of variables $\lambda = t - \tau$, Eq. (2.12) can be rewritten as

$$y(t) = \int_{-\infty}^{\infty} x(t - \lambda)\, h(\lambda)\, d\lambda \qquad (2.13)$$

If we assume that the input is zero for $t < 0$, the lower limit of integration can be changed to zero; and if we further assume that the system is causal, the upper limit of integration can be changed to t, thus yielding

$$y(t) = \int_{0}^{t} x(\tau)\, h(t - \tau)\, d\tau = \int_{0}^{t} x(t - \lambda)\, h(\lambda)\, d\lambda \qquad (2.14)$$

The integrals in (2.14) are known as *convolution integrals*, and the equation indicates that "$y(t)$ equals the *convolution* of $x(t)$ and $h(t)$." It is often more compact and convenient to denote this relationship as

$$y(t) = x(t) \otimes h(t) = h(t) \otimes x(t) \qquad (2.15)$$

Various texts use different symbols, such as stars or asterisks, in place of $\otimes$ to indicate convolution. The asterisk is probably favored by most printers, but in some contexts its usage to indicate convolution could be confused with the complex conjugation operator. A typical system's impulse response is sketched in Fig. 2.5.

Step response

The *step response* of a system is the output signal produced when a unit step $u(t)$ is applied to the input of the previously relaxed system. Since the unit step is simply the time integration of a unit impulse, it can easily be shown that the step response of a system can be obtained by integrating the impulse response. A typical system's step response is shown in Fig. 2.6.

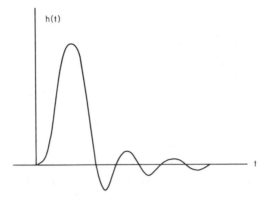

h(t)

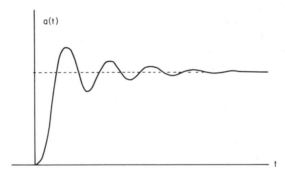

Figure 2.5 Impulse response of a typical system.

a(t)

t

Figure 2.6 Step response of a typical system.

2.3 Laplace Transform

The *Laplace transform* is a technique that is useful for transforming differential equations into algebraic equations that can be more easily manipulated to obtain desired results.

In most communications applications, the functions of interest will usually (but not always) be functions of time. The Laplace transform of a time function $x(t)$ is usually denoted as $X(s)$ or $\mathscr{L}[x(t)]$ and is defined by

$$X(s) = \mathscr{L}[x(t)] = \int_{-\infty}^{\infty} x(t)\,e^{-st}\,dt \qquad (2.16)$$

The complex variable s is usually referred to as *complex frequency* and is of the form $\sigma + j\omega$, where σ and ω are real variables sometimes referred to as *neper frequency* and *radian frequency*, respectively. The Laplace transform for a given function $x(t)$ is obtained by simply evaluating the given integral. Some mathematics texts (such as Spiegel 1965) denote the time function with an uppercase letter and the frequency function with a lowercase letter.

However, the use of lowercase for time functions is almost universal within the engineering literature.

If we transform both sides of a differential equation in t using the definition (2.16), we obtain an algebraic equation in s that can be solved for the desired quantity. The solved algebraic equation can then be transformed back into the time domain by using the inverse Laplace transform.

The inverse Laplace transform is defined by

$$x(t) = \mathcal{L}^{-1}[X(s)] = \frac{1}{2\pi j} \int_C X(s)\, e^{st}\, ds \qquad (2.17)$$

where C is a contour of integration chosen so as to include all singularities of $X(s)$. The inverse Laplace transform for a given function $X(s)$ can be obtained by evaluating the given integral. However, this integration is often a major chore—when tractable, it will usually involve application of the residue theorem from the theory of complex variables. Fortunately, in most cases of practical interest, direct evaluation of (2.16) and (2.17) can be avoided by using some well-known transform pairs, as listed in Table 2.2, along with a number of transform properties presented in Sec. 2.4.

TABLE 2.2 Laplace Transform Pairs

Ref. no.	$x(t)$	$X(s)$
1	1	$\dfrac{1}{s}$
2	$u_1(t)$	$\dfrac{1}{s}$
3	$\delta(t)$	1
4	t	$\dfrac{1}{s^2}$
5	t^n	$\dfrac{n!}{s^{n+1}}$
6	$\sin \omega t$	$\dfrac{\omega}{s^2 + \omega^2}$
7	$\cos \omega t$	$\dfrac{s}{s^2 + \omega^2}$
8	e^{-at}	$\dfrac{1}{s+a}$
9	$e^{-at} \sin \omega t$	$\dfrac{\omega}{(s+a)^2 + \omega^2}$
10	$e^{-at} \cos \omega t$	$\dfrac{s+a}{(s+a)^2 + \omega^2}$

Example 2.1 Find the Laplace transform of $x(t) = e^{-\alpha t}$.

solution

$$X(s) = \int_0^\infty e^{-\alpha t} e^{-st} \, dt \qquad (2.18)$$

$$= \int_0^\infty e^{-(\alpha + s)t} \, dt \qquad (2.19)$$

$$= \frac{1}{s + \alpha} \qquad (2.20)$$

Notice that this result agrees with entry 8 in Table 2.2.

Background

The Laplace transform defined by Eq. (2.16) is more precisely referred to as the *one-sided Laplace transform*, and it is the form generally used for the analysis of causal systems and signals. There is also a *two-sided transform* that is defined as

$$\mathscr{L}_{\text{II}}[x(t)] = \int_{-\infty}^\infty x(t) \, e^{-st} \, dt \qquad (2.21)$$

The Laplace transform is named for the French mathematician Pierre Simon de Laplace (1749–1827).

2.4 Properties of the Laplace Transform

Some properties of the Laplace transform are listed in Table 2.3. These properties can be used in conjunction with the transform pairs presented in Table 2.2, to obtain most of the Laplace transforms that will ever be needed in practical engineering situations. Some of the entries in the table require further explanation, which is provided below.

Time shifting

Consider the function $f(t)$ shown in Fig. 2.7a. The function has nonzero values for $t < 0$, but since the one-sided Laplace transform integrates only over positive time, these values for $t < 0$ have no impact on the evaluation of the transform. If we now shift $f(t)$ to the right by τ units as shown in Fig. 2.7b, some of the nonzero values from the left of the origin will be moved to the right of the origin, where they will be included in the evaluation of the transform. The Laplace transform's properties with regard to a time-shift right must be stated in such a way that these previously unincluded values will not be included in the transform of the shifted function either. This can be easily accomplished through multiplying the shifted function $f(t - \tau)$ by a shifted unit step function $u_1(t - \tau)$ as shown in Fig. 2.7c. Thus we have

$$\mathscr{L}[u_1(t - \tau)f(t - \tau)] = e^{-\tau s} F(s) \qquad a > 0 \qquad (2.22)$$

TABLE 2.3 Properties of the Laplace Transform

Property	Time function	Transform
1. Homogeneity	$a\,f(t)$	$a\,F(s)$
2. Additivity	$f(t) + g(t)$	$F(s) + G(s)$
3. Linearity	$a\,f(t) + b\,g(t)$	$a\,F(s) + b\,G(s)$
4. First derivative	$\dfrac{d}{dt} f(t)$	$s\,F(s) - f(0)$
5. Second derivative	$\dfrac{d^2}{dt^2} f(t)$	$s\,F(s) - s\,f(0) - \dfrac{d}{dt} f(0)$
6. kth derivative	$\dfrac{d^{(k)}}{dt^k} f(t)$	$s^k\,F(s) = \displaystyle\sum_{n=0}^{k-1} s^{k-1-n} f^{(n)}(0)$
7. Integration	$\displaystyle\int_{-\infty}^{t} f(\tau)\,d\tau$	$\dfrac{F(s)}{s} + \dfrac{1}{s}\left(\displaystyle\int_{-\infty}^{t} f(\tau)\,d\tau \right)_{t=0}$
	$\displaystyle\int_{0}^{t} f(\tau)\,d\tau$	$\dfrac{F(s)}{s}$
8. Frequency shift	$e^{-at} f(t)$	$X(s+a)$
9. Time shift right	$u_1(t-\tau) f(t-\tau)$	$e^{-\tau s}\,F(s) \qquad a > 0$
10. Time shift left	$f(t+r), f(t) = 0 \quad$ for $0 < t < \tau$	$e^{\tau s}\,F(s)$
11. Convolution	$y(t) = \displaystyle\int_{0}^{t} h(t-\tau)\,x(\tau)\,d\tau$	$Y(s) = H(s)\,X(s)$
12. Multiplication	$f(t)\,g(t)$	$\dfrac{1}{2\pi j} \displaystyle\int_{c-j\infty}^{c+j\infty} F(s-r)\,G(r)\,dr$ $\sigma_g < c < \sigma - \sigma_f$

Notes: $f^{(k)}(t)$ denotes the kth derivative of $f(t)$. $f^{(0)}(t) = f(t)$.

Consider now the case when $f(t)$ is shifted to the ~~right~~ left. Such a shift will move a portion of $f(t)$ from positive time, where it is included in the transform evaluation, into negative time, where it will not be included in the transform evaluation. The Laplace transform's properties with regard to a time shift left must be stated in such a way that all included values from the unshifted function will likewise be included in the transform of the shifted function. This can be accomplished by requiring that the original function be equal to zero for all values of t from zero to τ, if a shift to the left by τ units is to be made. Thus for a shift left by τ units

$$\mathscr{L}[f(t+\tau)] = F(s)\,e^{\tau s} \qquad \text{if } f(t) = 0 \qquad \text{for } 0 < t < \tau \qquad (2.23)$$

Multiplication

Consider the product of two time functions $f(t)$ and $g(t)$. The transform of the product will equal the complex convolution of $F(s)$ and $G(s)$ in the frequency

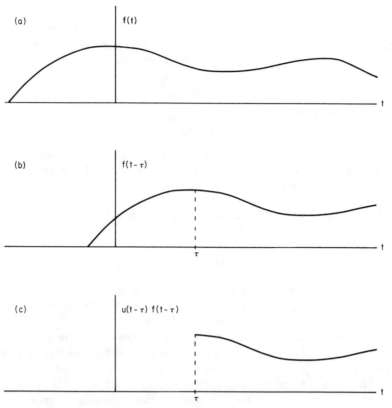

Figure 2.7 Signals for explanation of the Laplace transform's "time-shift-right" property.

domain.

$$\mathcal{L}[f(t)\,g(t)] = \frac{1}{2\pi j} \int_{c-j\infty}^{c+j\infty} F(s-r)\,G(r)\,dr \qquad \sigma_g < c < \sigma - \sigma_f \qquad (2.24)$$

2.5 Transfer Functions

The *transfer function H(s)* of a system is equal to the Laplace transform of the output signal divided by the Laplace transform of the input signal:

$$H(s) = \frac{Y(s)}{X(s)} = \frac{\mathcal{L}[y(t)]}{\mathcal{L}[x(t)]} \qquad (2.25)$$

It can be shown that the transfer function is also equal to the Laplace transform of the system's impulse response:

$$H(s) = \mathcal{L}[h(t)] \qquad (2.26)$$

Therefore,
$$y(t) = \mathscr{L}^{-1}\{H(s)\mathscr{L}[x(t)]\} \tag{2.27}$$

Equation (2.27) presents an alternative to the convolution defined by Eq. (2.14) for obtaining a system's response $y(t)$ to any input $x(t)$, given the impulse response $h(t)$. Simply perform the following steps:

1. Compute $H(s)$ as the Laplace transform of $h(t)$.
2. Compute $X(s)$ as the Laplace transform of $x(t)$.
3. Compute $Y(s)$ as the product of $H(s)$ and $X(s)$.
4. Compute $y(t)$ as the inverse Laplace transform of $Y(s)$. (The Heaviside expansion presented in Sec. 2.6 is a convenient technique for performing the inverse transform operation.)

A transfer function defined as in (2.25) can be put into the form

$$H(s) = \frac{P(s)}{Q(s)} \tag{2.28}$$

where $P(s)$ and $Q(s)$ are polynomials in s. For $H(s)$ to be stable and realizable in the form of a lumped-parameter network, it can be shown (Van Valkenburg 1974) that all of the coefficients in the polynomials $P(s)$ and $Q(s)$ must be real. Furthermore, all of the coefficients in $Q(s)$ must be positive. The polynomial $Q(s)$ must have a nonzero term for each degree of s from the highest to the lowest, unless all even-degree terms or all odd-degree terms are missing. If $H(s)$ is a voltage ratio or current ratio (that is, the input and output are either both voltages or both currents), the maximum degree of s in $P(s)$ cannot exceed the maximum degree of s in $Q(s)$. If $H(s)$ is a transfer impedance (that is, the input is a current and the output is a voltage) or a transfer admittance (that is, the input is a voltage and the output is a current), then the maximum degree of s in $P(s)$ can exceed the maximum degree of s in $Q(s)$ by at most 1. Note that these are only upper limits on the degree of s in $P(s)$; in either case, the maximum degree of s in $P(s)$ may be as small as zero. Also note that these are necessary but not sufficient conditions for $H(s)$ to be a valid transfer function. A candidate $H(s)$ satisfying all of these conditions may still not be realizable as a lumped-parameter network.

Example 2.2   Consider the following alleged transfer functions:

$$H_1(s) = \frac{s^2 - 2s + 1}{s^3 - 3s^2 + 3s + 1} \tag{2.29}$$

$$H_2(s) = \frac{s^4 + 2s^3 + 2s^2 - 3s + 1}{s^3 + 3s^2 + 3s + 2} \tag{2.30}$$

$$H_3(s) = \frac{s^2 - 2s + 1}{s^3 + 3s^2 + 1} \tag{2.31}$$

TABLE 2.4 System Characterizations Obtained from the Transfer Function

Starting with	Perform	To obtain
Transfer function $H(s)$	Compute roots of $H(s)$ denominator	Pole locations
	Compute roots of $H(s)$ numerator	Zero locations
	Compute $|H(j\omega)|$ over all ω	Magnitude response $A(\omega)$
	Compute $\arg[H(j\omega)]$ over all ω	Phase response $\theta(\omega)$
Phase response $\theta(\omega)$	Divide by ω	Phase delay $\tau_p(\omega)$
	Differentiate with respect to ω	Group delay $\tau_g(\omega)$

Equation (2.29) is not acceptable because the coefficient of s^2 in the denominator is negative. If Eq. (2.30) is intended as a voltage- or current-transfer ratio, it is not acceptable because the degree of the numerator exceeds the degree of the denominator. However, if Eq. (2.30) represents a transfer impedance or transfer admittance, it may be valid since the degree of the numerator exceeds the degree of the denominator by just 1. Equation (2.31) is not acceptable because the term for s is missing from the denominator.

A system's transfer function can be manipulated to provide a number of useful characterizations of the system's behavior. These characterizations are listed in Table 2.4 and examined in more detail in subsequent sections.

Some authors, such as Van Valkenburg (1974), use the term "network function" in place of "transfer function."

2.6 Heaviside Expansion

The Heaviside expansion provides a straightforward computational method for obtaining the inverse Laplace transform of certain types of complex-frequency functions. The function to be inverse-transformed must be expressed as a ratio of polynomials in s, where the order of the denominator polynomial exceeds the order of the numerator polynomial. If

$$H(s) = K_0 \frac{P(s)}{Q(s)} \tag{2.32}$$

where $Q(s) = \prod_{k=1}^{n} (s - s_k)^{m_k} = (s - s_1)^{m_1}(s - s_2)^{m_2} \cdots (s - s_n)^{m_n} \tag{2.33}$

then inverse transformation via the Heaviside expansion yields

$$\mathcal{L}^{-1}[H(s)] = K_0 \sum_{r=1}^{n} \sum_{k=1}^{m_r} [K_{rk} t^{m_r - k} \exp(s_r t)] \tag{2.34}$$

where $K_{rk} = \frac{1}{(k-1)!(m_r - k)!} \frac{d^{k-1}}{ds^{k-1}} \left[\frac{(s - s_r)^{m_r} P(s)}{Q(s)} \right]_{s = s_r} \tag{2.35}$

A method for computing the derivative in (2.35) can be found in Section 1.4.

Simple pole case

The complexity of the expansion is significantly reduced for the case of $Q(s)$ having no repeated roots. The denominator of (2.32) is then given by

$$Q(s) = \prod_{k=1}^{n} (s - s_k) = (s - s_1)(s - s_2) \cdots (s - s_n) \qquad s_1 \neq s_2 \neq s_3 \neq \cdots s_n \quad (2.36)$$

Inverse transformation via the Heaviside expansion then yields

$$\mathscr{L}^{-1}[H(s)] = K_0 \sum_{r=1}^{n} K_r e^{s_r t} \qquad (2.37)$$

where $K_r = \left[\dfrac{(s - s_r)P(s)}{Q(s)} \right]_{s = s_r}$ $\qquad (2.38)$

The Heaviside expansion is named for Oliver Heaviside (1850–1925), an English physicist and electrical engineer who was the nephew of Charles Wheatstone (as in Wheatstone bridge).

2.7 Poles and Zeros

As pointed out previously, the transfer function for a realizable linear time-invariant system can always be expressed as a ratio of polynomials in s:

$$H(s) = \frac{P(s)}{Q(s)} \qquad (2.39)$$

The numerator and denominator can each be factored to yield

$$H(s) = H_0 \frac{(s - z_1)(s - z_2)(s - z_3) \cdots (s - z_m)}{(s - p_1)(s - p_2)(s - p_3) \cdots (s - p_n)} \qquad (2.40)$$

Where the roots $z_1, z_2, \ldots, z_m$ of the numerator are called *zeros* of the transfer function, and the roots $p_1, p_2, \ldots, p_n$ of the denominator are called *poles* of the transfer function. Together, poles and zeros can be collectively referred to as *critical frequencies*. Each factor $(s - z_i)$ is called a *zero factor*, and each factor $(s - p_j)$ is called a *pole factor*. A repeated zero appearing n times is called either an nth-*order zero* or a *zero of multiplicity n*. Likewise, a repeated pole appearing n times is called either an nth-*order pole* or a *pole of multiplicity n*. Nonrepeated poles or zeros are sometimes described as *simple* or *distinct* to emphasize their nonrepeated nature.

Example 2.3 Consider the transfer function given by

$$H(s) = \frac{s^3 + 5s^2 + 8s + 4}{s^3 + 13s^2 + 59s + 87} \qquad (2.41)$$

The numerator and denominator can be factored to yield

$$H(s) = \frac{(s+2)^2(s+1)}{(s+5+2j)(s+5-2j)(s+3)}$$ (2.42)

Examination of (2.42) reveals that

$$s = -1 \text{ is a simple zero}$$

$$s = -2 \text{ is a second-order zero}$$

$$s = -5 + 2j \text{ is a simple pole}$$

$$s = -5 - 2j \text{ is a simple pole}$$

$$s = -3 \text{ is a simple pole}$$

A system's poles and zeros can be depicted graphically as locations in a complex plane as shown in Fig. 2.8. In mathematics, the complex plane itself is called the *gaussian plane*, while a plot depicting complex values as points in the plane is called an *Argand diagram* or a *Wessel-Argand-Gaussian diagram*. In the 1798 transactions of the Danish academy, Caspar Wessel (1745–1818) published a technique for graphical representation of complex numbers, and Jean Robert Argand published a similar technique in 1806. Geometric interpretation of complex numbers played a central role in the doctoral thesis of Gauss.

Pole locations can provide convenient indications of a system's behavior as indicated in Table 2.5. Furthermore, poles and zeros possess the following properties that can sometimes be used to expedite the analysis of a system:

1. For real $H(s)$, complex or imaginary poles and zeros will each occur in complex conjugate pairs that are symmetric about the σ axis.

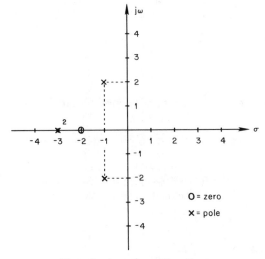

Figure 2.8 Plot of pole and zero locations.

TABLE 2.5 Impact of Pole Locations upon System Behavior

Pole type	Corresponding natural response component	Corresponding description of system behavior
Single real, negative	Decaying exponential	Stable
Single real, positive	Divergent exponential	Divergent instability
Real pair, negative, unequal	Decaying exponential	Overdamped (stable)
Real pair, negative equal	Decaying exponential	Critically damped (stable)
Complex conjugate pair with negative real parts	Exponentially decaying sinusoid	Underdamped (stable)
Complex conjugate pair with zero real parts	Sinusoid	Undamped (marginally stable)
Complex conjugate pair with positive real parts	Exponentially saturating sinusoid	Oscillatory instability

2. For $H(s)$ having even symmetry, the poles and zeros will exhibit symmetry about the $j\omega$ axis.

3. For nonnegative $H(s)$, any zeros on the $j\omega$ axis will occur in pairs.

In many situations, it is necessary to determine the poles of a given transfer function. For some systems, such as Chebyshev filters or Butterworth filters, explicit expressions have been found for evaluation of pole locations. For other systems, such as Bessel filters, the poles must be found by numerically solving for the roots of the transfer function's denominator polynomial. Several root-finding algorithms appear in the literature, but I have found the *Laguerre method* to be the most useful for approximating pole locations. The approximate roots can be subjected to small-step iterative refinement or polishing as needed.

Algorithm 2.1 Laguerre method for approximating one root of a polynomial $P(z)$

Step 1. Set z equal to an initial guess for the value of a root. Typically, z is set to zero so that the smallest root will tend to be found first.

Step 2. Evaluate the polynomial $P(z)$ and its first two derivatives $P'(z)$ and $P''(z)$ at the current value of z.

Step 3. If $P(z)$ evaluates to zero or to within some predefined epsilon of zero, exit with the current value of z as the root. Otherwise, continue on to step 4.

Step 4. Compute a correction term Δz, using

$$\Delta z = \frac{N}{F \pm \sqrt{(N-1)(NG - G^2)}}$$

where $F \triangleq P'(z)/P(z)$, $G \triangleq F^2 - P''(z)/P(z)$, and the sign in the denominator is taken so as to minimize the magnitude of the correction (or, equivalently, so as to maximize the denominator).

Step 5. If the correction term Δz has a magnitude smaller than some specified fraction of the magnitude of z, then take z as the value of the root and terminate the algorithm.

Step 6. If the algorithm has been running for a while (let's say six iterations) and the correction value has gotten bigger since the previous iteration, then take z as the value of the root and terminate the algorithm.

Step 7. If the algorithm was not terminated in step 3, 5, or 6, then subtract Δz from z and go back to step 2.

A C routine **laguerreMethod( )** that implements Algorithm 2.1 is provided in Listing 2.1.

2.8 Magnitude, Phase, and Delay Responses

A system's *steady-state response* $H(j\omega)$ can be determined by evaluating the transfer function $H(s)$ at $s = j\omega$:

$$H(j\omega) = |H(j\omega)| \, e^{j\theta(\omega)} = H(s)\big|_{s=j\omega} \tag{2.43}$$

The *magnitude response* is simply the magnitude of $H(j\omega)$:

$$|H(j\omega)| = (\{\mathrm{Re}[H(j\omega)]\}^2 + \{\mathrm{Im}[H(j\omega)]\}^2)^{1/2} \tag{2.44}$$

It can be shown that

$$|H(j\omega)|^2 = H(s)H(-s)\big|_{s=j\omega} \tag{2.45}$$

If $H(s)$ is available in factored form as given by

$$H(s) = H_0 \frac{(s - z_1)(s - z_2)(s - z_3) \cdots (s - z_m)}{(s - p_1)(s - p_2)(s - p_3) \cdots (s - p_n)} \tag{2.46}$$

then the magnitude response can be obtained by replacing each factor with its absolute value evaluated at $s = j\omega$:

$$|H(j\omega)| = H_0 \frac{|j\omega - z_1| \cdot |j\omega - z_2| \cdot |j\omega - z_3| \cdot \cdots \cdot |j\omega - z_m|}{|j\omega - p_1| \cdot |j\omega - p_2| \cdot |j\omega - p_3| \cdot \cdots \cdot |j\omega - p_n|} \tag{2.47}$$

The *phase response* $\theta(\omega)$ is given by

$$\theta(\omega) = \tan^{-1}\left\{\frac{\mathrm{Im}[H(j\omega)]}{\mathrm{Re}[H(j\omega)]}\right\} \tag{2.48}$$

Phase delay

The *phase delay* $\tau_p(\omega)$ of a system is defined as

$$\tau_p(\omega) = \frac{-\theta(\omega)}{\omega} \tag{2.49}$$

where $\theta(\omega)$ is the phase response defined in Eq. (2.48). When evaluated at any specific frequency ω_1, Eq. (2.49) will yield the time delay experienced by a sinusoid of frequency ω passing through the system. Some authors define $\tau_p(\omega)$ without the minus sign shown on the right-hand side of (2.49). As illustrated in Fig. 2.9, the phase delay at a frequency ω_1 is equal to the negative slope of a secant drawn from the origin to the phase response curve at ω_1.

Group delay

The *group delay* $\tau_g(\omega)$ of a system is defined as

$$\tau_g(\omega) = \frac{-d}{dt}\theta(\omega) \tag{2.50}$$

where $\theta(\omega)$ is the phase response defined in (2.48). In the case of a modulated carrier passing through the system, the modulation envelope will be delayed by an amount that is in general not equal to the delay $\tau_p(\omega)$ experienced by the carrier. If the system exhibits constant group delay over the entire bandwidth of the modulated signal, then the envelope will be delayed by an amount equal to τ_g. If the group delay is not constant over the entire bandwidth of the signal, the envelope will be distorted. As shown in Fig. 2.10, the group delay at a frequency ω_1 is equal to the negative slope of a tangent to the phase response at ω_1.

Assuming that the phase response of a system is sufficiently smooth, it can be approximated as

$$\theta(\omega + \omega_c) = \tau_p \omega_c + \tau_g \omega_c \tag{2.51}$$

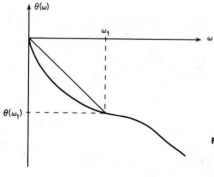

Figure 2.9 Phase delay.

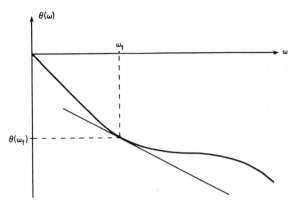

Figure 2.10 Group delay.

If an input signal $x(t) = a(t) \cos \omega_c t$ is applied to a system for which (2.51) holds, the output response will be given by

$$y(t) = Ka(t - \tau_g) \cos[\omega_c(t - \tau_p)] \qquad (2.52)$$

Since the envelope $a(t)$ is delayed by τ_g, the group delay is also called the *envelope delay*. Likewise, since the carrier is delayed by τ_p, the phase delay is also called the *carrier delay*.

2.9   Filter Fundamentals

Ideal filters would have rectangular magnitude responses as shown in Fig. 2.11. The desired frequencies are passed with no attenuation, while the undesired frequencies are completely blocked. If such filters could be implemented, they would enjoy widespread use. Unfortunately, ideal filters are noncausal and therefore not realizable. However, there are practical filter designs that approximate the ideal filter characteristics and which are realizable. Each of the major types—Butterworth, Chebyshev, and Bessel— optimizes a different aspect of the approximation.

Magnitude response features of lowpass filters

The magnitude response of a practical lowpass filter will usually have one of the four general shapes shown in Figs. 2.12 through 2.15. In all four cases the filter characteristics divide the spectrum into three general regions as shown. The *pass band* extends from direct current up to the cutoff frequency ω_c. The *transition band* extends from ω_c up to the beginning of the stop band at ω_1, and the *stop band* extends upward from ω_1 to infinity. The cutoff frequency ω_c is the frequency at which the amplitude response falls to a specified fraction (usually -3 dB, sometimes -1 dB) of the peak pass-band values. Defining the

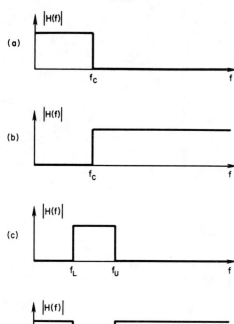

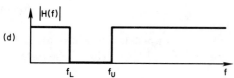

Figure 2.11 Ideal filter responses: (a) lowpass, (b) highpass, (c) bandpass, and (d) bandstop.

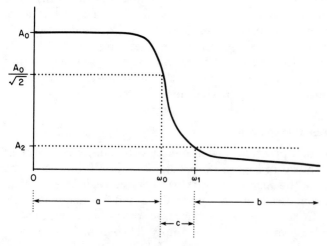

Figure 2.12 Monotonic magnitude response of a practical lowpass filter: (a) pass band, (b) stop band, and (c) transition band.

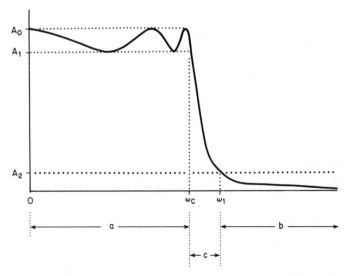

Figure 2.13 Magnitude response of a practical lowpass filter with ripples in the pass band: (a) pass band, (b) stop band, and (c) transition band.

frequency ω_1 which marks the beginning of the stop band is not quite so straightforward. In Fig. 2.12 or 2.13 there really isn't any particular feature that indicates just where ω_1 should be located. The usual approach involves specifying a *minimum stop-band loss* α_2 (or conversely a maximum stop-band amplitude A_2) and then defining ω_1 as the lowest frequency at which the loss

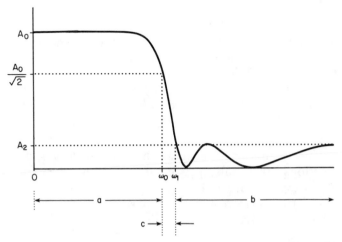

Figure 2.14 Magnitude response of a practical lowpass filter with ripples in the stop band: (a) pass band, (b) stop band, and (c) transition band.

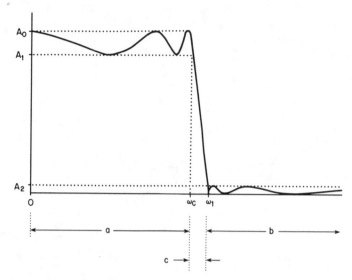

Figure 2.15 Magnitude response of a practical lowpass filter with ripples in the pass band and stop band: (*a*) pass band, (*b*) stop band, and (*c*) transition band.

exceeds and subsequently continues to exceed α_2. The width W_T of the transition band is equal to $\omega_c - \omega_1$. The quantity W_T/ω_c is sometimes called the *normalized transition width*. In the case of response shapes like those shown in Figs. 2.14 and 2.15, the minimum stop-band loss is clearly defined by the peaks of the stop-band ripples.

Scaling of lowpass filter responses

In plots of practical filter responses, the frequency axes are almost universally plotted on logarithmic scales. Magnitude response curves for lowpass filters are scaled so that the cutoff frequency occurs at a convenient frequency such as 1 rad/s (radian per second), 1 Hz, or 1 kHz. A single set of such normalized curves can then be denormalized to fit any particular cutoff requirement.

Transfer functions.   For common filter types such as Butterworth, Chebyshev, and Bessel, transfer functions are usually presented in a scaled form such that $\omega_c = 1$. Given such a response normalized for $\omega_c = 1$, we can scale the transfer function to yield the corresponding response for $\omega_c = \alpha$. If the normalized response for $\omega_c = 1$ is given by

$$H_N(s) = \frac{K \prod_{i=1}^{m} (s - z_i)}{\prod_{i=1}^{n} (s - p_i)}$$

then the corresponding response for $\omega_c = \alpha$ is given by

$$H_\alpha(s) = \frac{K \, \Pi_{i=1}^{m} (s - \alpha z_i)}{\alpha^{(m-n)} \, \Pi_{i=1}^{n} (s - \alpha p_i)}$$

Magnitude scaling. The vertical axes of a filter's magnitude response can be presented in several different forms. In theoretical presentations, the magnitude response is often plotted on a linear scale. In practical design situations it is convenient to work with plots of attenuation in decibels using a high-resolution linear scale in the pass band and a lower-resolution linear scale in the stop band. This allows details of the pass-band response to be shown as well as large attenuation values deep into the stop band. In nearly all cases, the data are normalized to present a 0-dB attenuation at the peak of the pass band.

Phase response. The phase response is plotted as a phase angle in degrees or radians versus frequency. By adding or subtracting the appropriate number of full-cycle offsets (that is, 2π rad or $360°$), the phase response can be presented either as a single curve extending over several full cycles (Fig. 2.16) or as an equivalent set of curves, each extending over a single cycle (Fig. 2.17). Phase calculations will usually yield results confined to a single 2π cycle. Listing 2.2 contains a C function, **unwrapPhase( )**, that can be used to convert such data into the multicycle form of Fig. 2.16.

Step response. Normalized step response plots are obtained by computing the step response from the normalized transfer function. The inherent scaling of the time axis will thus depend upon the transient characteristics of the normalized filter. The amplitude axis scaling is not dependent upon normal-

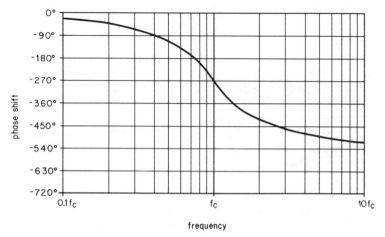

Figure 2.16 Phase response extending over multiple cycles.

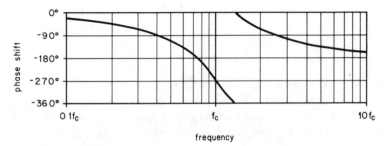

Figure 2.17 Phase response confined to a single-cycle range.

ization. The usual lowpass presentation will require that the response be
denormalized by dividing the frequency axis by some form of the cutoff
frequency.

Impulse response.   Normalized impulse response plots are obtained by computing the impulse response from the normalized-transfer function. Since an
impulse response will always have an area of unity, both the time axis and
the amplitude axis will exhibit inherent scaling that depends upon the
transient characteristics of the normalized filter. The usual lowpass presentation will require that the response be denormalized by multiplying the
amplitude by some form of the cutoff frequency and dividing the time axis by
the same factor.

Highpass filters

Highpass filters are usually designed via transformation of lowpass designs.
Normalized lowpass-transfer functions can be converted into corresponding
highpass-transfer functions by simply replacing each occurrence of s with $1/s$.
This will cause the magnitude response to be "flipped" around a line at f_c as
shown in Fig. 2.18. (Note that this flip works only when the frequency is
plotted on a logarithmic scale.) Rather than actually trying to draw a flipped
response curve, it is much simpler to take the reciprocals of all the important
frequencies for the highpass filter in question and then read the appropriate
response directly from the lowpass curves.

Bandpass filters

Bandpass filters are classified as wide band or narrow band based upon the
relative width of their pass bands. Different methods are used for obtaining
the transfer function for each type.

Wide-band bandpass filters.   Wide-band bandpass filters can be realized by
cascading a lowpass filter and a highpass filter. This approach will be
acceptable as long as the bandpass filters used exhibit relatively sharp

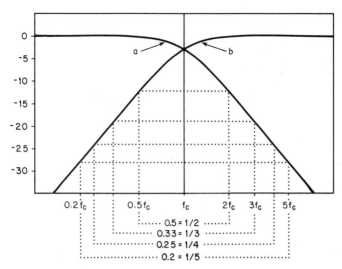

Figure 2.18 Relationship between lowpass and highpass magnitude responses: (*a*) lowpass response and (*b*) highpass response.

transitions from the pass band to cutoff. Relatively narrow bandwidths and/or gradual rolloffs that begin within the pass band can cause a significant center-band loss as shown in Fig. 2.19. In situations where such losses are unacceptable, other bandpass filter realizations must be used. A general rule of thumb is to use narrow-band techniques for pass bands that are an octave or smaller.

Narrow-band bandpass filters.   A normalized lowpass filter can be converted into a normalized narrow-band bandpass filter by substituting $[s - (1/s)]$ for s in

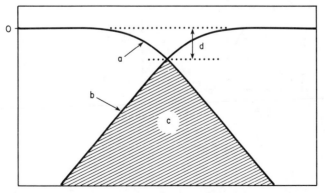

Figure 2.19 Center-band loss in a bandpass filter realized by cascading lowpass and highpass filters: (*a*) lowpass response, (*b*) highpass response, (*c*) pass band of BPF, and (*d*) center-band loss.

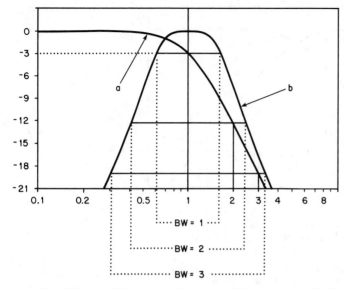

Figure 2.20 Relationship between lowpass and bandpass magnitude responses: (*a*) normalized lowpass response and (*b*) normalized bandpass response.

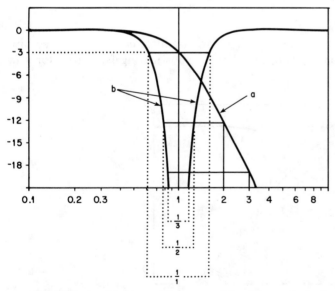

Figure 2.21 Relationship between lowpass and band-stop magnitude responses: (*a*) normalized lowpass response and (*b*) normalized band-stop response.

the lowpass-transfer function. The center frequency of the resulting bandpass filter will be at the cutoff frequency of the original lowpass filter, and the pass band will be symmetric about the center frequency when plotted on a logarithmic frequency scale. At any particular attenuation level, the bandwidth of the bandpass filter will equal the frequency at which the lowpass filter exhibits the same attenuation (see Fig. 2.20). This particular bandpass transformation preserves the magnitude response shape of the lowpass prototype but distorts the transient responses.

Bandstop filters. A normalized lowpass filter can be converted into a normalized bandstop filter by substituting $s/(s^2-1)$ for s in the lowpass-transfer function. The center frequency of the resulting bandstop filter will be at the cutoff frequency of the original lowpass filter, and the stop band will be symmetrical about the center frequency when plotted on a logarithmic frequency scale. At any particular attenuation level, the width of the stop band will be equal to the reciprocal of the frequency at which the lowpass filter exhibits the same attenuation (see Fig. 2.21).

Listing 2.1   laguerreMethod( )

```
/****************************************************/
/*                                                  */
/*  Listing 2.1                                     */
/*                                                  */
/*  laguerreMethod()                                */
/*                                                  */
/****************************************************/
#include "globDefs.h"
#include "protos.h"
extern FILE *fptr;

int laguerreMethod(
                    int order,
                    struct complex coef[],
                    struct complex *zz,
                    real epsilon,
                    real epsilon2,
                    int maxIterations)
{
int iteration, j;
struct complex d2P_dz2, dP_dz, P, f, g, fSqrd, radical, cwork;
struct complex z, fPlusRad, fMinusRad, delta2;
real error, mag2, oldMag2, fwork;
double dd1, dd2;

z = *zz;
oldMag2 = cAbs(z);

for( iteration=1; iteration<=maxIterations; iteration++)
    {
    d2P_dz2 = cmplx(0.0, 0.0);
    dP_dz = cmplx(0.0, 0.0);
    P = coef[order];
    error = cAbs(P);
    mag2 = cAbs(z);

for( j=order-1; j>=0; j--)
    {
    d2P_dz2 = cAdd(dP_dz, cMult(z, d2P_dz2));
    dP_dz = cAdd( P, cMult(dP_dz,z));
    cwork = cMult(P,z);
    P = cAdd( coef[j], cMult(P,z));
    error = cAbs(P) + mag2 * error;
    }
error = epsilon2 * error;
d2P_dz2 = sMult(2.0, d2P_dz2);
```

```
        if( cAbs(P) < error)
            {
            *zz = z;
            return 1;
            }
        f = cDiv( dP_dz,P);
        fSqrd = cMult( f, f);
        g = cSub( fSqrd, cDiv( d2P_dz2,P));
        radical = cSub( sMult( (real)order, g), fSqrd);
        fwork = (real)(order-1);
        radical = cSqrt( sMult(fwork, radical));
        fPlusRad = cAdd(f, radical);
        fMinusRad = cSub( f, radical);
        if( (cAbs(fPlusRad)) > (cAbs(fMinusRad)) )
            {
            deltaZ = cDiv( cmplx( (real)order, 0.0), fPlusRad);
            }
        else
            {
            deltaZ = cDiv( cmplx( (real)order, 0.0), fMinusRad);
            }
        z = cSub(z,deltaZ);
        if( (iteration > 6)  && (cAbs(deltaZ) > oldMagZ) )
            {
            *zz = z;
            return 2;
            }
        if( cAbs(deltaZ) < ( epsilon * cAbs(z)))
            {
            *zz = z;
            return 3;
            }
        }
fprintf(fptr,"Laguerre method failed to converge \n");
return -1;
}
```

Listing 2.2   unwrapPhase( )

```
/***********************************/
/*                             */
/*    Listing 2.2              */
/*                             */
/*    unwrapPhase()           */
/*                             */
/***********************************/
#include <math.h>

void unwrapPhase(int ix,
                 real *phase)
{
static real halfCircleOffset;
static real oldPhase;

if( ix==0)
    {
    halfCircleOffset = 0.0;
    oldPhase = *phase;
    }
else
    {
    *phase = *phase + halfCircleOffset;
    if( fabs(oldPhase - *phase) > (double)90.0)
        {
        if(oldPhase < *phase)
            {
            *phase = *phase - 360.0;
            halfCircleOffset = halfCircleOffset - 360.0;
            }
        else
            {
            *phase = *phase + 360.0;
            halfCircleOffset = halfCircleOffset + 360.0;
            }
        }
    oldPhase = *phase;
    }
return;
}
```

Butterworth Filters

Butterworth lowpass filters (LPF) are designed to have an amplitude response characteristic that is as flat as possible at low frequencies and that is monotonically decreasing with increasing frequency.

3.1 Transfer Function

The general expression for the transfer function of an nth-order Butterworth lowpass filter is given by

$$H(s) = \frac{1}{\Pi_{i=1}^{n}(s - s_i)} = \frac{1}{(s - s_1)(s - s_2) \cdots (s - s_n)} \tag{3.1}$$

where $s_i = e^{j\pi[(2i + n - 1)/2n]} = \cos\left(\pi \frac{2i + n - 1}{2n}\right) + j \sin\left(\pi \frac{2i + n - 1}{2n}\right)$ (3.2)

Example 3.1 Determine the transfer function for a lowpass third-order Butterworth filter.

solution The third-order transfer function will have the form

$$H(s) = \frac{1}{(s - s_1)(s - s_2)(s - s_3)}$$

The values for s_1, s_2, and s_3 are obtained from Eq. (3.2):

$$s_1 = \cos\left(\frac{2\pi}{3}\right) + j \sin\left(\frac{2\pi}{3}\right) = -0.5 + 0.866j$$

$$s_2 = e^{j\pi} = \cos(\pi) + j \sin(\pi) = -1$$

$$s_3 = \cos\left(\frac{4\pi}{3}\right) + j \sin\left(\frac{4\pi}{3}\right) = -0.5 - 0.866j$$

Thus,
$$H(s) = \frac{1}{(s + 0.5 - 0.866j)(s + 1)(s + 0.5 + 0.866j)}$$

$$= \frac{1}{s^3 + 2s^2 + 2s + 1}$$

The form of Eq. (3.1) indicates that an nth-order Butterworth filter will always have n poles and no finite zeros. Also true, but not quite so obvious, is the fact that these poles lie at equally spaced points on the left half of a circle in the s plane. As shown in Fig. 3.1 for the third-order case, any odd-order Butterworth LPF will have one real pole at $s = -1$, and all remaining poles will occur in complex conjugate pairs. As shown in Fig. 3.2 for the fourth-order case, the poles of any even-order Butterworth LPF will all occur in complex conjugate pairs. Pole values for orders 2 through 8 are listed in Table 3.1.

3.2 Frequency Response

A C function, **butterworthFreqResponse( )**, for generating Butterworth frequency response data is provided in Listing 3.1. Figures 3.3 through 3.5

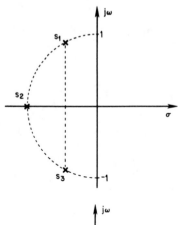

Figure 3.1 Pole locations for a third-order Butterworth LPF.

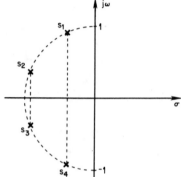

Figure 3.2 Pole locations for a fourth-order Butterworth LPF.

TABLE 3.1 Poles of Lowpass Butterworth Filters

n	Pole values
2	$-0.707107 \pm 0.707107j$
3	-1.0 $-0.5 \pm 0.866025j$
4	$-0.382683 \pm 0.923880j$ $-0.923880 \pm 0.382683j$
5	-1.0 $-0.809017 \pm 0.587785j$ $-0.309017 \pm 0.951057j$
6	$-0.258819 \pm 0.965926j$ $-0.707107 \pm 0.707107j$ $-0.965926 \pm 0.258819j$
7	-1.0 $-0.900969 \pm 0.433884j$ $-0.623490 \pm 0.781831j$ $-0.222521 \pm 0.974928j$
8	$-0.195090 \pm 0.980785j$ $-0.555570 \pm 0.831470j$ $-0.831470 \pm 0.555570j$ $-0.980785 \pm 0.195090j$

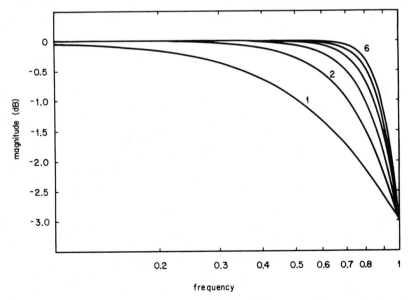

Figure 3.3 Pass-band amplitude response for lowpass Butterworth filters of orders 1 through 6.

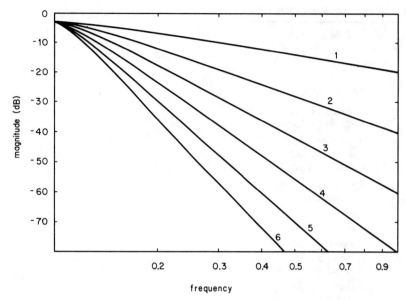

Figure 3.4 Stop-band amplitude response for lowpass Butterworth filters of orders 1 through 6.

show, respectively, the pass-band magnitude response, the stop-band magnitude response, and the phase response for Butterworth filters of various orders. These plots are normalized for a cutoff frequency of 1 Hz. To denormalize them, simply multiply the frequency axis by the desired cutoff frequency f_c.

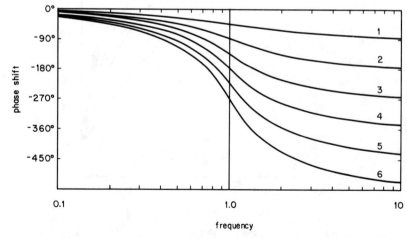

Figure 3.5 Phase response for lowpass Butterworth filters of orders 1 through 6.

Example 3.2 Use Figs. 3.4 and 3.5 to determine the magnitude and phase response at 800 Hz of a sixth-order Butterworth lowpass filter having a cutoff frequency of 400 Hz.

solution By setting $f_c = 400$, the $n = 6$ response of Fig. 3.4 is denormalized to obtain the response shown in Fig. 3.6. This plot shows that the magnitude at 800 Hz is approximately -36 dB. The corresponding response calculated by **butterworthFreqResponse( )** is -36.12466 dB. Likewise, the $n = 6$ response of Fig. 3.5 is denormalized to

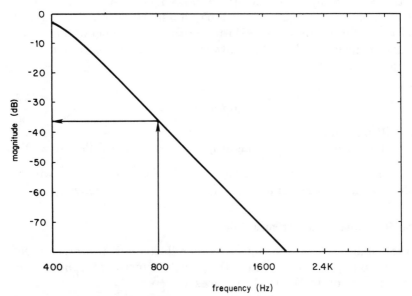

Figure 3.6 Denormalized amplitude response for Example 3.2.

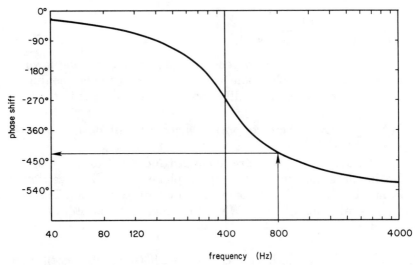

Figure 3.7 Denormalized phase response for Example 3.2.

obtain the response shown in Fig. 3.7. This plot shows that the phase response at 800 Hz is approximately $-425°$. The corresponding value calculated by **butterworthFreqResponse( )** is $-65.474°$, which "unwraps" to $-425.474°$.

3.3   Determination of Minimum Order for Butterworth Filters

Usually in the real world, the order of the desired filter is not given as in Example 3.2, but instead the order must be chosen based on the required performance of the filter. For lowpass Butterworth filters, the minimum order n that will ensure a magnitude of A_1 or lower at all frequencies ω_1 and above can be obtained by using

$$n = \frac{\log(10^{-A_1/10} - 1)}{2 \log(\omega_1/\omega_c)} \tag{3.3}$$

where ω_c = 3-dB frequency
$\quad\;\; \omega_1$ = frequency at which the magnitude response first falls below A_1

(*Note*: The value of A_1 is assumed to be in decibels. The value will be negative, thus canceling the minus sign in the numerator exponent.)

3.4   Impulse Response of Butterworth Filters

To obtain the impulse response for an nth-order Butterworth filter, we need to take the inverse Laplace transform of the transfer function. Application of the Heaviside expansion to Eq. (3.1) produces

$$h(t) = \mathcal{L}^{-1}[H(s)] = \sum_{r=1}^{n} K_r e^{s_r t} \tag{3.4}$$

where $K_r = \dfrac{(s - s_r)}{(s - s_1)(s - s_2) \cdots (s - s_n)} \bigg|_{s = s_r}$

The values of both K_r and s_r are, in general, complex, but for the lowpass Butterworth case all the complex pole values occur in complex conjugate pairs. When the order n is even, this will allow Eq. (3.4) to be put in the form

$$h(t) = \sum_{r=1}^{n/2} [2 \operatorname{Re}(K_r) e^{\sigma_r t} \cos(\omega_r t) - 2 \operatorname{Im}(K_r) e^{\sigma_r t} \sin(\omega_r t)] \tag{3.5}$$

where $s_r = \sigma_r + j\omega_r$ and the roots s_r are numbered such that for $r = 1, 2, \ldots,$ $n/2$ the s_r lie in the same quadrant of the s plane. [This last restriction prevents two members of the same complex conjugate pair from being used independently in evaluation of (3.5).] When the order n is odd, Eq. (3.4) can be put into the form

$$h(t) = K e^{-t} + \sum_{r=1}^{(n-1)/2} [2 \operatorname{Re}(K_r) e^{\sigma_r t} \cos(\omega_r t) - 2 \operatorname{Im}(K_r) e^{\sigma_r t} \sin(\omega_r t)] \tag{3.6}$$

where no two of the roots s_r, $r = 1, 2, \ldots, (n-1)/2$ form a complex conjugate pair. [Equations (3.5) and (3.6) form the basis for the C routine **butterworthImpulseResponse( )** provided in Listing 3.2.] This routine was used to generate the impulse responses for the lowpass Butterworth filters shown in Figs. 3.8 and 3.9. These responses are normalized for lowpass filters having a cutoff frequency equal to 1 rad/s. To denormalize the response, divide the time axis by the desired cutoff frequency $\omega_c = 2\pi f_c$ and multiply the time axis by the same factor.

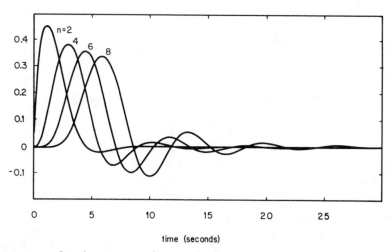

time (seconds)

Figure 3.8 Impulse response of even-order Butterworth filters.

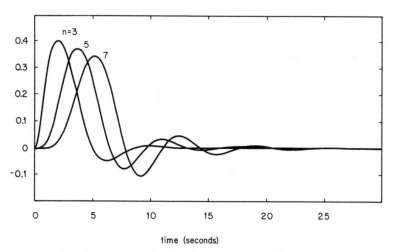

time (seconds)

Figure 3.9 Impulse response of odd-order Butterworth filters.

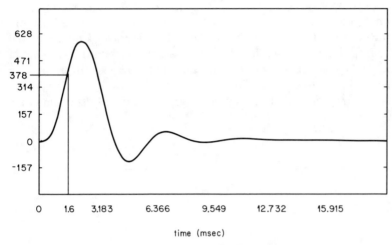

Figure 3.10 Denormalized impulse response for Example 3.3.

Example 3.3 Determine the instantaneous amplitude of the output 1.6 ms after a unit impulse is applied to the input of a fifth-order Butterworth LPF having $f_c = 250$ Hz.

solution The $n = 5$ response of Fig. 3.9 is denormalized as shown in Fig. 3.10. This plot shows that the response amplitude at $t = 1.6$ ms is approximately 378.

3.5 Step Response of Butterworth Filters

The step response can be obtained by integrating the impulse response. Step responses for lowpass Butterworth filters are shown in Figs. 3.11 and 3.12.

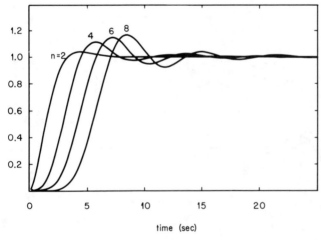

Figure 3.11 Step response of even-order lowpass Butterworth filters.

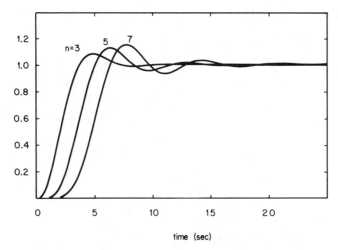

Figure 3.12   Step response of odd-order lowpass Butterworth filters.

These responses are normalized for lowpass filters having a cutoff frequency equal to 1 rad/s. To denormalize the response, divide the time axis by the desired cutoff frequency $\omega_c = 2\pi f_c$.

Example 3.4   Determine how long it will take for the step response of a third-order Butterworth LPF ($f_c = 4$ kHz) to first reach 100 percent of its final value.

solution   By setting $\omega_c = 2\pi f_c = 8000\pi = 25{,}132.7$, the $n = 3$ response of Fig. 3.12 is denormalized to obtain the response shown in Fig. 3.13. This plot indicates that the step response first reaches a value of 1 in approximately 150 µs.

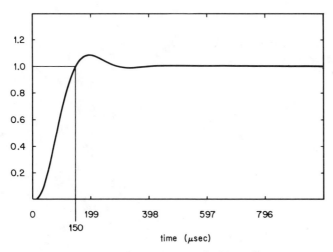

Figure 3.13   Denormalized step response for Example 3.4.

Listing 3.1   butterworthFreqResponse( )

```
/**********************************/
/*                              */
/*    Listing 3.1               */
/*                              */
/*    butterworthFreqResponse() */
/*                              */
/**********************************/
#include <math.h>
#include <stdio.h>
#include "globDefs.h"
#include "protos.h"

void butterworthFreqResponse( int order,
                              real frequency,
                              real *magnitude,
                              real *phase)
{
struct complex pole, s, numer, denom, transferFunction;
real x;
int k;
numer = cmplx(1.0,0.0);
denom = cmplx(1.0,0.0);

s = cmplx(0.0, frequency);
for( k=1; k<=order; k++)
    {
    x = PI * ((double)(order + (2*k)-1)) / (double)(2*order);
    pole = cmplx( cos(x), sin(x));
    denom = cMult(denom, cSub(s,pole));
    }
transferFunction = cDiv(numer, denom);
*magnitude = 20.0 * log10(cAbs(transferFunction));
*phase = 180.0 * arg(transferFunction) / PI;
return;
}
```

Listing 3.2   butterworthImpulseResponse( )

```
/****************************************************/
/*                                                  */
/*    Listing 3.2                                   */
/*                                                  */
/*    butterworthImpulseResponse()                  */
/*                                                  */
/****************************************************/
#include <math.h>
#include <stdio.h>
#include "globDefs.h"
#include "protos.h"


void butterworthImpulseResponse(   int order,
                                   real delta_t,
                                   int npts,
                                   real yval[])
{
real L, M, x, R, I, LT, MT, cosPart, sinPart, h_of_t;
real K, sigma, omega, t;
int ix, r, ii, iii;
real ymax, ymin;

for( ix=0; ix <= npts; ix++)
    {
    printf("%d/n",ix);
    h_of_t = 0.0;
    t = delta_t * ix;
    for( r=1; r <= (order>>1); r++)
        {
        x = PI * (double)(order + (2*r)-1) / (double)(2*order);
        sigma = cos(x);
        omega = sin(x);


/*  Compute Lr and Mr     */

L = 1.0;
M = 0.0;
for( ii=1; ii<=order; ii++)
    {
    if( ii == r ) continue;
    x = PI * (double)(order + (2*ii)-1) / (double)(2*order);
    R = sigma - cos(x);
    I = omega - sin(x);
```

```
        LT = L*R - M*I;
        MT = L*I + R*M;
        L = LT;
        M = MT;
        }
    L = LT / (LT*LT + MT*MT);
    M = -MT /(LT*LT + MT*MT);
    cosPart = 2.0 * L * exp(sigma*t) * cos(omega*t);
    sinPart = 2.0 * M * exp(sigma*t) * sin(omega*t);

    h_of_t = h_of_t + cosPart - sinPart;
    }
if( (order%2) == 0)
    {
    yval[ix] = h_of_t;
    if( (real) h_of_t > ymax) ymax = h_of_t;
    if( (real) h_of_t < ymin) ymin = h_of_t;
    continue;
    }
/* compute the real exponential component for odd-order responses */

    K = 1.0;
    L = 1.0;
    M = 0.0;
    r = (order+1)/2;
    x = PI * (double)(order + (2*r)-1) / (double)(2*order);
    sigma = cos(x);
    omega = sin(x);
    for( iii=1; iii<=order; iii++)
        {
        if( iii == r) continue;
        x = PI * (double)(order + (2*iii)-1) / (double)(2*order);
        R = sigma - cos(x);
        I = omega - sin(x);

        LT = L*R - M*I;
        MT = L*I + R*M;
        L = LT;
        M = MT;
        }
    K = LT / (LT*LT + MT*MT);
    h_of_t = h_of_t + K * exp(-t);
    yval[ix] = h_of_t;
    if( (real) h_of_t > ymax) ymax = h_of_t;
    if( (real) h_of_t < ymin) ymin = h_of_t;
    }
return;
```

Chebyshev Filters

Chebyshev filters are designed to have an amplitude response characteristic that has a relatively sharp transition from the pass band to the stop band. This sharpness is accomplished at the expense of ripples that are introduced into the response. Specifically, Chebyshev filters are obtained as an equiripple approximation to the pass band of an ideal lowpass filter. This results in a filter characteristic for which

$$|H(j\omega)|^2 = \frac{1}{1 + \epsilon^2 T_n^2(\omega)} \tag{4.1}$$

where $\quad \epsilon^2 = 10^{r/10} - 1$
$\qquad T_n(\omega) = $ Chebyshev polynomial of order n
$\qquad r = $ passband ripple, dB

Chebyshev polynomials are listed in Table 4.1.

TABLE 4.1 Chebyshev Polynomials

n	$T_n(\omega)$
0	1
1	ω
2	$2\omega^2 - 1$
3	$4\omega^3 - 3\omega$
4	$8\omega^4 - 8\omega^2 + 1$
5	$16\omega^5 - 20\omega^3 + 5\omega$
6	$32\omega^6 - 48\omega^4 + 18\omega^2 - 1$
7	$64\omega^7 - 112\omega^5 + 56\omega^3 - 7\omega$
8	$128\omega^8 - 256\omega^6 + 160\omega^4 - 32\omega^2 + 1$
9	$256\omega^9 - 576\omega^7 + 432\omega^5 - 120\omega^3 + 9\omega$
10	$512\omega^{10} - 1280\omega^8 + 1120\omega^6 - 400\omega^4 + 50\omega^2 + 1$

4.1 Transfer Function

The general shape of the Chebyshev magnitude response will be as shown in Fig. 4.1. This response can be normalized as in Fig. 4.2 so that the ripple bandwidth ω_r is equal to 1, or the response can be normalized as in Fig. 4.3 so that the 3-dB frequency ω_0 is equal to 1. Normalization based on the ripple bandwidth involves simpler calculations, but normalization based on the 3-dB point makes it easier to compare Chebyshev responses to those of other filter types.

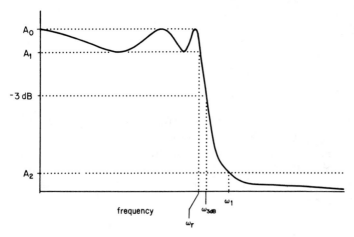

Figure 4.1 Magnitude response of a typical lowpass Chebyshev filter.

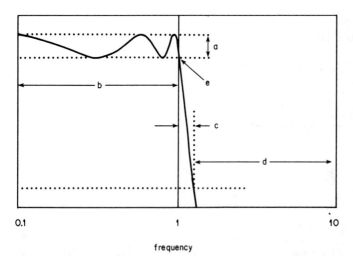

Figure 4.2 Chebyshev response normalized to have pass-band end at $\omega = 1$ rad/s. Features are: (*a*) ripple limits, (*b*) pass band, (*c*) transition band, (*d*) stop band, and (*e*) intersection of response and lower ripple limit at $\omega = 1$.

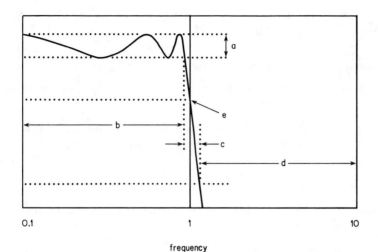

0.1   1   10

frequency

Figure 4.3 Chebyshev response normalized to have 3-dB point at $\hat{\omega} = 1$ rad/s. Features are: (*a*) ripple limits, (*b*) pass band, (*c*) transition band, (*d*) stop band, and (*e*) response that is 3 dB down at $\omega = 1$.

The general expression for the transfer function of an nth-order Chebyshev lowpass filter is given by

$$H(s) = \frac{H_0}{\prod_{i=1}^{n}(s - s_i)} = \frac{H_0}{(s - s_1)(s - s_2) \cdots (s - s_n)} \tag{4.2}$$

where $H_0 = \begin{cases} \displaystyle\prod_{i=1}^{n}(-s_i) & n \text{ odd} \\[2mm] \displaystyle 10^{r/20}\prod_{i=1}^{n}(-s_i) & n \text{ even} \end{cases}$ (4.3)

$$s_i = \sigma_i + j\omega_i \tag{4.4}$$

$$\sigma_i = \left[\frac{(1/\gamma) - \gamma}{2}\right] \sin \frac{(2i-1)\pi}{2n} \tag{4.5}$$

$$\omega_i = \left[\frac{(1/\gamma) + \gamma}{2}\right] \cos \frac{(2i-1)\pi}{2n} \tag{4.6}$$

$$\gamma = \left(\frac{1 + \sqrt{1 + \epsilon^2}}{\epsilon}\right)^{1/n} \tag{4.7}$$

$$\epsilon = \sqrt{10^{r/10} - 1} \tag{4.8}$$

The pole formulas are somewhat more complicated than for the Butterworth filter examined in Chap. 3, and several parameters—ϵ, γ, and r—must be determined before the pole values can be calculated. Also, all the poles are involved in the calculation of the numerator H_0.

Algorithm 4.1 Determining poles of a Chebyshev filter

This algorithm computes the poles of an nth-order Chebyshev lowpass filter normalized for a ripple bandwidth of 1 Hz.

Step 1. Determine the maximum amount (in decibels) of ripple that can be permitted in the pass-band magnitude response. Set r equal to or less than this value.

Step 2. Use Eq. (4.8) to compute ϵ.

Step 3. Select an order n for the filter that will ensure adequate performance.

Step 4. Use Eq. (4.7) to compute γ.

Step 5. For $i = 1, 2, \ldots, n$; use Eqs. (4.5) and (4.6) to compute the real part σ_i and imaginary part ω_i of each pole.

Step 6. Use Eq. (4.3) to compute H_0.

Step 7. Substitute the values of H_0 and s_1 through s_n into Eq. (4.2).

Example 4.1 Use Algorithm 4.1 to determine the transfer-function numerator and poles (normalized for ripple bandwidth equal to 1) for a third-order Chebyshev filter with 0.5-dB pass-band ripple.

solution Algorithm 5.1 produces the following results:

$$\epsilon = 0.349311 \qquad \gamma = 1.806477 \qquad s_1 = -0.313228 + 1.021928j$$

$$s_2 = -0.626457 \qquad s_3 = -0.313228 - 1.021928j \qquad H_0 = 0.715695$$

The form of Eq. (4.2) shows that an nth-order Chebyshev filter will always have n poles and no finite zeros. The poles will all lie on the left half of an ellipse in the s plane. The major axis of the ellipse lies on the $j\omega$ axis, and the minor axis lies on the σ axis. The dimensions of the ellipse and the locations of the poles will depend upon the amount of ripple permitted in the pass band. Values of pass-band ripple typically range from 0.1 to 1 dB. The smaller the pass-band ripple, the wider the transition band will be. In fact, for 0-dB ripple, the Chebyshev filter and Butterworth filter have exactly the same transfer-function and response characteristics. Pole locations for third-order Chebyshev filters having different ripple limits are compared in Fig. 4.4. Pole values for ripple limits of 0.1, 0.5, and 1 dB are listed in Tables 4.2, 4.3, and 4.4 for orders 2 through 8.

All the transfer functions and pole values presented so far are for filters normalized to have a ripple bandwidth of 1. Algorithm 4.2 can be used to renormalize the transfer function to have a 3-dB frequency of 1.

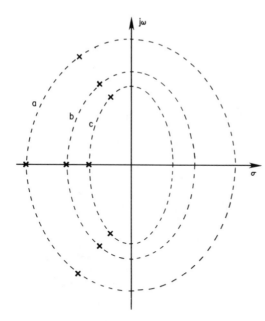

Figure 4.4 Comparison of pole locations for third-order low-pass Chebyshev filters with different amounts of pass-band ripple: (a) 0.01 dB, (b) 0.1 dB, and (c) 0.5 dB.

TABLE 4.2 Pole Values for Lowpass Chebyshev Filters with 0.1-dB Pass-Band Ripple

n	Pole values
2	$-1.186178 \pm 1.380948j$
3	-0.969406
	$-0.484703 \pm 1.206155j$
4	$-0.637730 \pm 0.465000j$
	$-0.264156 \pm 1.122610j$
5	-0.538914
	$-0.435991 \pm 0.667707j$
	$-0.166534 \pm 1.080372j$
6	$-0.428041 \pm 0.283093j$
	$-0.313348 \pm 0.773426j$
	$-0.114693 \pm 1.056519j$
7	-0.376778
	$-0.339465 \pm 0.463659j$
	$-0.234917 \pm 0.835485j$
	$-0.083841 \pm 1.041833j$
8	$-0.321650 \pm 0.205314j$
	$-0.272682 \pm 0.584684j$
	$-0.182200 \pm 0.875041j$
	$-0.063980 \pm 1.032181j$

TABLE 4.3 Pole Values for Lowpass Chebyshev Filters with 0.5-dB Pass-Band Ripple

n	Pole values
2	$-0.712812 \pm 1.00402j$
3	-0.626457
	$-0.313228 \pm 1.021928j$
4	$-0.423340 \pm 0.420946j$
	$-0.175353 \pm 1.016253j$
5	-0.362320
	$-0.293123 \pm 0.625177j$
	$-0.111963 \pm 1.011557j$
6	$-0.289794 \pm 0.270216j$
	$-0.212144 \pm 0.738245j$
	$-0.077650 \pm 1.008461j$
7	-0.256170
	$-0.230801 \pm 0.447894j$
	$-0.159719 \pm 0.807077j$
	$-0.057003 \pm 1.006409j$
8	$-0.219293 \pm 0.199907j$
	$-0.185908 \pm 0.569288j$
	$-0.124219 \pm 0.852000j$
	$-0.043620 \pm 1.005002j$

TABLE 4.4 Pole Values for Lowpass
Chebyshev Filters with 1.0-dB
Pass-Band Ripple

n	Pole values
2	$-0.548867 \pm 0.895129j$
3	-0.494171
	$-0.247085 \pm 0.965999j$
4	$-0.336870 \pm 0.407329j$
	$-0.139536 \pm 0.983379j$
5	-0.289493
	$-0.234205 \pm 0.611920j$
	$-0.089458 \pm 0.990107j$
6	$-0.232063 \pm 0.266184j$
	$-0.169882 \pm 0.727227j$
	$-0.062181 \pm 0.993411j$
7	-0.205414
	$-0.185072 \pm 0.442943j$
	$-0.128074 \pm 0.798156j$
	$-0.045709 \pm 0.995284j$
8	$-0.175998 \pm 0.198206j$
	$-0.149204 \pm 0.564444j$
	$-0.099695 \pm 0.844751j$
	$-0.035008 \pm 0.996451j$

**Algorithm 4.2   Renormalizing Chebyshev LPF
transfer functions**

This algorithm assumes that ϵ, H_0, and the pole values s_i have been obtained
for the transfer function having a ripple bandwidth of 1.

Step 1. Compute A using

$$A = \frac{\cosh^{-1}[(1/\epsilon)]}{n} = \frac{1}{n} \log\left(\frac{1 + \sqrt{1 - \epsilon^2}}{\epsilon}\right)$$

Step 2. Using the value of A obtained in step 1, compute R as

$$R = \cosh A = \frac{e^A + e^{-A}}{2}$$

(Table 4.5 lists R factors for various orders and ripple limits. If the required
combination can be found in this table, steps 1 and 2 can be skipped.)

Step 3. Use R to compute $H_{3\,\mathrm{dB}}(s)$ as

$$H_{3\,\mathrm{dB}}(s) = \frac{H_0/R^n}{\Pi_{i=1}^{n}\,[s - (s_i/R)]}$$

TABLE 4.5   Factors for Renormalizing Chebyshev Transfer Functions

Ripple	Order						
	2	3	4	5	6	7	8
0.1	1.94322	1.38899	1.21310	1.13472	1.09293	1.06800	1.05193
0.2	1.67427	1.28346	1.15635	1.09915	1.06852	1.05019	1.03835
0.3	1.53936	1.22906	1.12680	1.08055	1.05571	1.04083	1.03121
0.4	1.45249	1.19348	1.10736	1.06828	1.04725	1.03464	1.02649
0.5	1.38974	1.16749	1.09310	1.05926	1.04103	1.03009	1.02301
0.6	1.34127	1.14724	1.08196	1.05220	1.03616	1.02652	1.02028
0.7	1.30214	1.13078	1.07288	1.04644	1.03218	1.02361	1.01806
0.8	1.26955	1.11699	1.06526	1.04160	1.02883	1.02116	1.01618
0.9	1.24176	1.10517	1.05872	1.03745	1.02596	1.01905	1.01457
1.0	1.21763	1.09487	1.05300	1.03381	1.02344	1.01721	1.01316
1.1	1.19637	1.08576	1.04794	1.03060	1.02121	1.01557	1.01191
1.2	1.17741	1.07761	1.04341	1.02771	1.01922	1.01411	1.01079
1.3	1.16035	1.07025	1.03931	1.02510	1.01741	1.01278	1.00978
1.4	1.14486	1.06355	1.03558	1.02272	1.01576	1.01157	1.00886
1.5	1.13069	1.05740	1.03216	1.02054	1.01425	1.01046	1.00801

4.2   Frequency Response

Figures 4.5 through 4.8 show the magnitude and phase responses for Chebyshev filters with pass-band ripple limits of 0.5 dB. For comparison purposes, Figs. 4.9 and 4.10 show Chebyshev pass-band responses for ripple limits of 0.1 and 1.0 dB. These plots are normalized for a cutoff frequency of 1 Hz. To

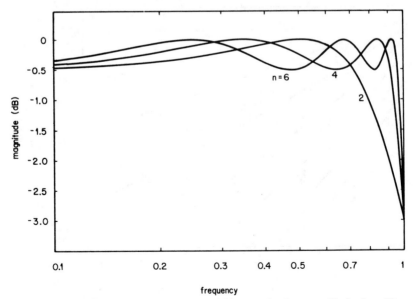

Figure 4.5   Pass-band magnitude response of even-order lowpass Chebyshev filters with 0.5-dB ripple.

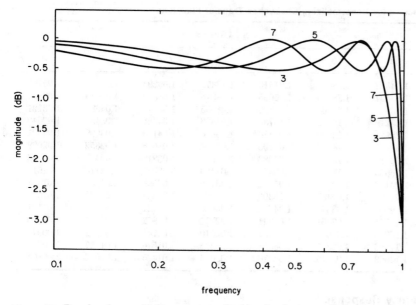

Figure 4.6 Pass-band magnitude response of odd-order lowpass Chebyshev filters with 0.5-dB ripple.

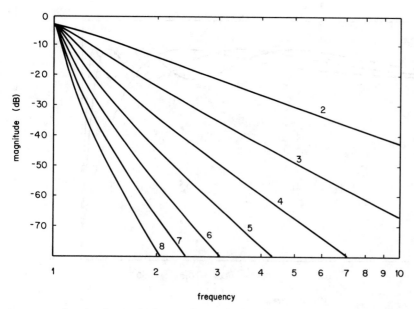

Figure 4.7 Stop-band magnitude response of lowpass Chebyshev filters with 0.5-dB ripple.

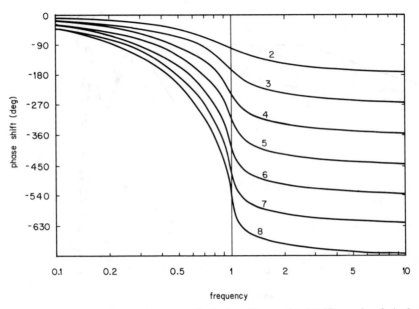

Figure 4.8 Phase response of lowpass Chebyshev filters with 0.5-dB pass-band ripple.

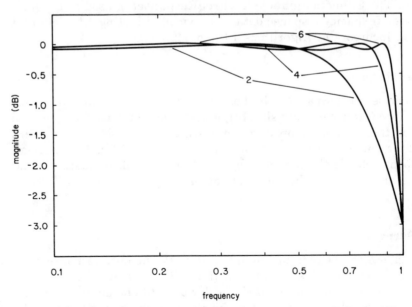

Figure 4.9 Pass-band magnitude response of even-order lowpass Chebyshev filters with 0.1-dB ripple.

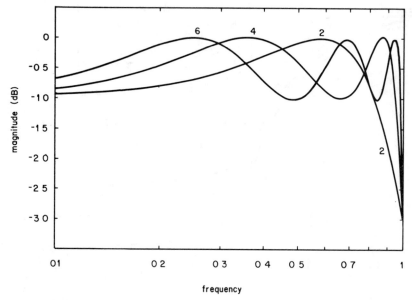

Figure 4.10 Pass-band magnitude response of even-order lowpass Chebyshev filters with 1.0-dB ripple.

denormalize them, simply multiply the frequency axis by the desired cutoff frequency f_c. The C function **chebyshevFreqResponse( )**, used to generate the Chebyshev frequency response data, is provided in Listing 4.1. Note that this function incorporates Algorithms 4.1 and 4.2.

4.3   Impulse Response

Impulse responses for lowpass Chebyshev filters with 0.5-dB ripple are shown in Fig. 4.11. The C routine **chebyshevImpulseResponse( )**, used to generate the data for these plots, is provided in Listing 4.2. These responses are normalized for lowpass filters having a 3-dB frequency of 1 Hz. To denormalize the response, divide the time axis by the desired cutoff frequency f_c and multiply the amplitude axis by the same factor.

4.4   Step Response

The step response can be obtained by integrating the impulse response. Step responses for lowpass Chebyshev filters with 0.5-dB ripple are shown in Fig. 4.12. These responses are normalized for lowpass filters having a cutoff frequency equal to 1 Hz. To denormalize the response, divide the time axis by the desired cutoff frequency f_c.

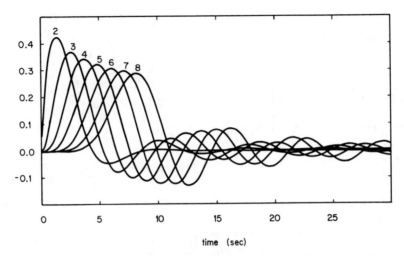

Figure 4.11 Impulse response of lowpass Chebyshev filters with 0.5-dB pass-band ripple.

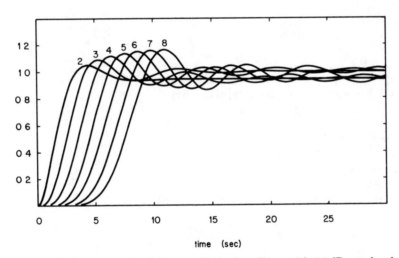

Figure 4.12 Step response of lowpass Chebyshev filters with 0.5-dB pass-band ripple.

Listing 4.1   chebyshevFreqResponse( )

```
/***********************************/
/*                                 */
/*    Listing 4.1                  */
/*                                 */
/*    chebyshevFreqResponse()      */
/*                                 */
/***********************************/
#include <math.h>
#define PI (double) 3.141592653589


void chebyshevFreqResponse(    int order,
                               float ripple,
                               char normalizationType,
                               float frequency,
                               float *magnitude,
                               float *phase)
{
double A, gamma, epsilon, work;
double rp, ip, x, i, r, rpt, ipt;
double normalizedFrequency, hSubZero;
int k, ix;

epsilon = sqrt( -1.0 + pow( (double)10.0, (double)(ripple/10.0) ));
gamma = pow( (( 1.0 + sqrt( 1.0 + epsilon*epsilon))/epsilon),
                 (double)(1.0/(float) order) );

if( normalizationType == '3' )
    {
    work = 1.0/epsilon;
    A = ( log( work + sqrt( work*work - 1.0) ) ) / order;
    normalizedFrequency = frequency * ( exp(A) + exp(-A))/2.0;
    }
else
    {
    normalizedFrequency = frequency;
    }

rp = 1.0;
ip = 0.0;

for( k=1; k<=order; k++)
    {
    x = (2*k-1) * PI / (2.0*order);
    i = 0.5 * (gamma + 1.0/gamma) * cos(x);
    r = -0.5 * (gamma - 1.0/gamma) * sin(x);
```

```
    rpt = ip * i - rp * r;
    ipt = -rp * i - r * ip;
    ip = ipt;
    rp = rpt;
    }
hSubZero = sqrt( ip*ip + rp*rp);
if( order%2 == 0 )
    {
    hSubZero = hSubZero / sqrt(1.0 + epsilon*epsilon);
    }


rp = 1.0;
ip = 0.0;
for( k=1; k<=order; k++)
    {
    x = (2*k-1)*PI/(2.0*order);
    i = 0.5 * (gamma + 1.0/gamma) * cos(x);
    r = -0.5 * (gamma - 1.0/gamma) * sin(x);
    rpt = ip*(i-normalizedFrequency) - rp*r;
    ipt = rp*(normalizedFrequency-i) - r*ip;
    ip=ipt;
    rp=rpt;
    }
*magnitude = 20.0 * log10(hSubZero/sqrt(ip*ip+rp*rp));
*phase = 180.0 * atan2( ip, rp) /PI;
return;
}
```

Listing 4.2   chebyshevImpulseResponse( )

```
/**************************************************/
/*                                                */
/*    Listing 4.2                                 */
/*                                                */
/*    chebyshevImpulseResponse()                  */
/*                                                */
/**************************************************/
#include <math.h>
#define PI (double) 3.141592653589


void chebyshevImpulseResponse(      int order,
                                    float ripple,
                                    char normalizationType,
                                    float delta_t,
                                    int npts,
                                    float yval[])
```

```
{
double m, p;
double A, gamma, epsilon, work, normFactor;
double rp, ip, x, i, r, rpt, ipt, ss;
double hSubZero, h_of_t, t, sigma, omega;
double K, L, M, LT, MT, I, R, cosPart, sinPart;
int k, ix, ii, iii, rrr;

epsilon = sqrt( -1.0 + pow( (double)10.0, (double)(ripple/10.0) ));

if( normalizationType == '3')
    {
    work = 1.0/epsilon;
    A = ( log( work + sqrt( work*work - 1.0) ) ) / order;
    normFactor = ( exp(A) + exp(-A))/2.0;
    }
else
    {
    normFactor = 1.0;
    }




gamma = pow( (( 1.0 + sqrt( 1.0 + epsilon*epsilon))/epsilon),
                (double)(1.0/(float) order) );

/*-----------------------------*/
/*   compute H_zero            */
rp = 1.0;
ip = 0.0;

for( k=1; k<=order; k++)
    {
    x = (2*k-1) * PI / (float)(2*order);
    i = 0.5 * (gamma + 1.0/gamma) * cos(x)/normFactor;
    r = -0.5 * (gamma - 1.0/gamma) * sin(x)/normFactor;
    rpt = ip * i - rp * r;
    ipt = -rp * i - r * ip;
    ip = ipt;
    rp = rpt;
    }
hSubZero = sqrt( ip*ip + rp*rp);
if( order%2 == 0 )
    {
    hSubZero = hSubZero / sqrt(1.0 + epsilon*epsilon);
    }
printf("hSubZero = %f\n",hSubZero);
/*-----------------------------------*/
```

```
for( ix=0; ix<npts; ix++)
    {
    printf("%d\n",ix);
    h_of_t = 0.0;
    t = delta_t * ix;
    for( rrr=1; rrr <= (order >> 1); rrr++)
        {
        x = (2*rrr-1)*PI/(2.0*order);
        sigma = -0.5 * (gamma - 1.0/gamma) * sin(x)/normFactor;
        omega = 0.5 * (gamma + 1.0/gamma) * cos(x)/normFactor;



    /*  compute Lr and Mr   */

    L = 1;
    M = 0;

    for(ii=1; ii<=order; ii++)
        {
        if( ii == rrr) continue;
        x = (2*ii-1) * PI /(float)(2*order);
        R = sigma -(-0.5*(gamma -1.0/gamma))*sin(x) / normFactor;
        I = omega -(0.5*(gamma +1.0/gamma))*cos(x) / normFactor;

        LT = L * R - M * I;
        MT = L * I + R * M;
        L = LT;
        M = MT;
        }
    L = LT / (LT * LT + MT * MT);
    M = -MT / (LT * LT + MT * MT);

    cosPart = 2.0 * L * exp(sigma*t) * cos(omega*t);
    sinPart = 2.0 * M * exp(sigma*t) * sin(omega*t);

    h_of_t = h_of_t + cosPart - sinPart;
    }
if( (order%2) == 0 )
    {
    yval[ix] = h_of_t * hSubZero;
    }
else
    {
    /*  compute the real exponential component    */
    /*  present in odd-order responses            */
```

```
K = 1;
L = 1;
M = 0;
rrr = (order+1) >> 1;

x = (2*rrr-1) * PI / (float)(2*order);


        sigma = -0.5 * (gamma - 1.0/gamma) * sin(x) / normFactor;
        omega = 0.5 * (gamma + 1.0/gamma) * cos(x) / normFactor;

        for( iii=1; iii<= order; iii++)
            {
            if(iii == rrr) continue;
            x = (2*iii-1) * PI / (float)(2*order);
            R = sigma -(-0.5*(gamma -1.0/gamma))*sin(x) / normFactor;
            I = omega -(0.5*(gamma +1.0/gamma))*cos(x) / normFactor;

            LT = L * R - M * I;
            MT = L * I + R * M;
            L = LT;
            M = MT;
            }
        K = LT / (LT*LT + MT*MT);
        h_of_t = h_of_t + K * exp(sigma*t);
        yval[ix] = h_of_t * hSubZero;
        }
    }
return;
}
```

Elliptical Filters

By allowing ripples in the pass band, Chebyshev filters obtain better selectivity than Butterworth filters do. Elliptical filters improve upon the performance of Chebyshev filters by permitting ripples in *both* the pass band and stop band. The response of an elliptical filter satisfies

$$|H(j\omega)|^2 = \frac{1}{1 + \epsilon^2 R_n^2(\omega, L)}$$

where $R_n(\omega, L)$ is an nth-order *Chebyshev rational function* with ripple parameter L. Elliptical filters are sometimes called *Cauer filters*.

5.1 Parameter Specification

As shown in Chap. 3, determination of the (amplitude-normalized) transfer function for a Butterworth lowpass filter requires specification of just two parameters—cutoff frequency ω_c and filter order n. Determination of the transfer function for a Chebyshev filter requires specification of these two parameters plus a third—pass-band ripple (or stop-band ripple for inverse Chebyshev). Determination of the transfer function for an elliptical filter requires specification of the filter order n plus the following four parameters, which are depicted in Fig. 5.1:

$$A_p = \text{maximum pass-band loss, dB}$$

$$A_s = \text{minimum stop-band loss, dB}$$

$$\omega_p = \text{pass-band cutoff frequency}$$

$$\omega_s = \text{stop-band cutoff frequency}$$

The design procedures presented in this chapter assume that the maximum pass-band amplitude is unity. Therefore, A_p is the size of the pass-band

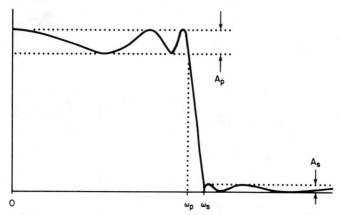

Figure 5.1 Frequency response showing parameters used to specify an elliptical filter.

ripples, and A_s is the size of the stop-band ripples. Any four of the five filter parameters can be specified independently, with the fifth then being fixed by the nature of the elliptical filter's response. The usual design strategy involves specifying A_p, A_s, ω_p, and ω_s based upon requirements of the intended application. Algorithm 5.1, as follows, can then be used to compute the minimum value of n for which an elliptical filter can yield the desired performance. Since n must be an integer, not all combinations of A_p, A_s, ω_p, and ω_s can be realized exactly. The design procedure presented in this chapter can yield a filter that meets the specified A_p, A_s, and ω_p and that meets *or exceeds* the specification on A_s.

Algorithm 5.1   Determining the required order for elliptical filters

Step 1.   Based upon requirements of the intended application, determine the maximum stop-band loss A_p and minimum stop-band loss A_s in decibels.

Step 2.   Based on requirements of the intended application, determine the pass-band cutoff frequency ω_p and stop-band cutoff frequency ω_s.

Step 3.   Using ω_p and ω_s, compute *selectivity factor* k as $k = \omega_p/\omega_s$.

Step 4.   Using the selectivity factor computed in step 3, compute the *modular constant* q using

$$q = u + 2u^5 + 15u^9 + 150u^{13} \qquad (5.1)$$

where $u = \dfrac{1 - \sqrt[4]{1 - k^2}}{2(1 + \sqrt[4]{1 - k^2})}$ \qquad (5.2)

Step 5. Using the values of A_p and A_s, determined in step 1, compute the *discrimination factor* D as

$$D = \frac{10^{A_s/10} - 1}{10^{A_p/10} - 1} \tag{5.3}$$

Step 6. Using the value of D from step 5 and the value of q from step 4, compute the minimum required order n as

$$n = \left\lceil \frac{\log 16D}{\log(1/q)} \right\rceil \tag{5.4}$$

where $\lceil x \rceil$ denotes the smallest integer equal to or greater than x.

The actual minimum stop-band loss provided by any given combination of A_p, ω_p, ω_s, and n is given by

$$A_s = 10 \log\left(1 + \frac{10^{A_p/10} - 1}{16q^n} \right) \tag{5.5}$$

where q is the modular constant given by Eq. (5.1).

Example 5.1 Use Algorithm 5.1 to determine the minimum order for an elliptical filter for which $A_p = 1$, $A_s \geq 50.0$, $\omega_p = 3000.0$, and $\omega_s = 3200.0$.

solution

$$k = \frac{3000}{3200} = 0.9375$$

$$u = 0.12897$$

$$q = 0.12904$$

$$D = \frac{10^5 - 1}{10^{0.01} - 1} = 4{,}293{,}093.82$$

$$n = \lceil 8.81267 \rceil = 9$$

A C function **cauerOrderEstim( )**, which implements Algorithm 5.1, is provided in Listing 5.1. This function also computes the actual minimum stop-band loss in accordance with Eq. (5.5).

5.2 Normalized-Transfer Function

The design of elliptical filters is greatly simplified by designing a frequency-normalized filter having the appropriate response characteristics, and then frequency-scaling this design to the desired operating frequency. The simplification comes about because of the particular type of normalizing that is performed. Instead of normalizing so that either a 3-dB bandwidth or the ripple bandwidth equals unity, an elliptical filter is normalized so that

$$\sqrt{\omega_{pN}\omega_{sN}} = 1 \tag{5.6}$$

where ω_{pN} and ω_{sN} are, respectively, the normalized pass-band cutoff frequency and the normalized stop-band cutoff frequency. If we let α represent the frequency-scaling factor such that

$$\omega_{pN} = \frac{\omega_p}{\alpha} \qquad \omega_{sN} = \frac{\omega_s}{\alpha} \tag{5.7}$$

then we can solve for the value of α by substituting (5.7) into (5.6) to obtain

$$\sqrt{\frac{\omega_p \omega_s}{\alpha^2}} = 1$$

$$\alpha = \sqrt{\omega_p \omega_s} \tag{5.8}$$

As it turns out, the only way that the frequencies ω_{pN} and ω_{sN} enter into the design procedure (given by Algorithm 5.2) is via the selectivity factor k that is given by

$$k = \frac{\omega_{pN}}{\omega_{sN}} = \frac{\omega_p / \alpha}{\omega_s / \alpha} = \frac{\omega_p}{\omega_s} \tag{5.9}$$

Since Eq. (5.9) indicates that k can be obtained directly from the desired ω_p and ω_s, we can design a *normalized* filter without having to determine the normalized frequencies ω_{pN} and ω_{sN}! However, once a normalized design is obtained, the frequency-scaling factor α as given by (5.8) *will* be needed to frequency-scale the design to the desired operating frequency.

Algorithm 5.2   Generating normalized-transfer functions for elliptical filters

Step 1.   Use Algorithm 5.1 or any other equivalent method to determine a viable combination of values for A_p, A_s, ω_p, ω_s, and n.

Step 2.   Using ω_p and ω_s, compute the *selectivity factor* k as $k = \omega_p / \omega_s$.

Step 3.   Using the selectivity factor computed in step 3, compute the *modular constant* q using

$$q = u + 2u^5 + 15u^9 + 150u^{13} \tag{5.10}$$

where $u = \dfrac{1 - \sqrt[4]{1 - k^2}}{2(1 + \sqrt[4]{1 - k^2})}$ \tag{5.11}

Step 4.   Using the values of A_p and n from step 1, compute V as

$$V = \frac{1}{2n} \ln\left(\frac{10^{A_p/20} + 1}{10^{A_p/20} - 1}\right) \tag{5.12}$$

Step 5. Using the value of q from step 3 and the value of V from step 4, compute p_0 as

$$p_0 = \left| \frac{q^{1/4} \sum\limits_{m=0}^{\infty} (-1)^m q^{m(m+1)} \sinh[(2m+1)V]}{0.5 + \sum\limits_{m=1}^{\infty} (-1)^m q^{m^2} \cosh 2mV} \right| \tag{5.13}$$

Step 6. Using the value of k from step 2 and the value of p_0 from step 5, compute W as

$$W = \left[\left(1 + \frac{p_0^2}{k} \right) (1 + kp_0^2) \right]^{1/2} \tag{5.14}$$

Step 7. Determine r, the number of quadratic sections in the filter, as $r = n/2$ for even n, and $r = (n-1)/2$ for odd n.

Step 8. For $i = 1, 2, \ldots, r$, compute X_i as

$$X_i = \frac{2q^{1/4} \sum\limits_{m=0}^{\infty} (-1)^m q^{m(m+1)} \sin[(2m+1)\mu\pi/n]}{1 + 2 \sum\limits_{m=1}^{\infty} (-1)^m q^{m^2} \cos(2m\mu\pi/n)} \tag{5.15}$$

where $\mu = \begin{cases} i & n \text{ odd} \\ i - \frac{1}{2} & n \text{ even} \end{cases}$

Step 9. For $i = 1, 2, \ldots, r$, compute Y_i as

$$Y_i \left[\left(1 - \frac{X_i^2}{k} \right) (1 - kX_i^2) \right]^{1/2} \tag{5.16}$$

Step 10. For $i = 1, 2, \ldots, r$, use the W, X_i, and Y_i from steps 6, 8, and 9; compute the coefficients a_i, b_i, and c_i as

$$a_i = \frac{1}{X_i^2} \tag{5.17}$$

$$b_i = \frac{2p_0 Y_i}{1 + p_0^2 X_i^2} \tag{5.18}$$

$$c_i = \frac{(p_0 Y_i)^2 + (X_i W)^2}{(1 + p_0^2 X_i^2)^2} \tag{5.19}$$

Step 11. Using a_i and c_i, compute H_0 as

$$H_0 = \begin{cases} p_0 \prod\limits_{i=1}^{r} \dfrac{c_i}{a_i} & n \text{ odd} \\[4ex] 10^{-A_p/20} \prod\limits_{i=1}^{r} \dfrac{c_i}{a_i} & n \text{ even} \end{cases} \tag{5.20}$$

Step 12. Finally, compute the normalized transfer function $H_N(s)$ as

$$H_N(s) = \frac{H_0}{d} \prod_{i=1}^{r} \frac{s^2 + a_i}{s^2 + b_i s + c_i} \qquad (5.21)$$

where $d = \begin{cases} s + p_0 & n \text{ odd} \\ 1 & n \text{ even} \end{cases}$

A C function **cauerCoeffs( )**, which implements steps 1 through 11 of Algorithm 5.2, is provided in Listing 5.2. Step 12 is implemented separately in the C function **cauerFreqResponse( )** shown in Listing 5.3, since Eq. (5.21) must be reevaluated for each value of frequency.

Example 5.2 Use Algorithm 5.2 to obtain the coefficients of the normalized-transfer function for the ninth-order elliptical filter having $A_p = 0.1$ dB, $\omega_p = 3000$ rad/s, and $\omega_s = 3200$ rad/s. Determine the actual minimum stop-band loss.

solution Using the formulas from Algorithm 5.2 plus Eq. (5.5), we obtain

$$q = 0.129041 \qquad V = 0.286525 \qquad p_0 = 0.470218$$

$$W = 1.221482 \qquad r = 4 \qquad A_s = 51.665651$$

The coefficients X_i, Y_i, a_i, b_i, and c_i obtained via steps 8 through 10 for $i = 1, 2, 3, 4$ are listed in Table 5.1. Using (5.20), we obtain $H_0 = 0.015317$. The normalized-frequency response of this filter is shown in Figs. 5.2, 5.3, and 5.4. (The phase response shown in Fig. 5.4 may seem a bit peculiar. At first glance, the discontinuities in the phase response

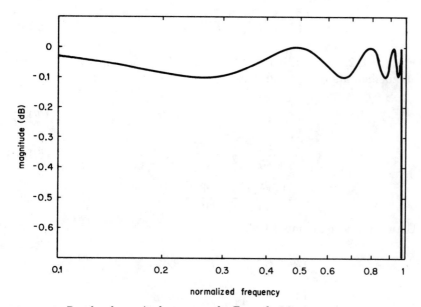

Figure 5.2 Pass-band magnitude response for Example 5.2.

TABLE 5.1 Coefficients for Example 5.2

i	X_i	Y_i	a_i	b_i	c_i
1	0.4894103	0.7598211	4.174973	0.6786235	0.4374598
2	0.7889940	0.3740371	1.606396	0.3091997	0.7415493
3	0.9196814	0.1422994	1.182293	0.1127396	0.8988261
4	0.9636668	0.0349416	1.076828	0.0272625	0.9538953

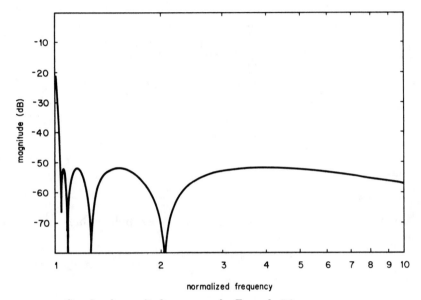

Figure 5.3 Stop-band magnitude response for Example 5.2.

might be taken for jumps of 2π caused by the $+\pi$ to $-\pi$ "wraparound" of the arctangent operation. However, this is not the case. The discontinuities in Fig. 5.4 are jumps of π that coincide with the nulls in the magnitude response.

5.3 Denormalized-Transfer Function

As noted in Sec. 2.9, if we have a response normalized for $\omega_{cN} = 1$, we can frequency-scale the transfer function to yield an identical response for $\omega_c = \alpha$ by multiplying each pole and each zero by α and dividing the overall transfer function by $\alpha^{(n_z - n_p)}$ where n_z is the number of zeros and n_p is the number of poles. An elliptical filter has a transfer function of the form given by (5.20). For odd n, there is a real pole at $s = p_0$ and r can conjugate pairs of poles that are roots of

$$s^2 + b_i s + c_i = 0 \qquad i = 1, 2, \dots, r$$

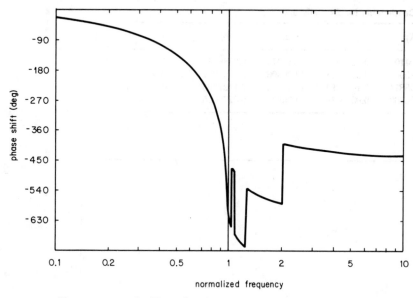

Figure 5.4 Phase response for Example 5.2.

Using the quadratic formula, the ith pair of complex pole values can be expressed as

$$p_i = \frac{-b_i \pm \sqrt{b_i^2 - 4c_i}}{2}$$

The zeros of the normalized-transfer function occur at $s = \pm j\sqrt{a_i}$, $i = 1, 2, \ldots, r$. For even n, the number of poles equals the number of zeros so $\alpha^{(n_z - n_p)} = 1$. For odd n, $n_z - n_p = -1$, so the transfer function must be divided by $1/\alpha$ or multiplied by α. If we multiply the poles and zeros by α and multiply the overall transfer function by 1 or α as appropriate, we obtain the frequency-scaled transfer function $H(s)$ as

$$H(s) = K \prod_{i=1}^{r} \frac{s^2 + \alpha^2 a_i}{s^2 + \alpha b_i s + \alpha^2 c_i} \tag{5.22}$$

where $K = \begin{cases} \dfrac{H_0 \alpha}{s + \alpha p_0} & n \text{ odd} \\ H_0 & n \text{ even} \end{cases}$

Comparison of Eqs. (5.21) and (5.22) indicates that the frequency rescaling consists of making the following substitutions in (5.21):

$$\alpha^2 a_i \text{ replaces } a_i$$

$$\alpha^2 c_j \text{ replaces } c_i$$

$$\alpha b_i \text{ replaces } b_i$$

$$H_0 \alpha \text{ replaces } H_0 \ (n \text{ odd})$$

$$\alpha p_0 \text{ replaces } p_0 \ (n \text{ odd})$$

A C function **cauerRescale( )**, which makes these substitutions, is given in Listing 5.4.

Listing 5.1   cauerOrderEstim( )

```
/***********************************/
/*                                 */
/*    Listing 5.1                  */
/*                                 */
/*    cauerOrderEstim()            */
/*                                 */
/***********************************/

void cauerOrderEstim( real omegaPass,
                      real omegaStop,
                      real maxPassLoss,
                      real minStopLoss,
                      int *order,
                      real *actualMinStopLoss)
{
real k, u, q, dd, kk, lambda, w, mu, om;
real sum, term, denom, numer, sigma, v;
int i, m, r;

k=omegaPass/omegaStop;                /* Alg. 5.1, step 3 */

kk=sqrt(sqrt(1.0 - k*k));      /* Eq (5.2) */
u=0.5*(1.0-kk)/(1.0+kk);

q = 150.0 * ipow(u,13);            /* Eq (5.1) */
q = q + 15.0 * ipow(u,9);
q = q + 2.0 * ipow(u,5);
q = q + u;

dd = pow(10.0, minStopLoss/10.0) - 1.0;       /* Eq (5.3) */
dd = dd/ (pow(10.0,maxPassLoss/10.0) - 1.0);

*order = ceil( log10(16.0*dd) / log10(1.0/q));   /* Eq (5.4) */

                                            /* Eq (5.5) */
numer = pow(10.0, (maxPassLoss/10.0))-1.0;
*actualMinStopLoss = 10.0 * log10(numer/(16*ipow(q,*order))+1.0);
return;
}
```

Listing 5.2   cauerCoeffs( )

```
/***********************************/
/*                                 */
/*    Listing 5.2                  */
/*                                 */
/*    cauerCoeffs()                */
/*                                 */
/***********************************/

void cauerCoeffs(real omegaPass,
                 real omegaStop,
                 real maxPassLoss,
                 int order,
                 real aa[],
                 real bb[],
                 real cc[],
                 int *numSecs,
                 real *hZero,
                 real *pZero)
{
real k, kk, u, q, vv, ww, mu, xx, yy;
real sum, term, denom, numer;
int i, m, r;

k=omegaPass/omegaStop;              /* Alg 5.2, step 2 */

kk=sqrt(sqrt(1.0 - k*k));    /* Eq (5.11) */
u=0.5*(1.0-kk)/(1.0+kk);

q = 150.0 * ipow(u,13);             /* Eq (5.10) */
q = q + 15.0 * ipow(u,9);
q = q + 2.0 * ipow(u,5);
q = q + u;

                                    /* Eq (5.12) */
numer = pow(10.0,maxPassLoss/20.0)+1.0;
vv = log( numer / (pow(10.0, maxPassLoss/20.0)-1))/(2.0*order);

sum = 0.0;                    /* Eq (5.13) */
for( m=0; m<5; m++) {
    term = ipow(-1.0,m);
    term = term * ipow(q, m*(m+1));
    term = term * sinh((2*m+1) * vv);
    fprintf(dumpFile,"for m=%d, term = %e\n",m,term);
    sum = sum + term;
    }
numer = 2.0 * sum * sqrt(sqrt(q));
```

```
sum = 0.0;
for( m=1; m<5; m++) {
    term = ipow(-1.0,m);
    term = term * ipow(q,m*m);
    term = term * cosh(2.0 * m * vv);
    sum = sum + term;
    }
denom = 1.0 + 2.0*sum;
*pZero = fabs(numer/denom);


ww = 1.0 + k * *pZero * *pZero;            /* Eq (5.14) */
ww = sqrt(ww * (1.0 + *pZero * *pZero/k));


r = (order-(order%2))/2;      /* Alg 5.2, step 7 */
*numSecs = r;


for(i=1; i<=r; i++) {      /* loop for Alg 5.2, steps 8, 9, 10 */
    if(order%2)
        {mu = i;}
    else
        {mu = i - 0.5;}
    sum = 0.0;                   /* Eq (5.15) numerator */
    for(m=0; m<5; m++) {
        term = ipow(-1.0,m);
        term = term * ipow(q, m*(m+1));
        term = term * sin( (2*m+1) * PI * mu / order);
        sum = sum + term;
        }
    numer = 2.0 * sum * sqrt(sqrt(q));

sum = 0.0;                    /* Eq (5.15) denominator */
for(m=1; m<5; m++) {
    term = ipow(-1.0,m);
    term = term * ipow(q,m*m);
    term = term * cos(2.0 * PI * m * mu / order);
    fprintf(dumpFile,"for m=%d, term = %e\n",m,term);
    sum = sum + term;
    }
denom = 1.0 + 2.0 * sum;
xx = numer/denom;


yy = 1.0 - k * xx*xx;                /* Eq (5.16) */
yy = sqrt(yy * (1.0-(xx*xx/k)));


aa[i] = 1.0/(xx*xx);                 /* Eq (5.17) */


denom = 1.0 + ipow(*pZero*xx, 2);    /* Eq (5.18) */
bb[i] = 2.0 * *pZero * yy/denom;
```

```
        denom = ipow(denom,2);                      /* Eq (5.19) */
        numer = ipow(*pZero*yy,2) + ipow(xx*ww,2);
        cc[i] = numer/denom;
    }

    term = 1.0;                              /* Eq (5.20) */
    for(i=1; i<=r; i++) {
        term = term * cc[i]/aa[i];
        }
    if(order%2)
        {term = term * *pZero;}
    else
        {term = term * pow(10.0, maxPassLoss/(-20.0));}
    *hZero = term;
    return;
    }
```

Listing 5.3   cauerFreqResponse( )

```
/***********************************/
/*                                 */
/*    Listing 5.3                  */
/*                                 */
/*    cauerFreqResponse()          */
/*                                 */
/***********************************/

void cauerFreqResponse(    int order,
                           real aa[],
                           real bb[],
                           real cc[],
                           real hZero,
                           real pZero,
                           real frequency,
                           real *magnitude,
                           real *phase)
{
double normalizedFrequency;
int r, k, ix, i;
struct complex s, cProd, cTermNumer, cTermDenom;

r = (order-(order%2))/2;
s = cmplx(0.0, frequency);

if(order%2) {
    cTermDenom = cAdd(s, cmplx(pZero, 0.0));
    cProd = cDiv(cmplx(1.0,0.0), cTermDenom);
    cProd = sMult(hZero, cProd);
    }
```

```
else {
    cProd = cmplx(hZero,0.0);
    }
for (i=1; i<=r; i++) {
    cTermNumer=cMult(s,s);
    cTermDenom=cAdd(cTermNumer,sMult(bb[i],s));
    cTermNumer.Re = cTermNumer.Re + aa[i];
    cTermDenom.Re = cTermDenom.Re + cc[i];
    cProd = cMult(cProd, cTermNumer);
    cProd = cDiv(cProd, cTermDenom);
    }
*magnitude = 20.0* log10(cAbs( cProd));
*phase = 180.0 * arg(cProd)/PI;
return;
}
```

Listing 5.4   cauerRescale( )

```
/**********************************/
/*                                */
/*   Listing 5.4                  */
/*                                */
/*   cauerRescale()               */
/*                                */
/**********************************/

void cauerRescale(    int order,
                      real aa[],
                      real bb[],
                      real cc[],
                      real *hZero,
                      real *pZero,
                      real alpha)
{
real alphaSqrd;
int r, i;

alphaSqrd = alpha*alpha;

if( order%2) {
    r = (order-1)/2;
    *hZero = *hZero * alpha;
    *pZero = *pZero * alpha;
    }
```

```
else {
    r = order/2;
    }
for(i=1; i<=r; i++) {
    aa[i] = aa[i] * alphaSqrd;
    cc[i] = cc[i] * alphaSqrd;
    bb[i] = bb[i] * alpha;
    }
}
```

Bessel Filters

Bessel filters are designed to have maximally flat group-delay characteristics. As a consequence, there is no ringing in the impulse and step responses.

6.1 Transfer Function

The general expression for the transfer function of an nth-order Bessel lowpass filter is given by

$$H(s) = \frac{b_0}{q_n(s)} \qquad (6.1)$$

where $q_n(s) = \sum_{k=1}^{n} b_k s^k$

$$b_k = \frac{(2n-k)!}{2^{n-k} k!(n-k)!}$$

The following recursion can be used to determine $q_n(s)$ from $q_{n-1}(s)$ and $q_{n-2}(s)$:

$$q_n = (2n-1)q_{n-1} + s^2 q_{n-2}$$

Table 6.1 lists $q_n(s)$ for $n = 2$ through $n = 8$. These values were generated by the C function **besselCoefficients( )** provided in Listing 6.1. This function is used by other Bessel filter routines presented later in this section.

Unlike the transfer function for Butterworth and Chebyshev filters, Eq. (6.1) does not provide an explicit expression for the poles of the Bessel filter. The numerator of (6.1) will be a polynomial in s, upon which numerical root-finding methods (such as Algorithm 2.1) must be used to determine the pole locations for $H(s)$. Table 6.2 lists approximate pole locations for $n = 2$ through $n = 8$.

TABLE 6.1 Denominator Polynomials for Transfer Functions of Bessel Filters Normalized to Have Unit Delay at $\omega = 0$

n	$q_n(s)$
2	$s^2 + 3s + 3$
3	$s^3 + 6s^2 + 15s + 15$
4	$s^4 + 10s^3 + 45s^2 + 105s + 105$
5	$s^5 + 15s^4 + 105s^3 + 420s^2 + 945s + 945$
6	$s^6 + 21s^5 + 210s^4 + 1260s^3 + 4725s^2 + 10{,}395s + 10{,}395$
7	$s^7 + 28s^6 + 378s^5 + 3150s^4 + 17{,}325s^3 + 62{,}370s^2 + 135{,}135s + 135{,}135$
8	$s^8 + 36s^7 + 630s^6 + 6930s^5 + 9450s^4 + 270{,}270s^3 + 945{,}945s^2 + 2{,}027{,}025s + 2{,}027{,}025$

TABLE 6.2 Poles of Bessel Filter Normalized to Have Unit Delay at $\omega = 0$

n	Pole values
2	$-1.5 \pm 0.8660j$
3	-2.3222
	$-1.8390 \pm 1.7543j$
4	$-2.1039 \pm 2.6575j$
	$-2.8961 \pm 0.8672j$
5	-3.6467
	$-2.3247 \pm 3.5710j$
	$-3.3520 \pm 1.7427j$
6	$-2.5158 \pm 4.4927j$
	$-3.7357 \pm 2.6263j$
	$-4.2484 \pm 0.8675j$
7	-4.9716
	$-2.6857 \pm 5.4206j$
	$-4.0701 \pm 3.5173j$
	$-4.7584 \pm 1.7393j$
8	$-5.2049 \pm 2.6162j$
	$-4.3683 \pm 4.4146j$
	$-2.8388 \pm 6.3540j$
	$-5.5878 \pm 0.8676j$

The transfer functions given by (6.1) are for Bessel filters normalized to have unit delay at $\omega = 0$. The poles p_k and denominator coefficients b_k can be renormalized for a 3-dB frequency of $\omega = 1$ using

$$p'_k = A p_k \qquad b'_k = A^{n-k} b_k$$

where the value of A appropriate for n is selected from Table 6.3. (The values from the table have been incorporated in the **besselCoefficient( )** function.)

TABLE 6.3 Factors for Renormalizing Bessel
Filter Poles from Unit Delay at $\omega = 0$ to
3-dB Attenuation at $\omega = 1$

n	A
2	1.35994
3	1.74993
4	2.13011
5	2.42003
6	2.69996
7	2.95000
8	3.17002

6.2   Frequency Response

Figures 6.1 and 6.2 show the magnitude responses for Bessel filters of several
different orders. The frequency response data was generated by the C routine
besselFreqResponse( ), which is provided in Listing 6.2.

6.3   Group Delay

Group delays for lowpass Bessel filters of several different orders are plotted
in Fig. 6.3. The data for these plots was generated by the C function
besselGroupDelay( ), provided in Listing 6.3, which performs numerical
differentiation of the phase response to evaluate the group delay.

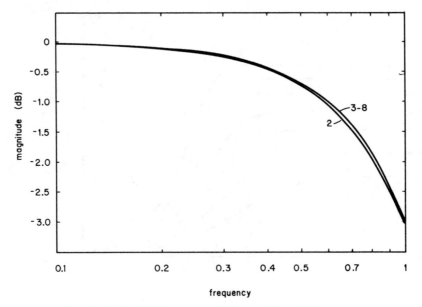

Figure 6.1   Pass-band magnitude response of lowpass Bessel filters.

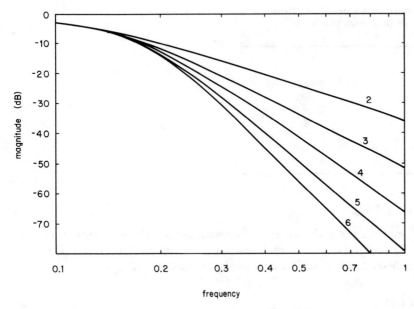

Figure 6.2 Stop-band magnitude response of lowpass Bessel filters.

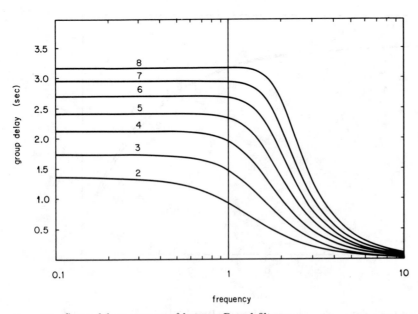

Figure 6.3 Group-delay response of lowpass Bessel filters.

Listing 6.1   besselCoefficients( )

```
/**********************************/
/*                                */
/*    Listing 6.1                 */
/*                                */
/*    besselCoefficients()        */
/*                                */
/**********************************/
#include <math.h>
#include "globDefs.h"

void besselCoefficients(  int order,
                          char typeOfNormalization,
                          real coef[])
{
int i, N, index, indexM1, indexM2;
real B[3][MAXORDER];
real A, renorm[MAXORDER];

renorm[2] = 0.72675;
renorm[3] = 0.57145;
renorm[4] = 0.46946;
renorm[5] = 0.41322;
renorm[6] = 0.37038;
renorm[7] = 0.33898;
renorm[8] = 0.31546;
A = renorm[order];

index = 1;
indexM1 = 0;
indexM2 = 2;

for( i=0; i<(3*MAXORDER); i++) B[0][i] = 0;
B[0][0] = 1.0;
B[1][0] = 1.0;
B[1][1] = 1.0;

for( N=2; N<=order; N++)
    {
    index = (index+1)%3;
    indexM1 = (indexM1 + 1)%3;
    indexM2 = (indexM2 + 1)%3;

    for( i=0; i<N; i++)
        {
        B[index][i] = (2*N-1) * B[indexM1][i];
        }
    for( i=2; i<=N; i++)
```

```
        {
        B[index][i] = B[index][i] + B[indexM2][i-2];
        }
    }
if(typeOfNormalization == 'D')
    {
    for( i=0; i<=order; i++) coef[i] = B[index][i];
    }
else
    {
    for( i=0; i<=order; i++)
        {
        coef[i] = B[index][i] * pow(A, (order - i) );
        }
    }
return;
}
```

Listing 6.2   besselFreqResponse( )

```
/**********************************/
/*                                */
/*    Listing 6.2                 */
/*                                */
/*    besselFreqResponse()        */
/*                                */
/**********************************/
#include <math.h>
#include "globDefs.h"
#include "protos.h"


void besselFreqResponse(    int order,
                            real coef[],
                            real frequency,
                            real *magnitude,
                            real *phase)
{
struct complex numer, omega, denom, transferFunction;
int i;

numer = cmplx( coef[0], 0.0);
omega = cmplx( 0.0, frequency);
denom = cmplx( coef[order], 0.0);

for( i=order-1; i>=0; i--)
    {
```

```
        denom = cMult(omega,denom);
        denom.Re = denom.Re + coef[i];
        }
transferFunction = cDiv( numer, denom);

*magnitude = 20.0 * log10(cAbs(transferFunction));
*phase = 180.0 * arg(transferFunction) / PI;
return;
}
```

Listing 6.3   besselGroupDelay( )

```
/*********************************/
/*                               */
/*    Listing 6.3                */
/*                               */
/*    besselGroupDelay()         */
/*                               */
/*********************************/

void besselGroupDelay(    int order,
                          real coef[],
                          real frequency,
                          real delta,
                          real *groupDelay)
{
struct complex numer, omega, omegaPlus, denom, transferFunction;
int i;
real phase, phase2;

numer = cmplx( coef[0], 0.0);
denom = cmplx( coef[order], 0.0);
omega = cmplx( 0.0, frequency);

for( i=order-1; i>=0; i--) {
    denom = cMult(omega,denom);
    denom.Re = denom.Re + coef[i];
    }
transferFunction = cDiv( numer, denom);
phase = arg(transferFunction);

denom = cmplx( coef[order], 0.0);
omegaPlus = cmplx(0.0, frequency + delta);

for( i=order-1; i>=0; i--) {
    denom = cMult(omegaPlus,denom);
```

```
      denom.Re = denom.Re + coef[i];
      }
transferFunction = cDiv( numer, denom);
phase2 = arg(transferFunction);
*groupDelay = (phase2 - phase)/delta;
return;
}
```

Fundamentals of Digital
Signal Processing

Digital signal processing (DSP) is based on the fact that an analog signal can be digitized and input to a general-purpose digital computer or special-purpose digital processor. Once this is accomplished, we are free to perform all sorts of mathematical operations on the sequence of digital data samples inside the processor. Some of these operations are simply digital versions of classical analog techniques, while others have no counterpart in analog circuit devices or processing methods. This chapter covers digitization and introduces the various types of processing that can be performed on the sequence of digital values once they are inside the processor.

7.1 Digitization

Digitization is the process of converting an analog signal such as a time-varying voltage or current into a sequence of digital values. Digitization actually involves two distinct parts—*sampling* and *quantization*—which are usually analyzed separately for the sake of convenience and simplicity. Three basic types of sampling, shown in Fig. 7.1, are *ideal*, *instantaneous*, and *natural*. From the illustration we can see that the sampling process converts a signal that is defined over a continuous time interval into a signal that has nonzero amplitude values only at discrete instants of time (as in ideal sampling) or over a number of discretely separate but internally continuous subintervals of time (as in instantaneous and natural sampling). The signal that results from a sampling process is called a *sampled-data signal*. The signals resulting from ideal sampling are also referred to as *discrete-time signals*.

Each of the three basic sampling types occurs at different places within a DSP system. The output from a sample-and-hold amplifier or a digital-to-analog converter (DAC) is an instantaneously sampled signal. In the output

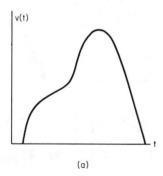

(a)

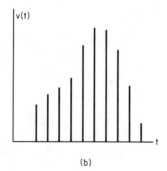

(b)

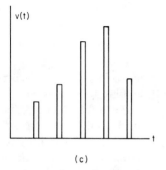

(c)

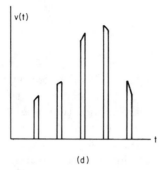

(d)

Figure 7.1   An analog signal (*a*) and three different types of sampling: (*b*) ideal, (*c*) instantaneous, and (*d*) natural.

of a practical analog-to-digital converter (ADC) used to sample a signal, each sample will of course exist for some nonzero interval of time. However, within the software of the digital processor, these values can still be interpreted as the amplitudes for a sequence of ideal samples. In fact, this is almost always the best approach since the ideal sampling model results in the simplest processing for most applications. Natural sampling is encountered in the analysis of the analog multiplexing that is often performed prior to A/D conversion in multiple-signal systems. In all three of the sampling approaches presented, the sample values are free to assume any appropriate value from the continuum of possible analog signal values.

Quantization is the part of digitization that is concerned with converting the amplitudes of an analog signal into values that can be represented by binary numbers having some finite number of bits. A quantized, or *discrete-valued*, signal is shown in Fig. 7.2. The sampling and quantization processes will introduce some significant changes in the spectrum of a digitized signal. The details of the changes will depend upon both the precision of the quantization operation and the particular sampling model that most aptly fits the actual situation.

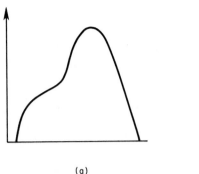 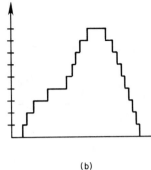

(a)   (b)

Figure 7.2 An analog signal (a) and the corresponding quantized signal (b).

Ideal sampling

In *ideal sampling*, the sampled-data signal, as shown in Fig. 7.3, comprises a sequence of uniformly spaced impulses, with the weight of each impulse equal to the amplitude of the analog signal at the corresponding instant in time. Although not mathematically rigorous, it is convenient to think of the sampled-data signal as the result of multiplying the analog signal $x(t)$ by a periodic train of unit impulses:

$$x_s(\cdot) = x(t) \sum_{n=-\infty}^{\infty} \delta(t - nT)$$

Based upon property 11 from Table 1.5, this means that the spectrum of the sampled-data signal could be obtained by convolving the spectrum of the analog signal with the spectrum of the impulse train:

$$\mathscr{F}\left[x(t) \sum_{n=-\infty}^{\infty} \delta(t - nT) \right] = X(f) * \left[f_s \sum_{m=-\infty}^{\infty} \delta(f - mf_s) \right]$$

As illustrated in Fig. 7.4, this convolution produces copies, or *images*, of the original spectrum that are periodically repeated along the frequency axis. Each of the images is an exact (to within a scaling factor) copy of the

 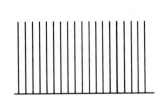 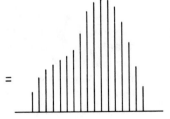

Figure 7.3 Ideal sampling.

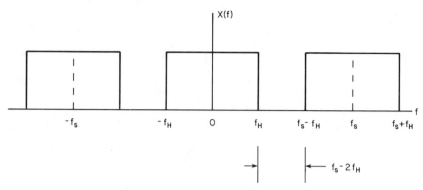

Figure 7.4   Spectrum of an ideally sampled signal.

original spectrum. The center-to-center spacing of the images is equal to the sampling rate f_s, and the edge-to-edge spacing is equal to $f_s - 2f_H$. As long as f_s is greater than 2 times f_H, the original signal can be recovered by a lowpass filtering operation that removes the extra images introduced by the sampling.

Sampling rate selection

If f_s is less than $2f_H$, the images will overlap, or *alias*, as shown in Fig. 7.5, and recovery of the original signal will not be possible. The minimum alias-free sampling rate of $2f_H$ is called the *Nyquist rate*. A signal sampled exactly at its Nyquist rate is said to be *critically sampled*.

Uniform sampling theorem.   If the spectrum $X(f)$ of a function $x(t)$ vanishes beyond an upper frequency of f_H Hz or ω_H rad/s, then $x(t)$ can be completely determined by its values at uniform intervals of less than $1/(2f_H)$ or π/ω. If sampled within these constraints, the original function $x(t)$ can be reconstructed from the samples by

$$x(t) = \sum_{n=-\infty}^{\infty} x(nT) \frac{\sin[2f_s(t-nT)]}{2f_s(t-nT)}$$

where T is the sampling interval.

Since practical signals cannot be strictly band-limited, sampling of a real-world signal must be performed at a rate greater than $2f_H$ where the signal is known to have negligible (that is, typically less than 1 percent) spectral energy above the frequency of f_H. When designing a signal processing system, we will rarely, if ever, have reliable information concerning the exact spectral occupancy of the noisy real-world signals that our system will eventually face. Consequently, in most practical design situations, a value is selected for f_H based upon the requirements of the particular application, and

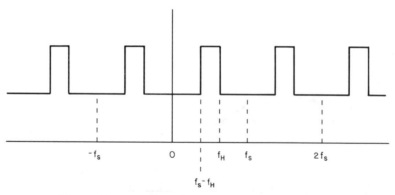

Figure 7.5 Aliasing due to overlap of spectral images.

then the signal is lowpass-filtered prior to sampling. Filters used for this purpose are called *antialiasing filters* or *guard filters*. The sample-rate selection and guard filter design are coordinated so that the filter provides attenuation of 40 dB or more for all frequencies above $f_s/2$. The spectrum of an ideally sampled practical signal is shown in Fig. 7.6. Although some aliasing does occur, the aliased components are suppressed at least 40 dB below the desired components. Antialias filtering must be performed prior to sampling. In general, there is no way to eliminate aliasing once a signal has been improperly sampled. The particular type (Butterworth, Chebyshev, Bessel, Cauer, and so on) and order of the filter should be chosen to provide the necessary stop-band attenuation while preserving the pass-band characteristics most important to the intended application.

Instantaneous sampling

In instantaneous sampling, each sample has a nonzero width and a flat top. As shown in Fig. 7.7, the sampled-data signal resulting from instantaneous sampling can be viewed as the result of convolving a sample pulse $p(t)$ with an ideally sampled version of the analog signal. The resulting sampled-data signal can thus be expressed as

$$x_s(\cdot) = p(t) * \left[x(t) \sum_{n=-\infty}^{\infty} \delta(t - nT) \right]$$

where $p(t)$ is a single rectangular sampling pulse and $x(t)$ is the original analog signal. Based upon property 10 from Table 1.5, this means that the spectrum of the instantaneous sampled-data signal can be obtained by multiplying the spectrum of the sample pulse with the spectrum of the ideally sampled signal:

$$\mathscr{F}\left\{ p(t) * \left[x(t) \sum_{n=-\infty}^{\infty} \delta(t - nT) \right] \right\} = P(f) \cdot \left\{ X(f) * \left[f_s \sum_{m=-\infty}^{\infty} \delta(f - mf_s) \right] \right\}$$

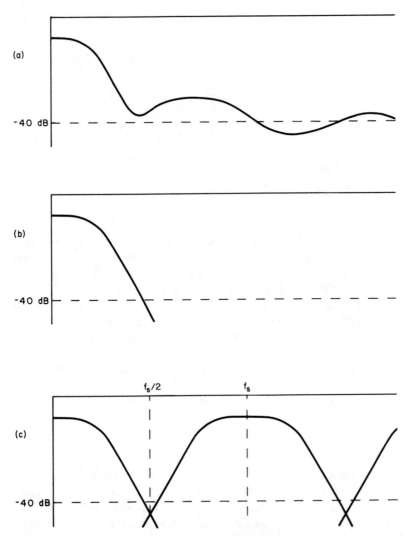

Figure 7.6 Spectrum of an ideally sampled practical signal: (*a*) spectrum of raw analog signal, (*b*) spectrum after lowpass filtering, and (*c*) spectrum after sampling.

As shown in Fig. 7.8, the resulting spectrum is similar to the spectrum produced by ideal sampling. The only difference is the amplitude distortion introduced by the spectrum of the sampling pulse. This distortion is sometimes called the *aperture effect*. Notice that distortion is present in all the images, including the one at base-band. The distortion will be less severe for narrow sampling pulses. As the pulses become extremely narrow, instantaneous sampling begins to look just like ideal sampling, and distortion due to the aperture effect all but disappears.

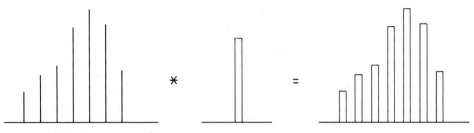

Figure 7.7 Instantaneous sampling.

(a)
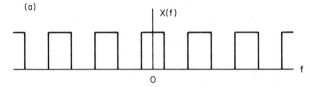

(b)
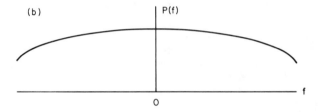

(c)
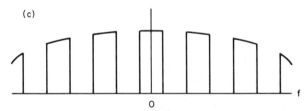

Figure 7.8 Spectrum of an instantaneously sampled signal is equal to the spectrum (*a*) of an ideally sampled signal multiplied by the spectrum (*b*) of 1 sampling pulse.

Natural sampling

In natural sampling, each sample's amplitude follows the analog signal's amplitude throughout the sample's duration. As shown in Fig. 7.9, this is mathematically equivalent to multiplying the analog signal by a periodic train of rectangular pulses:

$$x_s(\cdot) = x(t) \cdot \left\{ p(t) * \left[\sum_{n=-\infty}^{\infty} \delta(t - nT) \right] \right\}$$

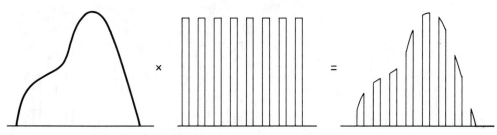

Figure 7.9 Natural sampling.

The spectrum of a naturally sampled signal is found by convolving the spectrum of the analog signal with the spectrum of the sampling pulse train:

$$\mathscr{F}[x_s(\cdot)] = X(f) * \left[P(f)\, f_s \sum_{m=-\infty}^{\infty} \delta(f - mf_s) \right]$$

As shown in Fig. 7.10, the resulting spectrum will be similar to the spectrum produced by instantaneous sampling. In instantaneous sampling, all frequen-

(a)

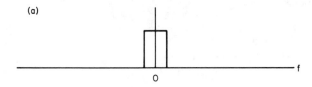

(b)

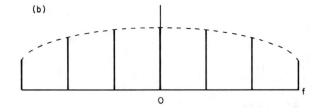

(c)

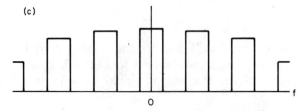

Figure 7.10 Spectrum (c) of a naturally sampled signal is equal to the spectum (a) of the analog signal multiplied by the spectrum (b) of the sampling pulse train.

cies of the sampled signal's spectrum are attenuated by the spectrum of the sampling pulse, while in natural sampling each image of the basic spectrum will be attenuated by a factor that is equal to the value of the sampling pulse's spectrum at the center frequency of the image. In communications theory, natural sampling is called *shaped-top pulse amplitude modulation.*

Discrete-time signals

In the discussion so far, weighted impulses have been used to represent individual sample values in a discrete-time signal. This was necessary in order to use continuous mathematics to connect continuous-time analog signal representations with their corresponding discrete-time digital representations. However, once we are operating strictly within the digital or discrete-time realms, we can dispense with the Dirac delta impulse and adopt in its place the unit sample function, which is much easier to work with. The unit sample function is also referred to as a *Kronecker delta impulse* (Cadzow 1973). Figure 7.11 shows both the Dirac delta and Kronecker delta representations for a typical signal. In the function sampled using a Dirac impulse train, the independent variable is continuous time t, and integer multiples of the sampling interval T are used to explicitly define the discrete sampling instants. On the other hand, the Kronecker delta notation assumes uniform

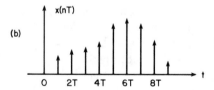

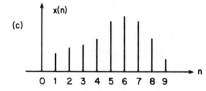

Figure 7.11 Sampling with Dirac and Kronecker impulses: (*a*) continuous signal, (*b*) sampling with Dirac impulses, and (*c*) sampling with Kronecker impulses.

sampling with an implicitly defined sampling interval. The independent variable is the integer-valued index n whose values correspond to the discrete instants at which samples can occur. In most theoretical work, the implicitly defined sampling interval is dispensed with completely by treating all the discrete-time functions as though they have been normalized by setting $T = 1$.

Notation

Writers in the field of digital-signal processing are faced with the problem of finding a convenient notational way to distinguish between continuous-time functions and discrete-time functions. Since the early 1970s, a number of different approaches have appeared in the literature, but none of the schemes advanced so far have been perfectly suited for all situations. In fact, some authors use two or more different notational schemes within different parts of the same book. In keeping with long-established mathematical practice, functions of a continuous variable are almost universally denoted with the independent variable enclosed in parentheses: $x(t)$, $H(e^{j\omega})$, $\phi(f)$ and so on. Many authors, such as Oppenheim and Schafer (1975), Rabiner and Gold (1975), and Roberts and Mullis (1987), make no real notational distinction between functions of continuous variables and functions of discrete variables, and instead rely on context to convey the distinction. This approach, while easy for the writer, can be very confusing for the reader. Another approach involves using subscripts for functions of a discrete variable:

$$x_k \triangleq x(kT)$$

$$H_n \triangleq H(e^{jn\theta})$$

$$\phi_m \triangleq \phi(mF)$$

This approach quickly becomes typographically unwieldy when the independent variable is represented by a complicated expression. A fairly recent practice (Oppenheim and Schafer 1989) uses parentheses ( ) to enclose the independent variable of continuous-variable functions and brackets [ ] to enclose the independent variable of discrete-variable functions:

$$x[k] = x(kT)$$

$$H[n] = H(e^{jn\theta})$$

$$\phi[m] = \phi(mF)$$

For the remainder of this book, we will adopt this practice and just remind ourselves to be careful in situations where the bracket notation for discrete-variable functions could be confused with the bracket notation used for arrays in the C language.

7.2   Discrete-Time Fourier Transform

The Fourier series given by Eq. (1.140) can be rewritten to make use of the discrete sequence notation that was introduced in Sec. 7.1:

$$x(t) = \sum_{n=-\infty}^{\infty} X[n]\, e^{j2\pi nFt}$$

where $F = \dfrac{1}{t_0} = $ sample spacing in the frequency domain

$t_0 = $ period of $x(t)$

Likewise, Eq. (1.141) can be written as

$$X[n] = \frac{1}{t_0} \int_{t_0} x(t)\, e^{-jn2\pi Ft}\, dt$$

The fact that the signal $x(t)$ and sequence $F[n]$ form a Fourier series pair with a frequency domain sampling interval of F can be indicated as

$$x(t) \xleftrightarrow{\text{FS};\, F} X[n]$$

Discrete-time Fourier transform

In Sec. 7.1 the results concerning the impact of sampling upon a signal's spectrum were obtained using the *continuous-time* Fourier transform in conjunction with a periodic train of Dirac impulses to model the sampling of the continuous-time signal $x(t)$. Once we have defined a discrete-time sequence $x[n]$, the *discrete-time Fourier transform* (DTFT) can be used to obtain the corresponding spectrum directly from the sequence without having to resort to impulses and continuous-time Fourier analysis.

The discrete-time Fourier transform, which links the discrete-time and continuous-frequency domain, is defined by

$$X(e^{j\omega T}) = \sum_{n=-\infty}^{\infty} x[n]\, e^{-j\omega nT} \tag{7.1}$$

and the corresponding inverse is given by

$$x[n] = \frac{1}{2\pi} \int_{-\pi}^{\pi} X(e^{j\omega})\, e^{j\omega nT}\, d\omega \tag{7.2}$$

If Eqs. (7.1) and (7.2) are compared to the DTFT definitions given by certain texts (Oppenheim and Schafer 1975; Oppenheim and Schafer 1989; Rabiner and Gold 1975), an apparent disagreement will be found. The cited texts define the DTFT and its inverse as

$$X(e^{j\omega}) = \sum_{n=-\infty}^{\infty} x[n]\, e^{-j\omega n} \tag{7.3}$$

$$x[n] = \frac{1}{2\pi} \int_{-\pi}^{\pi} X(e^{j\omega})\, e^{j\omega nT}\, d\omega \tag{7.4}$$

The disagreement is due to the notation used by these texts, in which ω is used to denote the *digital* frequency given by

$$\omega = \frac{\Omega}{F_s} = \Omega T$$

where Ω = analog frequency
F_s = sampling frequency
T = sampling interval

In most DSP books other than the three cited above, the analog frequency is denoted by ω rather than by Ω. Whether ω or Ω is the "natural" choice for denoting analog frequency depends upon the overall approach taken in developing Fourier analysis of sequences. Books that begin with sequences, and then proceed on to Fourier analysis of sequences, and finally tie sequences to analog signals via sampling tend to use ω for the first frequency variable encountered which is *digital* frequency. Other books that begin with analog theory and then move on to sampling and sequences, tend to use ω for the first frequency variable encountered which is *analog* frequency. In this book, we will adopt the convention used by Peled and Liu (1976) denoting analog frequency by ω and digital frequency by $\lambda = \omega T$. The function $X(e^{j\omega T})$ is periodic with a period of $\omega_p = 2\pi/T$, and $X(e^{j\lambda})$ is periodic with a period of $\lambda_p = 2\pi$.

Independent of the ω versus Ω controversy, the notation $X(e^{j\omega T})$ or $X(e^{j\lambda})$ is commonly used rather than $X(\omega)$ or $X(\lambda)$ so that the form of (7.1) remains similar to the form of the z transform given in Sec. 5.1 which is

$$X(z) = \sum_{n=-\infty}^{\infty} x[n]\, z^{-n} \tag{7.5}$$

If $e^{j\omega}$ is substituted for z in (7.5), the result is identical to (7.1). This indicates that the DTFT is nothing more than the z transform evaluated on the unit circle. [Note: $e^{j\omega} = \cos\omega + j\sin\omega$, $0 \le \omega \le 2\pi$, does in fact define the unit circle in the z plane since $|e^{j\omega}| = (\cos^2\omega + \sin^2\omega)^{1/2} \equiv 1$].

Convergence conditions

If the time sequence $x[n]$ satisfies

$$\sum_{n=-\infty}^{\infty} |x[n]| < \infty$$

then $X(e^{j\omega T})$ exists and the series in (7.1) converges uniformly to $X(e^{j\omega T})$. If $x[n]$ satisfies

$$\sum_{n=-\infty}^{\infty} |x[n]|^2 < \infty$$

then $X(e^{j\omega T})$ exists and the series in (7.1) converges in a mean-square sense to $X(e^{j\omega T})$, that is,

$$\lim_{M\to\infty} \int_{-\pi}^{\pi} |X(e^{j\omega T}) - X_M(e^{j\omega T})|^2 \, d\omega = 0$$

where $X_M(e^{j\omega T}) = \sum_{n=-M}^{M} x[n] \, e^{-j\omega n T}$

The function $X_M(e^{j\omega T})$ is a form of the Dirichlet kernel discussed in Sec. 11.2.

Relationship to Fourier series

Since the Fourier series represents a periodic continuous-time function in terms of a discrete-frequency function, and the DTFT represents a discrete-time function in terms of a periodic continuous-frequency function, we might suspect that some sort of duality exists between the Fourier series and DTFT. It turns out that such a duality does indeed exist. Specifically if

$$f[k] \xleftarrow{\text{DTFT}} F(e^{j\omega T})$$

and we set

$$\omega_0 = T$$

$$x(t) = F(e^{j\omega T})\big|_{\omega = T}$$

$$X[n] = f[k]\big|_{k = -n}$$

then
$$x(t) \xleftarrow{\text{FS; } \omega_0} X[n]$$

7.3 Discrete-Time Systems

In Chap. 2 we saw how continuous-time systems such as filters and amplifiers can accept analog input signals and operate upon them to produce different analog output signals. *Discrete-time systems* perform essentially the same role for digital or discrete-time signals.

Difference equations

Although I have deliberately avoided discussing differential equations and their accompanying headaches in the analysis of analog systems, *difference* equations are much easier to work with, and they play an important role in the analysis and synthesis of discrete-time systems. A discrete-time, linear, time-invariant (or if you prefer, shift-invariant) (DTLTI or DTLSI) system, which accepts an input sequence $x[n]$ and produces an output sequence $y[n]$, can be described by a linear difference equation of the form

$$y[n] + a_1\,y[n-1] + a_2\,y[n-2] + \cdots + a_k\,y[n-k]$$
$$= b_0\,x[n] + b_1\,x[n-1] + b_2\,x[n-2] + \cdots + b_k\,x[n-k] \qquad (7.6)$$

Such a difference equation can describe a DTLTI system having any initial conditions as long as they are specified. This is in contrast to the discrete-convolution and discrete-transfer function that are limited to describing digital filters that are initially relaxed (that is, all inputs and outputs are initially zero). In general, the computation of the output $y[n]$ at point n using Eq. (7.6) will involve previous outputs $y[n-1]$, $y[n-2]$, $y[n-3]$, and so on. However, in some filters, all of the coefficients $a_1, a_2, \ldots, a_k$ are equal to zero, thus yielding

$$y[n] = b_0\,x[n] + b_1\,x[n-1] + b_2\,x[n-2] + \cdots + b_k\,x[n-k] \qquad (7.7)$$

in which the computation of $y[n]$ does not involve previous output values. Difference equations involving previous output values are called *recursive difference equations*, and equations in the form of (7.7) are called *nonrecursive difference equations*.

Example 7.1   Determine a nonrecursive difference equation for a simple moving-average lowpass filter in which the output at $n = i$ is equal to the arithmetic average of the five inputs from $n = i - 4$ through $n = i$.

solution   The desired difference equation is given by

$$y[n] = \frac{x[n] + x[n-1] + x[n-2] + x[n-3] + x[n-4]}{5}$$
$$= 0.2x[n] + 0.2x[n-1] + 0.2x[n-2] + 0.2x[n-3] + 0.2x[n-4] \qquad (7.8)$$

Relating this to the standard form of Eq. (7.7), we find $k = 4$, $b_i = 0$ for all i, and $a_0 = a_1 = a_2 = a_3 = a_4 = 0.2$.

Discrete convolution

A discrete-time system's impulse response is the output response produced when a unit sample function is applied to the input of the previously relaxed system. As we might expect from our experiences with continuous systems, we can obtain the output $y[n]$ due to any input by performing a *discrete convolution* of the input signal $x[n]$ and the impulse response $h[n]$. This discrete convolution is given by

$$y[n] = \sum_{m=0}^{\infty} h[m]\,x[n-m]$$

If the impulse response has nonzero values at an infinite number of points along the discrete-time axis, a digital filter having such an impulse response is called an *infinite-impulse response* (IIR) filter. On the other hand, if $h[m] = 0$ for all $m \geq M$, the filter is called a *finite-impulse response* (FIR) filter, and the convolution summation can be rewritten as

$$y[n] = \sum_{m=0}^{M-1} h[m]\, x[n-m]$$

FIR filters are also called *transversal filters*.

Example 7.2 For the moving-average filter described in Example 7.1, obtain the filter's impulse response.

solution The filter's impulse response $h[n]$ can be obtained by direct evaluation of Eq. (7.8) for the case of $x[n]$ equal to the unit sample function:

$$h[n] = y[n] \quad \text{for} \quad x[n] = \begin{cases} 1 & n = 0 \\ 0 & n \neq 0 \end{cases}$$

Thus,
$$h[n] = \begin{cases} 0.2 & 0 \leq n \leq 4 \\ 0 & \text{otherwise} \end{cases}$$

The following summation identities will often prove useful in the evaluation of convolution summations:

$$\sum_{n=0}^{N} \alpha^n = \frac{1 - \alpha^{N+1}}{1 - \alpha} \qquad \alpha \neq 1 \tag{7.9}$$

$$\sum_{n=0}^{N} n\alpha^n = \frac{\alpha}{(1-\alpha)^2} \left(1 - \alpha^N - N\alpha^N + N\alpha^{N+1}\right) \qquad \alpha \neq 1 \tag{7.10}$$

$$\sum_{n=0}^{N} n^2 \alpha^n = \frac{\alpha}{(1-\alpha)^3} \left[(1+\alpha)(1-\alpha^N) - 2(1-\alpha)N\alpha^N - (1-\alpha)^2 N^2 \alpha^N\right] \qquad \alpha \neq 1$$

$$\tag{7.11}$$

7.4 Diagramming Discrete-Time Systems

Block diagrams

As is the case for continuous-time systems, block diagrams are useful in the design and analysis of discrete-time systems. Construction of block diagrams for discrete time systems involves three basic building blocks: the unit-delay element, multiplier, and summer.

Unit-delay element. As its name implies, a *unit-delay element* generates an output that is identical to its input delayed by 1 sample interval:

$$y[k] = x[k-1]$$

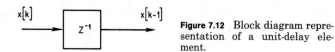

Figure 7.12 Block diagram representation of a unit-delay element.

The unit-delay element is usually drawn as shown in Fig. 7.12. The term z^{-1} is used to denote a unit delay because delaying a discrete-time signal by 1 sample time multiplies the signal's z transform by z^{-1}. (See property 5 in Table 9.4.) Delays of p sample times may be depicted as p unit delays in series or as a box enclosing z^{-p}.

Multiplier. A *multiplier* generates as output the product of a fixed constant and the input signal

$$y[k] = a\,x[k]$$

A multiplier can be drawn in any of the ways shown in Fig. 7.13. The form shown in Fig. 7.13c is usually reserved for adaptive filters and other situations where the factor a is not constant. [Note that a system containing multiplication by a nonconstant factor would not be a *linear time-invariant* (LTI) system!]

Summer. A *summer* adds two or more discrete-time signals to generate the discrete-time output signal:

$$y[k] = x_1[k] + x_2[k] + \cdots + x_n[k]$$

a)

b)

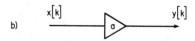

c)

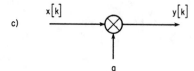

Figure 7.13 Block diagram representations of a multiplier.

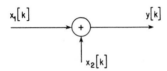

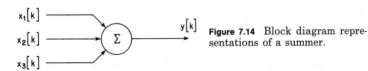

Figure 7.14 Block diagram representations of a summer.

A summer is depicted using one of the forms shown in Fig. 7.14. A negative sign can be placed next to a summer's input paths as required to indicate a signal that is to be subtracted rather than added.

Example 7.3 Draw a block diagram for a simple moving-average lowpass filter in which the output at $k = i$ is equal to the arithmetic average of the three inputs for $k = i - 2$ through $k = i$.

solution The difference equation for the desired filter is

$$y[k] = \tfrac{1}{3}x[k] + \tfrac{1}{3}x[k-1] + \tfrac{1}{3}x[k-2]$$

The block diagram for this filter will be as shown in Fig. 7.15. It should be noted that block diagram representations are in general not unique and that a given system can be represented in several different ways.

Example 7.4 Draw alternative block diagrams for the filter of Example 7.3.

solution Since multiplication distributes over addition, the difference equation can be rewritten as

$$y[k] = \tfrac{1}{3}\{x[k] + x[k-1] + x[k-2]\}$$

and the block diagram can be redrawn as shown in Fig. 7.16.

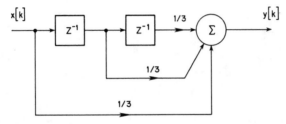

Figure 7.15 Block diagram for Example 7.3.

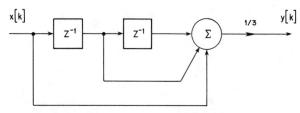

Figure 7.16 Block diagram for Example 7.4.

Signal flow graphs

A modified form of a directed graph, called a *signal flow graph* (SFT), can be used to depict all the same information as a block diagram but in a more compact form. Consider the block diagram in Fig. 7.17 which has some labeled points added for ease of reference. The *oriented graph*, or *directed graph*, for this system is obtained by replacing each multiplier, each connecting branch, and each delay element with a directed line segment called an *edge*. Furthermore, each branching point and each adder is replaced by a point called a *node*. The resulting graph is shown in Fig. 7.18. A signal flow graph is obtained by associating a signal with each node and a linear operation with each edge of the directed graph. The node weights correspond to signals present within the discrete-time system. Associated with each edge is the linear operation (delay or constant gain) that must be performed upon the signal associated with the edge's *from* node in order to obtain the signal associated with the edge's *to* node. For a node which is the *to* node for two or more edges, the signal associated with the node is the sum of all the signals produced by the incoming edges. For the graph shown in Fig. 7.18, the

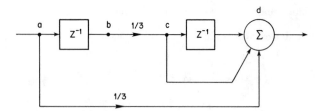

Figure 7.17 Block diagram of a discrete-time system.

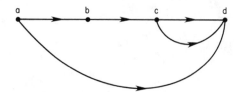

Figure 7.18 Directed graph corresponding to the block diagram of Fig. 7.17.

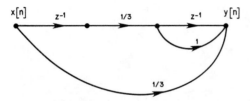

Figure 7.19 Signal flow graph derived from the directed graph of Fig. 7.18.

following correpondences can be identified:

Node a: $x[k]$

Node b: $x[k-1]$

Node c: $\frac{1}{3}x[k-1]$

Node d: summer producing $y[k]$

Edge (a, b):   first delay element

Edge (c, d):   second delay element

Edge (a, d):   bottom multiplier

Edge (b, c):   top multiplier

Edge (c, d):   unity gain connection from point c to summer

The resulting signal flow graph is shown in Fig. 7.19. It is customary to use multiplication by z^{-1} as a shorthand notation for unit delay, even though the signals in an SFG are time domain signals, and multiplication by z^{-1} is a frequency domain operation.

Discrete Fourier Transform

The *Fourier series* (FS), introduced in Chap. 1, links the continuous-time domain to the discrete-frequency domain; and the *Fourier transform* (FT) links the continuous-time domain to the continuous-frequency domain. The *discrete-time Fourier transform* (DTFT), introduced in Sec. 7.2, links the discrete-time domain to the continuous-frequency domain. In this chapter, we examine the *discrete Fourier transform* (DFT) which links the discrete-time and discrete-frequency domains. A complete treatment of the design and coding of DFT algorithms can fill volumes (see Brigham 1975; Burrus and Parks 1984; Nussbaumer 1981). Rather than attempt complete coverage of DFTs, this chapter presents only those aspects that are germane to the design of digital filters. Coverage of the so-called fast algorithms for implementation of the DFT is limited to one specific type of algorithm along with an examination of the computational savings that fast algorithms can provide.

8.1 Discrete Fourier Transform

The discrete Fourier transform and its inverse are given by

$$X[m] = \sum_{n=0}^{N-1} x[n]\, e^{-j2\pi mnFT} \qquad m = 0, 1, \ldots, N-1 \tag{8.1a}$$

$$= \sum_{n=0}^{N-1} x[n]\, \cos(2\pi mnFT) + j \sum_{n=0}^{N-1} x[n]\, \sin(2\pi mnFT) \tag{8.1b}$$

$$x[n] = \sum_{m=0}^{N-1} X[m]\, e^{j2\pi mnFT} \qquad n = 0, 1, \ldots, N-1 \tag{8.2a}$$

$$= \sum_{m=0}^{N-1} X[m]\, \cos(2\pi mnFT) + j \sum_{m=0}^{N-1} X[m]\, \sin(2\pi mnFT) \tag{8.2b}$$

It is a common practice in the DSP literature to "bury the details" of Eqs.

(8.1) and (8.2) by defining $W_N = e^{j2\pi/N} = e^{j2\pi FT}$ and rewriting (8.1a) and (8.2a) as

$$X[m] = \sum_{n=0}^{N-1} x[n]\ W_N^{-mn} \tag{8.3}$$

$$x[n] = \sum_{m=0}^{N-1} X[m]\ W_N^{mn} \tag{8.4}$$

Since the exponents in (8.3) and (8.4) differ only in sign, another common practice in writing DFT software is to write only a single routine that can evaluate either (8.3) or (8.4) depending upon the value of an input flag being equal to $+1$ or -1. Back in the "olden days," when memory and disk space were expensive, this was a big deal; but these days, having two separate routines may pay for itself in terms of clarity, execution speed, and simplified calling sequences.

Parameter selection

In designing a DFT for a particular application, values must be chosen for the parameters N, T, and F. N is the number of time sequence values $x[n]$ over which the DFT summation is performed to compute each frequency sequence value. It is also the total number of frequency sequence values $X[m]$ produced by the DFT. For convenience, the complete set of N consecutive time sequence values is referred to as the *input record*, and the complete set of N consecutive frequency sequence values is called the *output record*. T is the time interval between two consecutive samples of the input sequence, and F is the frequency interval between two consecutive samples of the output sequence. The selection of values for N, F, and T is subject to the following constraints, which are a consequence of the sampling theorem and the inherent properties of the DFT:

1. The inherent properties of the DFT require that $FNT = 1$.

2. The sampling theorem requires that $T \le 1/(2f_H)$, where f_H is the highest significant frequency component in the continuous-time signal.

3. The record length in time is equal to NT or $1/F$.

4. Many fast DFT algorithms (such as the one discussed in Sec. 8.5) require that N be an integer power of 2.

Example 8.1 Choose values of N, F, and T given that F must be 5 Hz or less, N must be an integer power of 2, and the bandwidth of the input signal is 300 Hz. For the values chosen, determine the longest signal that can fit into a single input record.

solution From constraint 2 above, $T \le 1/(2f_H)$. Since $f_H = 300$ Hz, $T \le 1.66$ ms. If we select $F = 5$ and $T = 0.0016$, then $N \ge 125$. Since N must be an integer power of 2, then we choose $N = 128 = 2^7$, and F becomes 4.883 Hz. Using these values, the input record will span $NT = 204.8$ ms.

Example 8.2 Assuming that $N = 256$ and F must be 5 Hz or less, determine the highest input-signal bandwidth that can be accommodated without aliasing.

solution Since $FNT = 1$, then $T \geq 781.25\ \mu$s. This corresponds to a maximum f_H of 640 Hz.

Periodicity

A periodic function of time will have a discrete-frequency spectrum, and a discrete-time functon will have a spectrum that is periodic. Since the DFT relates a discrete-time function to a corresponding discrete-frequency function, this implies that both the time function and frequency function are periodic as well as discrete. This means that some care must be exercised in selecting DFT parameters and in interpreting DFT results, but it does not mean that the DFT can be used only on periodic digital signals. Based on the DFT's inherent periodicity, it is a common practice to regard the points from $n = 1$ through $n = N/2$ as positive and the points from $n = N/2$ through $n = N - 1$ as negative. Since both the time and frequency sequences are periodic, the values at points $n = N/2$ through $n = N - 1$ are in fact equal to the values at points $n = N/2$ through $n = -1$. Under this convention, it is convenient to redefine the concept of even and odd sequences: If $x[N - n] = x[n]$, the $x[n]$ is even symmetric, and if $x[N - n] = -x[n]$, then $x[n]$ is odd symmetric or antisymmetric.

8.2 Properties of the DFT

The DFT exhibits a number of useful properties and operational relationships that are similar to the properties of the continuous Fourier transform discussed in Chap. 1.

Linearity

The DFT relating $x[n]$ and $X[m]$:

$$x[n] \underset{\text{IDFT}}{\overset{\text{DFT}}{\rightleftharpoons}} X[m]$$

is homogeneous

$$a\,X[n] \underset{\text{IDFT}}{\overset{\text{DFT}}{\rightleftharpoons}} a\,X[m]$$

additive

$$x[n] + y[n] \underset{\text{IDFT}}{\overset{\text{DFT}}{\rightleftharpoons}} X[m] + Y[m]$$

and therefore linear

$$a\,x[n] + b\,y[n] \underset{\text{IDFT}}{\overset{\text{DFT}}{\rightleftharpoons}} a\,X[m] + b\,Y[m]$$

Symmetry

A certain symmetry exists between a time sequence and the corresponding frequency sequence produced by the DFT. Given that $x[n]$ and $X[m]$ constitute a DFT pair, that is,

$$x[n] \underset{\text{IDFT}}{\overset{\text{DFT}}{\rightleftharpoons}} X[m]$$

then

$$\frac{1}{N} X[n] \underset{\text{IDFT}}{\overset{\text{DFT}}{\rightleftharpoons}} x[-m]$$

Time shifting

A time sequence $x[n]$ can be shifted in time by subtracting an integer from n. Shifting the time sequence will cause the corresponding frequency sequence to be phase-shifted. Specifically, given

$$x[n] \underset{\text{IDFT}}{\overset{\text{DFT}}{\rightleftharpoons}} X[m]$$

then

$$x[n-k] \underset{\text{IDFT}}{\overset{\text{DFT}}{\rightleftharpoons}} X[m] \, e^{-j2\pi mk/N}$$

Frequency shifting

Time sequence modulation is accomplished by multiplying the time sequence by an imaginary exponential term $e^{j2\pi nk/N}$. This will cause a frequency shift of the corresponding spectrum. Specifically, given

$$x[n] \underset{\text{IDFT}}{\overset{\text{DFT}}{\rightleftharpoons}} X[m]$$

then

$$x[n] \, e^{j2\pi mk/N} \underset{\text{IDFT}}{\overset{\text{DFT}}{\rightleftharpoons}} X[m-k]$$

Even and odd symmetry

Consider a time sequence $x[n]$ and the corresponding frequency sequence $X[m] = X_R[m] + jX_I[m]$, where $X_R[m]$ and $X_I[m]$ are real valued. If $x[n]$ is even, then $X[m]$ is real valued and even:

$$x[-n] = x[n] \; \Leftrightarrow \; X[m] = X_R[m] = X_R[-m]$$

If $x[n]$ is odd, then $X[m]$ is imaginary and odd:

$$x[-n] = -x[n] \; \Leftrightarrow \; X[m] = jX_I[m] = -jX_I[-m]$$

Real and imaginary properties

In general, the DFT of a real-valued time sequence will have an even real component and an odd imaginary component. Conversely, an imaginary-valued time sequence will have an odd real component and an even imaginary component. Given a time sequence $x[n] = x_R[n] + jx_I[n]$ and the corresponding frequency sequence $X[m] = X_R[m] + jX_I[m]$, then

$$x[n] = x_R[n] \;\Leftrightarrow\; X_R[m] = X_R[-m] \qquad X_I[m] = -X_I[-m]$$

$$x[n] = jx_I[n] \;\Leftrightarrow\; X_R[m] = -X_R[-m] \qquad X_I[m] = X_I[-m]$$

8.3 Implementing the DFT

The C function shown in Listing 8.1 is the "brute-force" implementation of Eq. (8.1). This function is an example of grossly inefficient code. The sine and cosine operations are each performed N^2 times to compute an N-point DFT. Since

$$\exp\!\left(\frac{-2\pi jk}{N}\right) = \exp\!\left[\frac{-2\pi j(k \bmod N)}{N}\right] \tag{8.5}$$

it follows that there are only N different values of **phi** that need be computed in **dft( )**. We can trade space for speed by precomputing and storing the values of **sin(phi)** and **cos(phi)** for **phi** $= 0, 1, \ldots, N-1$. The resulting modified function **dft2( )** is presented in Listing 8.2.

8.4 Fast Fourier Transforms

Consider the operation of **dft2( )** for the case of $N = 8$. The computation of **sumRe** involves the product of **x[n].Re** and **cosVal[k]** for $n = 0, 1, \ldots, 7$. For any given value of n, the value of k is determined by the value of m using

$$k = mn \text{ modulo } N$$

For $N = 8$, there are 64 possible combinations of (m, n) and only 8 possible values of k. Obviously, more than 1 combination of (m, n) will map into each value of k as indicated in Table 8.1.

TABLE 8.1 Values of k as a Function of (m, n) for an 8-point DFT

n	$k(0, n)$	$k(1, n)$	$k(2, n)$	$k(3, n)$	$k(4, n)$	$k(5, n)$	$k(6, n)$	$k(7, n)$
0	0	0	0	0	0	0	0	0
1	0	1	2	3	4	5	6	7
2	0	2	4	6	0	2	4	6
3	0	3	6	1	4	7	2	5
4	0	4	0	4	0	4	0	4
5	0	5	2	7	4	1	6	3
6	0	6	4	2	0	6	4	2
7	0	7	6	5	4	3	2	1

For $N = 8$, the function **dft2( )** computes the product **x[0].Re*cosVal[0]** a total of eight times—once for each different value of m. Similarly, the product **x[4].Re*cosVal[0]** is computed a total of four times—once for each odd value of m. A variety of different fast DFT algorithms has been developed by reordering and regrouping hhe DFT computations so as to minimize or eliminate the need for multiple calculation of the same product.

The expanded equations for computation of $X(0)$ through $X(7)$ for an 8-point DFT are listed in Table 8.2. Making use of Eq. (8.5) along with the commutative, associative, and distributive properties of addition and multiplication, the equations of Table 8.2 can be rewritten in the form shown in Table 8.3. Examination of these equations reveals that they share many common terms that can be computed once and then used as needed without having to be computed over again. Use of these common terms is easier to understand if the equations are presented in the form of a signal flow graph as in Fig. 8.1. The format of this signal flow graph has been slightly modified from the format of Sec. 7.6 in order to reduce the clutter somewhat. In the modified format, each circle represents one (possibly complex) addition and one (possibly complex) multiplication. The term corresponding to the line with the arrowhead entering the circle is multiplied by the constant within the circle and then added to the term correeesponding to the other line entering the circle. The notation W^n represents $\exp(-j2\pi/N)$. The computa-

TABLE 8.2   Equations for Computation of an 8-point DFT

$X(0) = x(0)W^0 + x(1)W^0 + x(2)W^0 + x(3)W^0 + x(4)W^0 + x(5)W^0 + x(6)W^0 + x(7)W^0$

$X(1) = x(0)W^0 + x(1)W^1 + x(2)W^2 + x(3)W^3 + x(4)W^4 + x(5)W^5 + x(6)W^6 + x(7)W^7$

$X(2) = x(0)W^0 + x(1)W^2 + x(2)W^4 + x(3)W^6 + x(4)W^8 + x(5)W^{10} + x(6)W^{12} + x(7)W^{14}$

$X(3) = x(0)W^0 + x(1)W^3 + x(2)W^6 + x(3)W^9 + x(4)W^{12} + x(5)W^{15} + x(6)W^{18} + x(7)W^{21}$

$X(4) = x(0)W^0 + x(1)W^4 + x(2)W^8 + x(3)W^{12} + x(4)W^{16} + x(5)W^{20} + x(6)W^{24} + x(7)W^{28}$

$X(5) = x(0)W^0 + x(1)W^5 + x(2)W^{10} + x(3)W^{15} + x(4)W^{20} + x(5)W^{25} + x(6)W^{30} + x(7)W^{35}$

$X(6) = x(0)W^0 + x(1)W^6 + x(2)W^{12} + x(3)W^{18} + x(4)W^{24} + x(5)W^{30} + x(6)W^{36} + x(7)W^{42}$

$X(7) = x(0)W^0 + x(1)W^7 + x(2)W^{14} + x(3)W^{21} + x(4)W^{28} + x(5)W^{35} + x(6)W^{42} + x(7)W^{49}$

TABLE 8.3   Factored Equations for Computation of an 8-point DFT

$X(0) = \{[x(0) + x(4)W^0] + W_0[x(2) + x(6)W^0]\} + W_0\{[x(1) + x(5)W^0] + W_0[x(3) + x(7)W^0]\}$

$X(1) = \{[x(0) + x(4)W^4] + W^2[x(2) + x(6)W^4]\} + W^1\{[x(1) + x(5)W^4] + W^2[x(3) + x(7)W^4]\}$

$X(2) = \{[x(0) + x(4)W^0] + W^4[x(2) + x(6)W^0]\} + W^2\{[x(1) + x(5)W^0] + W^4[x(3) + x(7)W^0]\}$

$X(3) = \{[x(0) + x(4)W^4] + W^6[x(2) + x(6)W^4]\} + W^3\{[x(1) + x(5)W^4] + W^6[x(3) + x(7)W^4]\}$

$X(4) = \{[x(0) + x(4)W^0] + W^0[x(2) + x(6)W^0]\} + W^4\{[x(1) + x(5)W^0] + W^0[x(3) + x(7)W^0]\}$

$X(5) = \{[x(0) + x(4)W^4] + W^2[x(2) + x(6)W^4]\} + W^5\{[x(1) + x(5)W^4] + W^2[x(3) + x(7)W^4]\}$

$X(6) = \{[x(0) + x(4)W^0] + W^4[x(2) + x(6)W^0]\} + W^6\{[x(1) + x(5)W^0] + W^4[x(3) + x(7)W^0]\}$

$X(7) = \{[x(0) + x(4)W^4] + W^6[x(2) + x(6)W^4]\} + W^7\{[x(1) + x(5)W^4] + W^6[x(3) + x(7)W^4]\}$

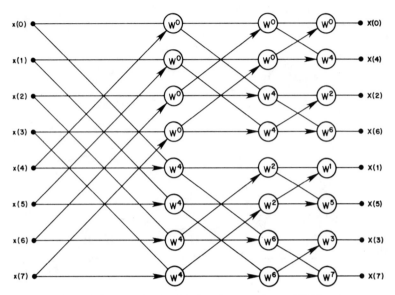

Figure 8.1 Signal flow graph representing the equations of Table 8.3.

tion scheme depicted by Fig. 8.1 can be extended for any value of N that is an integer power of 2. A C function **fft( )** that implements this scheme is given in Listing 8.3. Listings of the support functions **bitRev( )**, **ipow( )**, and **log2( )** are provided in App. A.

8.5 Applying the Discrete Fourier Transform

Short time-limited signals

Consider the time-limited continuous-time signal and its continuous spectrum shown in Figs. 8.2a and 8.2b. (Remember that a signal cannot be both strictly time limited and strictly band limited.) We can sample this signal to produce the time sequence shown in Fig. 8.2c for input to a DFT. If the input record length N is chosen to be longer than the length of the input time sequence, the entire sequence can fit within the input record as shown. As discussed in Sec. 8.2, the DFT will treat the input sequence as though it is the periodic sequence shown in Fig. 8.2d. This will result in a periodic discrete-frequency spectrum as shown in Fig. 8.2e. The actual output produced by the DFT algorithm will be the sequence of values from $m = 0$ to $m = N - 1$. Of course, there will be some aliasing due to the time-limited nature (and consequently unlimited bandwidth) of the input-signal pulse.

Periodic signals

Consider the band-limited and periodic continuous-time signal and its spectrum shown in Fig. 8.3. We can sample this signal to produce the time

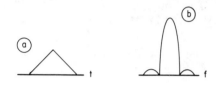

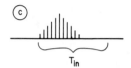

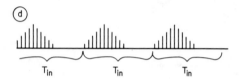

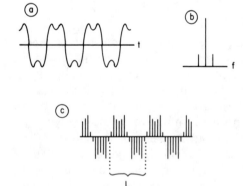

Figure 8.2 Signals and sequences for the DFT of a short time-limited signal.

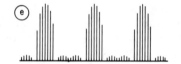

Figure 8.3 Signal and sequences for the DFT of a periodic signal. The length L of the DFT input record equals the period of the signal.

sequence shown in Fig. 8.3c for input to the DFT. If the input record length *N* of the DFT is chosen to be exactly equal to the length of 1 period of this sequence, the periodic assumption implicit in the DFT will cause the DFT to treat the single input record as though it were the complete sequence. The corresponding periodic discrete-frequency spectrum is shown in Fig. 8.3d. The DFT output sequence will actually consist of just 1 period that matches *exactly* the spectrum of Fig. 8.3b. We could not hope for (or find) a more convenient situation. Unfortunately, this realtionship exists only in an *N*-point DFT where the input signal is both band limited and periodic with a period of exactly *N*.

Long aperiodic signals

So far we have covered the use of the DFT under relatively favorable conditions that are not likely to exist in many important signal processing applications. Often the signal to be analyzed will be neither periodic nor reasonably time limited. The corresponding sequence of digitized-signal values will be longer than the DFT input record and will therefore have to be truncated to just *N* samples before the DFT can be applied. The periodic nature of the DFT will cause the truncated sequence of Fig. 8.4b to be interpreted as though it were the sequence shown in Fig. 8.4c. Notice that in this sequence there is a large discontinuity in the signal at the points corresponding to the ends of the input record. This will introduce additional high-frequency components into the spectrum produced by the DFT. This

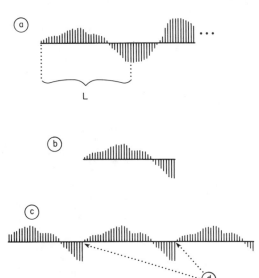

Figure 8.4 Discontinuities caused by truncating the input sequence of a DFT: (a) long input sequence, (b) truncated input sequence; (c) input sequence as interpreted by the DFT, and (d) resulting discontinuities.

phenomenon is called *leakage*. To reduce the leakage effects, it is a common practice to multiply the truncated input sequence by a tapering window prior to application of the DFT. A good window shape will taper off at the ends of the input record but still have a reasonably compact and narrow spectrum. This is important since multiplying the time sequence by the window will cause the corresponding frequency sequence to be convolved with the spectrum of the window. A narrow window spectrum will cause minimum smearing of the signal spectrum. Several popular windowing functions and their spectra are treated at length in Chap. 11.

Listing 8.1   dft( )

```
/***********************************/
/*                                 */
/*    Listing 8.1                  */
/*                                 */
/*    dft()                        */
/*                                 */
/***********************************/

void dft(    struct complex x[],
             struct complex xx[],
             int N)
{
int n, m;
real sumRe, sumIm, phi;

for( m=0; m<N; m++) {
    sumRe = 0.0;
    sumIm = 0.0;
    for( n=0; n<N; n++) {
        phi = 2.0 * PI * m * n /N;
        sumRe += x[n].Re * cos(phi) + x[n].Im * sin(phi);
        sumIm += x[n].Im * cos(phi) - x[n].Re * sin(phi);
        }
    xx[m] = cmplx(sumRe, sumIm);
    }
return;
}
```

Listing 8.2   dft2( )

```
/***********************************/
/*                                 */
/*    Listing 8.2                  */
/*                                 */
/*    dft2()                       */
/*                                 */
/***********************************/

void dft2(    struct complex x[],
              struct complex xx[],
              int N)
{
int n, m, k;
real sumRe, sumIm, phi;
static real cosVal[DFTSIZE], sinVal[DFTSIZE];
```

```
for( k=0; k<N; k++) {
    cosVal[k] = cos(2.0 * PI * k /N);
    sinVal[k] = sin(2.0 * PI * k /N);
    }

for( m=0; m<N; m++) {
    sumRe = 0.0;
    sumIm = 0.0;

    for(n=0; n<N; n++) {
        k = (m*n)%N;
        sumRe += x[n].Re * cosVal[k] + x[n].Im * sinVal[k];
        sumIm += x[n].Im * cosVal[k] - x[n].Re * sinVal[k];
        }
    xx[m] = cmplx(sumRe, sumIm);
    }
return;
}
```

Listing 8.3   fft( )

```
/***********************************/
/*                                 */
/*    Listing 8.3                  */
/*                                 */
/*    fft()                        */
/*                                 */
/***********************************/

void fft(    struct complex xIn[],
             struct complex xOut[],
             int N)
{
static struct complex x[2][DFTSIZE];
static real cc[DFTSIZE], ss[DFTSIZE];
static char inString[81];
int ping, pong, n, L, nSkip, level, nG, nB, kt, kb, nBot;

for( n=0; n<N; n++) {
    x[0][n] = xIn[n];
    cc[n] = cos(2.0 * PI * n /N);
    ss[n] = sin(2.0 * PI * n /N);
    }
```

```
pong = 0;
ping = 1;
L = log2(N);
nSkip = N;

for(level=1; level<=L; level++) {
    nSkip /= 2;
    n = 0;
    for(nG=0; nG<ipow(2,(level-1)); nG++) {
        kt = bitRev(L,2*nG);
        kb = bitRev(L,2*nG+1);

        for(nB=0; nB<nSkip; nB++) {
            nBot = n + nSkip;
            x[ping][n].Re =  x[pong][n].Re
                                 + cc[kt] * x[pong][nBot].Re
                                 + ss[kt] * x[pong][nBot].Im;
            x[ping][n].Im =  x[pong][n].Im
                                 + cc[kt] * x[pong][nBot].Im
                                 - ss[kt] * x[pong][nBot].Re;
            x[ping][nBot].Re =   x[pong][n].Re
                                 + cc[kb] * x[pong][nBot].Re
                                 + ss[kb] * x[pong][nBot].Im;
            x[ping][nBot].Im =   x[pong][n].Im
                                 + cc[kb] * x[pong][nBot].Im
                                 - ss[kb] * x[pong][nBot].Re;
            n++;
            }
        n += nSkip;
        }
    ping = !ping;
    pong = !pong;
    }
for(n=0; n<N; n++) xOut[bitRev(L,n)] = x[pong][n];
return;
}
```

The z Transform

The *two-sided*, or *bilateral*, z transform of a discrete-time sequence $x[n]$ is defined by

$$X(z) = \sum_{n=-\infty}^{\infty} x[n]\, z^{-n} \tag{9.1}$$

and the *one-sided*, or *unilateral*, z transform is defined by

$$X(z) = \sum_{n=0}^{\infty} x[n]\, z^{-n} \tag{9.2}$$

Some authors (for example, Rabiner and Gold 1975) use the unqualified term "z transform" to refer to (9.1), while others (for example, Cadzow 1973) use the unqualified term to refer to (9.2). In this book, "z transform" refers to the two-sided transform, and the one-sided transform is explicitly identified as such. For causal sequences (that is, $x[n] = 0$ for $n < 0$) the one-sided and two-sided transforms are equivalent. Some of the material presented in this chapter may seem somewhat abstract, but rest assured that the z transform and its properties play a major role in many of the design and realization methods that appear in later chapters.

9.1 Region of Convergence

For some values of z, the series in (9.1) does not converge to a finite value. The portion of the z plane for which the series does converge is called the *region of convergence* (ROC). Whether or not (9.1) converges depends upon the magnitude of z rather than a specific complex value of z. In other words, for a given sequence $x[n]$, if the series in (9.1) converges for a value of $z = z_1$, then the series will converge for all values of z for which $|z| = |z_1|$. Conversely, if the series diverges for $z = z_2$, then the series will diverge for all values of z for which $|z| = |z_2|$. Because convergence depends on the magni-

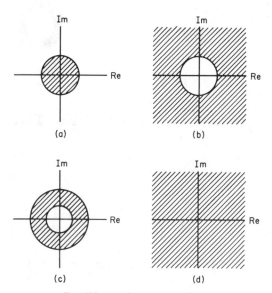

Figure 9.1 Possible configurations of the region of convergence for the z transform.

tude of z, the region or convergence will always be *bounded* by circles centered at the origin of the z plane. This is not to say that the region of convergence is always a circle—it can be the interior of a circle, the exterior of a circle, an annulus, or the entire z plane as shown in Fig. 9.1. Each of these four cases can be loosely viewed as an annulus—a circle's interior being an annulus with an inner radius of zero and a finite outer radius, a circle's exterior being an annulus with nonzero inner radius and infinite outer radius, and the entire z plane being an annulus with an inner radius of zero and an infinite outer radius. In some cases, the ROC has an inner radius of zero, but the origin itself is not part of the region. In other cases, the ROC has an infinite outer radius, but the series diverges *at* $|z| = \infty$.

By definition, the ROC cannot contain any poles since the series becomes infinite at the poles. The ROC for a z transform will always be a simply connected region in the z plane. If we assume that the sequence $x[n]$ has a finite magnitude for all finite values of n, the nature of the ROC can be related to the nature of the sequence in several ways as discussed in the paragraphs that follow and as summarized in Table 9.1.

Finite-duration sequences

If $x[n]$ is nonzero over only a finite range of n, then the z transform can be rewritten as

$$X(z) = \sum_{n = N_1}^{N_2} x[n] \, z^{-n}$$

TABLE 9.1   Properties of the Region of Convergence for the z Transform

$x[n]$	ROC for $X(z)$
All	Includes no poles
All	Simply connected region
Single sample at $n = 0$	Entire z plane
Finite-duration, causal, $x[n] = 0$ for all $n < 0$, $x[n] \neq 0$ for some $n > 0$	z plane except for $z = 0$
Finite-duration, with $x[n] \neq 0$ for some $n < 0$, $x[n] = 0$ for all $n > 0$	z plane except for $z = \infty$
Finite-duration, with $x[n] \neq 0$ for some $n < 0$, $x[n] \neq 0$ for some $n > 0$	z plane except for $z = 0$ and $z = \infty$
Right-sided, $x[n] = 0$ for all $n < 0$	Outward from outermost pole
Right-sided, $x[n] \neq 0$ for some $n < 0$	Outward from outermost pole, $z = \infty$ is excluded
Left-sided, $x[n] = 0$ for all $n > 0$	Inward from innermost pole
Left-sided, $x[n] \neq 0$ for some $n > 0$	Inward from innermost pole, $z = 0$ is excluded
Two-sided	Annulus

This series will converge provided that $|x[n]| < \infty$ for $N_1 \leq n \leq N_2$ and $|z^{-n}| < \infty$ for $N_1 \leq n \leq N_2$. For negative values of n, $|z^{-n}|$ will be infinite for $z = \infty$; and for positive values of n, $|z^{-n}|$ will be infinite for $z = 0$. Therefore, a sequence having nonzero values only for $n = N_1$ through $n = N_2$ will have a z transform that converges everywhere in the z plane except for $z = \infty$ when $N_1 < 0$ and $z = 0$ when $N_2 > 0$. Note that a single sample at $n = 0$ is the only finite-duration sequence defined over the entire z plane.

Infinite-duration sequences

The sequence $x[n]$ is a *right-sided sequence* if $x[n]$ is zero for all n less than some finite value N_1. It can be shown (see Oppenheim and Schafer 1975 or 1989) that the z transform $X(z)$ of a right-sided sequence will have an ROC that extends outward from the outermost finite pole of $X(z)$. In other words, the ROC will be the area outside a circle whose radius equals the magnitude of the pole of $X(z)$ having the largest magnitude (see Fig. 9.2). If $N_1 < 0$, this ROC will not include $z = \infty$.

The sequence $x[n]$ is a *left-sided sequence* if $x[n]$ is zero for all n greater than some finite value N_2. The z transform $X(z)$ of a left-sided sequence will have an ROC that extends inward from the innermost pole of $X(z)$. The ROC will be the interior of a circle whose radius equals the magnitude of the pole of $X(z)$ having the smallest magnitude (see Fig. 9.3). If $N_2 > 0$, this ROC will not include $z = 0$.

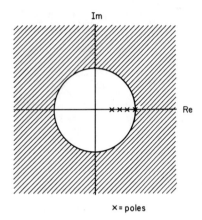

× = poles

Figure 9.2 Region of convergence for the z transform of a right-sided sequence.

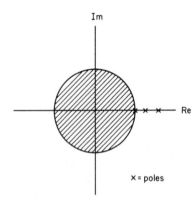

× = poles

Figure 9.3 Region of convergence for the z transform of a left-sided sequence.

The sequence $x[n]$ is a *two-sided sequence* if $x[n]$ has nonzero values extending to both $-\infty$ and $+\infty$. The ROC for the z transform of a two-sided sequence will be an annulus.

Convergence of the unilateral z transform

Note that all of the properties discussed above are for the two-sided z transform defined by (9.1). Since the one-sided z transform is equivalent to the two-sided transform when $x[n] = 0$ for $n < 0$, the ROC for a one-sided transform will always look like the ROC for the two-sided transform of either a causal finite-duration sequence or a causal right-sided sequence. For all causal systems, the ROC for the bilateral transform always consists of the area outside a circle of radius $R \geq 0$. Therefore, for two-sided transforms of causal sequences and for all one-sided transforms, the ROC can be (and frequently is) specified in terms of a *radius of convergence* R such that the transform converges for $|z| > R$.

9.2 Relationship between the Laplace and z Transforms

The z transform can be related to both the Laplace and Fourier transforms. As noted in Chap. 7, a sequence can be obtained by sampling a function of continuous time. Specifically, for a causal sequence

$$x[n] = \sum_{n=0}^{\infty} x_a(nT)\,\delta(t - nT) \tag{9.3}$$

the Laplace transform is given by

$$X(s) = \sum_{n=0}^{\infty} x_a(nT)\,e^{-nTs} \tag{9.4}$$

Let $X_a(s)$ denote the Laplace transform of $x_a(t)$. The pole-zero pattern for $X(s)$ consists of the pole-zero pattern for $X_a(s)$ replicated at intervals of $\omega_s = 2\pi/T$ along the $j\omega$ axis in the s plane. If we modify (9.4) by substituting

$$z = e^{sT} \tag{9.5}$$

$$x[n] = x_a(nT) \tag{9.6}$$

we obtain the z transform defined by Eq. (9.1).

Relationships between features in the s plane and features in the z plane can be established using (9.5). Since $s = \sigma + j\omega$ with σ and ω real, we can expand (9.5) as

$$z = e^{sT} = e^{\sigma T}e^{j\omega T} = e^{\sigma T}(\cos \omega T + j \sin \omega T)$$

Because $|e^{j\omega T}| = (\cos^2 \omega T + \sin^2 \omega T)^{1/2} = 1$, and $T > 0$, we can conclude that $|z| < 1$ for $\sigma < 0$. Or, in other words, the left half of the s plane maps into the interior of the unit circle in the z plane. Likewise, $|z| = 1$ for $\sigma = 0$, so the $j\omega$ axis of the s plane maps onto the unit circle in the z plane. The "extra" replicated copies of the pole-zero pattern for $X(s)$ will all map into a single pole-zero pattern in the z plane. When evaluated around the unit circle (that is, $z = e^{j\lambda}$), the z transform yields the discrete-time Fourier transform (DTFT) (see Sec. 7.2).

9.3 System Functions

Given the relationships between the Laplace transform and the z transform that were noted in the previous section, we might suspect that the z transform of a discrete-time system's unit sample response (that is, digital impulse response) plays a major role in the analysis of the system in much the same way that the Laplace transform of a continuous-time system's impulse response yields the system's transfer function. This suspicion is indeed correct. The z transform of a discrete-time system's unit sample response is called the *system function*, or *transfer function*, of the system and is denoted by $H(z)$.

The system function can also be derived from the linear difference equation that describes the filter. If we take the z transform of each term in Eq. (7.6), we obtain

$$Y(z) + a_1 z^{-1} Y(z) + a_2 z^{-2} Y(z) + \cdots + a_k z^{-k} Y(z)$$

$$= b_0 X(z) + b_1 z^{-1} X(z) + b_2 z^{-2} X(z) + b_k z^{-k} X(z)$$

Factoring out $Y(z)$ and $X(z)$ and then solving for $H(z) = Y(z)/X(z)$ yields

$$H(z) = \frac{Y(z)}{X(z)} = \frac{b_0 + b_1 z^{-1} + b_2 z^{-2} + \cdots + b_k z^{-k}}{1 + a_1 z^{-1} + a_2 z^{-2} + \cdots + a_k z^{-k}}$$

Both the numerator and denominator of $H(z)$ can be factored to yield

$$H(z) = \frac{b_0(z - q_1)(z - q_2) \cdots (z - q_k)}{(z - p_1)(z - p_2)(z - p_3) \cdots (z - p_k)}$$

The poles of $H(z)$ are $p_1, p_2, \ldots, p_k$, and the zeros are $q_1, q_2, \ldots, q_m$.

9.4   Common z-Transform Pairs and Properties

The use of the unilateral z transform by some authors and the use of the bilateral transform by others does not present as many problems as we might expect, because in the field of digital filters, most of the sequences of interest are causal sequences or sequences that can easily be made causal. As we noted previously, for causal sequences the one-sided and two-sided transforms are equivalent. It really just comes down to a matter of being careful about definitions. An author using the unilateral default (that is, "z transform" means "unilateral z transform") might say that the z transform of $x[n] = a^n$ is given by

$$X(z) = \frac{z}{z - a} \qquad \text{for } |z| > |a| \tag{9.7}$$

On the other hand, an author using the bilateral default might say that (9.7) represents the z transform of $x[n] = a^n u[n]$, where $u[n]$ is the unit step sequence. Neither author is concerned with the values of a^n for $n < 0$—the first author is eliminating these values by the way the transform is defined, and the second author is eliminating these values by multiplying them with a unit step sequence that is zero for $n < 0$. There are a few useful bilateral transform pairs that consider values of $x[n]$ for $n < 0$. These pairs are listed in Table 9.2. However, the majority of the most commonly used z-transform pairs involve values of $x[n]$ only for $n \geq 0$. These pairs are most conveniently

TABLE 9.2   Common Bilateral z-Transform Pairs

$x[n]$	$X(z)$	ROC
$\delta[n]$	1	all z
$\delta[n-m], m>0$	z^{-m}	$z \neq 0$
$\delta[n-m], m<0$	z^{-m}	$z \neq \infty$
$u[n]$	$\dfrac{z}{z-1}$	$|z|>1$
$-u[-n-1]$	$\dfrac{z}{z-1}$	$|z|<1$
$-a^n u[-n-1]$	$\dfrac{z}{z-a}$	$|z|<|a|$
$-na^n u[-n-1]$	$\dfrac{az}{(z-a)^2}$	$|z|<|a|$

tabulated as unilateral transforms with the understanding that any unilateral transform pair can be converted into a bilateral transform pair by replacing $x[n]$ with $x[n]\,u[n]$. Some common unilateral z-transform pairs are listed in Table 9.3. Some useful properties exhibited by both the unilateral and bilateral z transforms are listed in Table 9.4.

9.5   Inverse z Transform

The inverse z transform is given by the contour integral

$$x[n] = \frac{1}{2\pi j} \oint_C X(z)\, z^{n-1}\, dz \tag{9.8}$$

where the integral notation indicates a counterclockwise closed contour that encircles the origin of the z plane and that lies within the region of convergence for $X(z)$. If $X(z)$ is rational, the residue theorem can be used to evaluate (9.8). However, direct evaluation of the inversion integral is rarely performed in actual practice. In practical situations, inversion of the z transform is usually performed indirectly, using established transform pairs and transform properties.

9.6   Inverse z Transform via Partial Fraction Expansion

Consider a system function of the general form given by

$$H(z) = \frac{b_0 z^m + b_1 z^{m-1} + \cdots + b_{m-1} z^1 + b_m}{z_m + a_1 z^{m-1} + \cdots + a_{m-1} z^1 + a_m} \tag{9.9}$$

TABLE 9.3 Common Unilateral z-Transform Pairs
(R = radius of convergence)

$x[n]$	$X(z)$	R
1	$\dfrac{z}{z-1}$	1
$u_1[n]$	$\dfrac{z}{z-1}$	1
$\delta[n]$	1	$0 \quad (z=0 \text{ included})$
nT	$\dfrac{Tz}{(z-1)^2}$	1
$(nT)^2$	$\dfrac{T^2 z(z+1)}{(z-1)^3}$	1
$(nT)^3$	$\dfrac{T^3 z(z^2+4z+1)}{(z-1)^4}$	1
a^n	$\dfrac{z}{z-a}$	$|a|$
$(n+1)a^n$	$\dfrac{z^2}{(z-a)^2}$	$|a|$
$\dfrac{(n+1)(n+2)}{2!}a^n$	$\dfrac{z^3}{(z-a)^3}$	$|a|$
$\dfrac{(n+1)(n+2)(n+3)}{3!}a^n$	$\dfrac{z^4}{(z-a)^4}$	$|a|$
$\dfrac{(n+1)(n+2)(n+3)(n+4)}{4!}a^n$	$\dfrac{z^5}{(z-a)^5}$	$|a|$
na^n	$\dfrac{az}{(z-a)^2}$	$|a|$
$n^2 a^n$	$\dfrac{az(z+a)}{(z-a)^3}$	$|a|$
$n^3 a^n$	$\dfrac{az(z^2+4az+a^2)}{(z-a)^4}$	$|a|$
$\dfrac{a^n}{n!}$	$e^{a/z}$	0
e^{-anT}	$\dfrac{z}{z-e^{-aT}}$	$|e^{-aT}|$
$a^n \sin n\omega T$	$\dfrac{az \sin \omega T}{z^2 - 2az \cos \omega T + a^2}$	$|a|$
$a^n \cos n\omega T$	$\dfrac{z^2 - za \cos \omega T}{z^2 - 2az \cos \omega T + a^2}$	$|a|$
$e^{-anT} \sin \omega_0 nT$	$\dfrac{ze^{-aT} \sin \omega_0 T}{z^2 - 2ze^{-aT} \cos \omega_0 T + e^{-2aT}}$	$|e^{-aT}|$
$e^{-anT} \cos \omega_0 nT$	$\dfrac{z^2 - ze^{-aT} \cos \omega_0 T}{z^2 - 2ze^{-aT} \cos \omega_0 T + e^{-2aT}}$	$|e^{-aT}|$

TABLE 9.4 Properties of the *z* Transform

Property no.	Time function	Transform
	$x[n]$	$X(z)$
	$y[n]$	$Y(z)$
1	$a\,x[n]$	$a\,X(z)$
2	$x[n] + y[n]$	$X(z) + Y(z)$
3	$e^{-anT}\,x[n]$	$X(e^{at}z)$
4	$\alpha^n\,x[n]$	$X\!\left(\dfrac{z}{\alpha}\right)$
5	$x[n-m]$	$z^{-m}\,X(z)$
6	$x[n] * y[n]$	$X(z)\,Y(z)$
7	$n\,x[n]$	$-z\dfrac{d}{dz}X(z)$
8	$x[-n]$	$X(z^{-1})$
9	$x^*[n]$	$X^*(z^*)$

Such a system function can be expanded into a sum of simpler terms that can be more easily inverse-transformed. Linearity of the *z* transform allows us to then sum the simpler inverse transforms to obtain the inverse of the original system function. The method for generating the expansion differs slightly depending upon whether the system function's poles are all distinct or if some are multiple poles. Since most practical filter designs involve system functions with distinct poles, the more complicated multiple-pole procedure is not presented. For a discussion of the multiple-pole case, see Cadzow (1973).

**Algorithm 9.1 Partial fraction expansion for *H(z)*
having simple poles**

Step 1. Factor the denominator of $H(z)$ to produce

$$H(z) = \frac{b_0 z^m + b_1 z^{m-1} + \cdots + b_{m-1}z^1 + b_m}{(z - p_1)(z - p_2)(z - p_3)\cdots(z - p_k)}$$

Step 2. Compute c_0 as given by

$$c_0 = H(z)\big|_{z=0} = \frac{b_m}{(-p_1)(-p_2)(-p_3)\cdots(-p_m)}$$

Step 3. Compute c_i for $1 \le i \le m$ using

$$c_i = \frac{z - p_i}{z} H(z)\Big|_{z = p_i}$$

Step 4. Formulate the discrete-time function $h[n]$ as given by

$$h(n) = c_0\delta(n) + c_1(p_1)^n + c_2(p_2)^n + \cdots + c_m(p_m)^n \qquad \text{for } n = 0, 1, 2, \ldots$$

The function $h[n]$ is the inverse z transform of $H(z)$.

Example 9.1 Use the partial fraction expansion to determine the inverse z transform of

$$H(z) = \frac{z^2}{z^2 + z - 2}$$

solution

Step 1. Factor the denominator of $H(z)$ to produce

$$H(z) = \frac{z^2}{(z - 1)(z + 2)}$$

Step 2. Compute c_0 as

$$c_0 = H(z)\big|_{z = 0} = 0$$

Step 3. Compute c_1, c_2 as

$$c_1 = \left[\frac{(z - 1)}{z}\frac{z^2}{(z - 1)(z + 2)}\right]\Bigg|_{z = 1} = \frac{z^2}{z^2 + 2z}\Bigg|_{z = 1} = \frac{1}{3}$$

$$c_2 = \left[\frac{(z + 2)}{z}\frac{z^2}{(z - 1)(z + 2)}\right]\Bigg|_{z = -2} = \frac{z^2}{z^2 - z}\Bigg|_{z = -2} = \frac{2}{3}$$

Step 4. The inverse transform $h[n]$ is given by

$$h[n] = \tfrac{1}{3}(1)^n + \tfrac{1}{3}(-2)^n$$
$$= 1 + \tfrac{1}{3}(-2)^n \qquad n = 0, 1, 2, \ldots$$

FIR Filter Fundamentals

Digital filters are usually classified by the duration of their impulse response, which can be either finite or infinite. The methods for designing and implementing these two filter classes differ considerably. *Finite impulse response* (FIR) filters are digital filters whose response to a unit impulse (unit sample function) is finite in duration. This is in contrast to *infinite impulse response* (IIR) filters whose response to a unit impulse (unit sample function) is infinite in duration. FIR and IIR filters each have advantages and disadvantages, and neither is best in all situations. FIR filters can be implemented using either recursive or nonrecursive techniques, but usually nonrecursive techniques are used.

10.1 Introduction to FIR Filters

The general form for a linear time-invariant FIR system's output $y[k]$ at time k is given by

$$y[k] = \sum_{n=0}^{N-1} h[n]\, x[k-n] \tag{10.1}$$

where $h[n]$ is the system's inpulse response. As Eq. (10.1) indicates, the output is a linear combination of the present input and the N previous inputs. The remainder of this chapter is devoted to basic properties and realization issues for FIR filters. Specific design approaches for selecting the coefficients b_n are covered in Chaps. 11, 12, and 13.

FIR advantages

FIR filters have the following advantages:

- FIR filters can easily be designed to have constant phase delay and/or constant group delay.

- FIR filters implemented with nonrecursive techniques will always be stable and free from the limit-cycle oscillations that can plague IIR designs.
- Round-off noise (which is due to finite precision arithmetic performed in the digital processor) can be made relatively small for nonrecursive implementations.
- FIR filters can also be implemented using recursive techniques if this is desired.

FIR disadvantages

Despite their advantages, FIR filters still exhibit some significant disadvantages:

- An FIR filter's impulse response duration, although finite, may have to be very long to obtain sharp cutoff characteristics.
- The design of FIR filters to meet specific performance objectives is generally more difficult than the design of IIR filters for similar applications.

10.2   Evaluating the Frequency Response of FIR Filters

A digital filter's impulse response $h[n]$ is related to the frequency response $H(e^{j\lambda})$ via the DTFT:

$$H(e^{j\lambda}) = \sum_{n=-\infty}^{\infty} h[n]\, e^{-jn\lambda} \tag{10.2}$$

For an FIR filter, $h[n]$ is nonzero only for $0 \leq n < N$. Therefore, the limits of the summation can be changed to yield

$$H(e^{j\lambda}) = \sum_{n=0}^{N-1} h[n]\, e^{-jn\lambda} \tag{10.3}$$

Equation (10.3) can be evaluated directly at any desired value of λ.

We now take note of the fact that $\lambda = \omega T$ and that the value of continuous-radian frequency ω_m corresponding to the discrete-frequency index m is given by

$$\omega_m = 2\pi m F \tag{10.4}$$

Substituting $2\pi m FT$ for λ, and $H[m]$ for $H(e^{j\lambda})$ in (10.2) yields the discrete Fourier transform:

$$H[m] = \sum_{n=0}^{N-1} h[n]\, \exp(-2\pi jnmFT) \tag{10.5}$$

Thus, the DTFT can be evaluated at a set of discrete frequencies $\omega = \omega_m$, $0 \leq m < N$, by using the DFT, which in turn may be evaluated in a computationally efficient fashion using one of the various FFT algorithms.

10.3   Linear Phase FIR Filters

As discussed in Sec. 2.8, constant group delay is a desirable property for filters to have since nonconstant group delay will cause envelope distortion in modulated-carrier signals and pulse-shape distortion in base-band digital signals. A filter's frequency response $H(e^{j\omega})$ can be expressed in terms of amplitude response $A(\omega)$ and phase response $\theta(\omega)$ as

$$H(e^{j\omega}) = A(\omega)\, e^{j\theta(\omega)}$$

If a filter has a linear phase response of the form

$$\theta(\omega) = -\alpha\omega \qquad -\pi \le \omega \le \pi \tag{10.6}$$

it will have both constant phase delay τ_p and constant group delay τ_g. In fact, in this case $\tau_p = \tau_g = \alpha$. It can be shown (for example, Rabiner and Gold 1975) that for $\alpha = 0$, the impulse response is an impulse of arbitrary strength:

$$h[n] = \begin{cases} c & n = 0 \\ 0 & n \ne 0 \end{cases}$$

For nonzero α, it can be shown that Eq. (10.6) is satisfied if and only if

$$\alpha = \frac{N-1}{2} \tag{10.7a}$$

$$h[n] = h[N-1-n] \qquad 0 \le n \le N-1 \tag{10.7b}$$

Within the constraints imposed by (10.7), the possible filters are usually separated into two types. Type 1 filters satisfy (10.7) with N odd, and type 2 filters satisfy (10.7) with N even. For type 1 filters, the axis of symmetry for $h[n]$ lies at $n = (N-1)/2$ as shown in Fig. 10.1. For type 2 filters, the axis of symmetry lies midway between $n = N/2$ and $n = (N-2)/2$ as shown in Fig. 10.2.

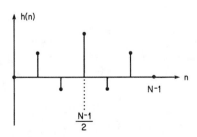

Figure 10.1 Impulse response for a type 1 linear phase FIR filter showing even symmetry about $n = (N-1)/2$.

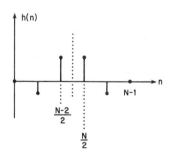

Figure 10.2 Impulse response for a type 2 linear phase FIR filter showing even symmetry about the abscissa midway between $n = (N-2)/2$ and $n = N/2$.

Filters can have constant group delay without having constant phase delay if the phase response is a straight line that does not pass through the origin. Such a phase response is defined as

$$\theta(\omega) = \beta + \alpha\omega \qquad (10.8)$$

The phase response of a filter will satisfy (10.8) if

$$\alpha = \frac{N-1}{2} \qquad (10.9a)$$

$$\beta = \pm\frac{\pi}{2} \qquad (10.9b)$$

$$h[n] = -h[N-1-n] \qquad 0 \le n \le N-1 \qquad (10.9c)$$

An impulse response satisfying (10.9c) is said to be *odd symmetric*, or *antisymmetric*. Within the constraints imposed by (10.9), the possible filters can be separated into two types that are commonly referred to as type 3 and type 4 *linear phase* filters despite the fact that the phase response is *not truly linear*. [The phase response is a straight line, but it does not pass through the origin, and consequently $\theta(\omega_1 + \omega_2)$ does not equal $\theta(\omega_1) + \theta(\omega_2)$.] Type 3 filters satisfy (10.9) with N odd, and type 4 filters satisfy (10.9) with N even. For type 3 filters, the axis of antisymmetry for $h[n]$ lies at $n = (N-1)/2$ as shown in Fig. 10.3. When $n = (N-1)/2$, with N even, Eq. (10.9c) gives

$$h\left[\frac{N-1}{2}\right] = -h\left[\frac{N-1}{2}\right]$$

Therefore, $h[(N-1)/2]$ must always equal zero in type 3 filters. For type 4 filters, the axis of antisymmetry lies midway between $n = N/2$ and $n = (N-2)/2$ as shown in Fig. 10.4.

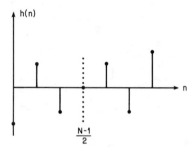

Figure 10.3 Impulse response for a type 3 linear phase FIR filter showing odd symmetry about $n = (N-1)/2$.

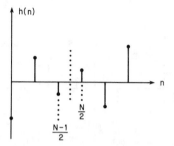

Figure 10.4 Impulse response for a type 4 linear phase FIR filter showing odd symmetry about the abscissa midway between $n = (N-2)/2$ and $n = N/2$.

The discrete-time Fourier transform (DTFT) can be used directly to obtain the frequency response of any FIR filter. However, for the special case of linear phase FIR filters, the symmetry and "realness" properties of the impulse response can be used to modify the general DTFT to obtain dedicated formulas having reduced computational burdens.

The frequency response $H(e^{j\omega T})$ and amplitude response $A(e^{j\omega T})$ are listed in Table 10.1 for the four types of linear phase FIR filters. The properties of these four types are summarized in Table 10.2. A C function, **cgdFirResponse( )**, which implements the equations of Table 10.1 is provided in Listing 10.1. The function **normalizeResponse( )** in Listing 10.2 can be used to normalize the response so that the peak pass-band value is at 0 dB.

At first glance, the fact that $A(\omega)$ is periodic with a period of 4π for type 2 and type 4 filters seems to contradict the fundamental relationship between sampling rate and folding frequency that was established in Chap. 7. The difficulty lies in how we have defined $A(\omega)$. The frequency response $H(\omega)$ is in fact periodic in 2π for all four types as we would expect. Both $\text{Re}[H(\omega)]$ and $\text{Im}[H(\omega)]$ are periodic in 2π, but factors of -1 are allocated between $A(\omega)$ and $\theta(\omega)$ differently over the intervals $(0, 2\pi)$ and $(2\pi, 4\pi)$ so that $\theta(\omega)$ can be made linear [and $A(\omega)$ can be made analytic].

TABLE 10.1 Frequency Response Formulas for Linear Phase FIR Filters

$h(nT)$ symmetry	N	$H(e^{j\omega T})$	$A(e^{j\omega T})$
Even	Odd	$e^{-j\omega(N-1)T/2} A(e^{j\omega T})$	$\sum\limits_{k=0}^{(N-1)/2} a_k \cos \omega k T$
Even	Even	$e^{-j\omega(N-1)T/2} A(e^{j\omega T})$	$\sum\limits_{k=1}^{N/2} b_k \cos[\omega(k-\frac{1}{2})T]$
Odd	Odd	$e^{-j[\omega(N-1)T/2 - \pi/2]} A(e^{j\omega T})$	$\sum\limits_{k=1}^{(N-1)/2} a_k \sin \omega k T$
Odd	Even	$e^{-j[\omega(N-1)T/2 - \pi/2]} A(e^{j\omega T})$	$\sum\limits_{k=1}^{N/2} b_k \sin[\omega(k-\frac{1}{2})T]$

$$a_0 = h\left[\frac{(N-1)T}{2}\right] \quad a_k = 2h\left[\left(\frac{N-1}{2}-k\right)T\right] \quad b_k = 2h\left[\left(\frac{N}{2}-k\right)T\right]$$

TABLE 10.2 Properties of FIR Filters Having Constant Group Delay

	Type			
	1	2	3	4
Length, N	Odd	Even	Odd	Even
Symmetry about $\omega = 0$	Even	Even	Odd	Odd
Symmetry about $\omega = \pi$	Even	Odd	Odd	Even
Periodicity	2π	4π	2π	4π

Some of the properties listed in Table 10.2 have an impact on which types can be used in particular applications. As a consequence of odd symmetry about $\omega = 0$, types 3 and 4 always have $A(0) = 0$ and should therefore not be used for lowpass or bandstop filters. As a consequence of their odd symmetry about $\omega = \pi$, types 2 and 3 always have $A(\pi) = 0$ and should therefore not be used for highpass or bandstop filters. Within the bounds of these restrictions, the choice between an odd-length or even-length filter is often made so that the desired transition frequency falls as close as possible to the midpoint between two sampled frequencies. The phase response of types 3 and 4 includes a constant component of 90° in addition to the linear component. Therefore, these types are suited for use as differentiators and Hilbert transformers (see Rabiner and Gold 1975).

Listing 10.1 cgdFirResponse( )

```
/**********************************/
/*                                */
/*    Listing 10.1                */
/*                                */
/*    cgdFirResponse()            */
/*                                */
/**********************************/

void cgdFirResponse( int firType,
                     int numbTaps,
                     real hh[],
                     logical dbScale,
                     int numberOfPoints,
                     real Hd[])
{
int index, L, n;
real lambda, work;
/*printf("in symFirResponse\n");*/

for( L=0; L<=numberOfPoints-1; L++)
    {
    lambda = L * PI / (real) numberOfPoints;
    switch (firType) {
        case 1:          /* symmetric and odd */
            work = hh[(numbTaps-1)/2];
            for( n=1; n<=((numbTaps-1)/2); n++) {
                index = (numbTaps-1)/2 - n;
                work = work + 2.0 * hh[index] * cos(n*lambda);
                }
            break;
        case 2:          /* symmetric and even */
            work = 0.0;
            for( n=1; n<=(numbTaps/2); n++) {
                index = numbTaps/2-n;
                work = work + 2.0 * hh[index] * cos((n-0.5)*lambda);
                }
            break;
        case 3:          /* antisymmetric and odd */
            work = 0.0;
            for( n=1; n<=((numbTaps-1)/2); n++) {
                index = (numbTaps-1)/2 - n;
                work = work + 2.0 * hh[index] * sin(n*lambda);
                }
            break;
        case 4:          /* symmetric and even */
            work = 0.0;
```

```
                for( n=1; n<=(numbTaps/2); n++) {
                    index = numbTaps/2-n;
                    work = work + 2.0 * hh[index] * sin((n-0.5)*lambda);
                    }
                break;
            }

    if(dbScale)
        {Hd[L] = 20.0 * log10(fabs(work));}
    else
        {Hd[L] = fabs(work);}
    if(!(L%10)) printf("%3d\r",numberOfPoints-L);
    }
return;
}
```

Listing 10.2   normalizeResponse( )

```
/**********************************/
/*                                */
/*    Listing 10.2                */
/*                                */
/*    normalizeResponse()         */
/*                                */
/**********************************/

void normalizeResponse(    logical dbScale,
                           int numPts,
                           real H[])
{
int n;
real biggest;

if(dbScale)
    {
    biggest = -100.0;
    for( n=0; n<=numPts-1; n++)
        {if(H[n]>biggest) biggest = H[n];}
    for( n=0; n<=numPts-1; n++)
        {H[n] = H[n]-biggest;}
    }
else
    {
    biggest = 0.0;
    for( n=0; n<=numPts-1; n++)
```

```
            {if(H[n]>biggest) biggest = H[n];}
        for( n=0; n<=numPts-1; n++)
            {H[n] = H[n]/biggest;}
        }
return;
}
```

Fourier Series Method
of FIR Filter Design

11.1 Basis of the Fourier Series Method

This Fourier series method of FIR filter design is based on the fact that the frequency response of a digital filter is periodic and is therefore representable as a Fourier series. A desired "target" frequency response is selected and expanded as a Fourier series. This expansion is truncated to a finite number of terms that are then used as the filter coefficients or tap weights. The resulting filter has a frequency response that approximates the original desired target response.

Algorithm 11.1 Designing FIR filters via the Fourier series method

Step 1. Specify a desired frequency response $H_d(\lambda)$.

Step 2. Specify the desired number of filter taps N.

Step 3. Compute the filter coefficients $h[n]$ for $n = 0, 1, 2, \ldots, N-1$ using

$$h[n] = \frac{1}{2\pi} \int_{2\pi} H_d(\lambda)[\cos(m\lambda) + j \sin(m\lambda)] \, d\lambda \qquad (11.1)$$

where $m = n - (N-1)/2$.

[Simplifications of (11.1) are presented below for the cases in which H_d is the magnitude response of ideal lowpass, highpass, bandpass, or bandstop filters.]

Step 4. Using the techniques presented in Secs. 10.2 and 10.3, compute the actual frequency response of the resulting filter. If the performance is not adequate, change N or $H_d(\lambda)$ and go back to step 3.

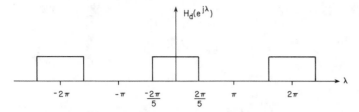

Figure 11.1 Desired frequency response for Example 11.1.

Example 11.1 Use the Fourier series method to design a 21-tap FIR filter that approximates the amplitude response of an ideal lowpass filter with a cutoff frequency of 2 kHz assuming a sampling frequency of 5 kHz.

solution The normalized cutoff is $\lambda = 2\pi/5$. The desired frequency response is depicted in Fig. 11.1. Using Eq. (11.1), we can immediately write

$$h[n] = \frac{1}{2\pi} \int_{-2\pi/5}^{2\pi/5} \cos(m\lambda)\, d\lambda + j\frac{1}{2\pi} \int_{-2\pi/5}^{2\pi/5} \sin(m\lambda)\, d\lambda$$

Since the second integrand is an odd function and the limits of integration are symmetric about zero, the second integral equals zero. Therefore,

$$h[n] = \frac{\sin(m\lambda)}{2m\pi} \Bigg|_{\lambda = -2\pi/5}^{2\pi/5}$$

$$= \frac{\sin(2m\pi/5)}{m\pi} \tag{11.2}$$

where $m = n - 10$.

L'Hospital's rule can be used to evaluate (11.2) for the case of $m = 0$ (that is, $n = 10$):

$$h[10] = \frac{(d/dm)\sin(2m\pi/5)}{(d/dm)m\pi} \Bigg|_{m=0}$$

$$= \frac{(2\pi/5)\cos(2m\pi/5)}{\pi} \Bigg|_{m=0}$$

$$= \frac{2}{5} = 0.4$$

Evaluation of (11.2) for $m \neq 0$ is straightforward. The values of $h[n]$ are listed in Table 11.1, and the corresponding magnitude response is shown in Figs. 11.2 and 11.3. Usually, the pass-band ripples are more pronounced when the vertical axis is in linear units such as numeric magnitude or percentage of peak magnitude as in Fig. 11.2. On the other hand, details of the stop-band response are usually more clearly displayed when the vertical axis is in decibels as in Fig. 11.3.

Properties of the Fourier series method

1. Filters designed using Algorithm 11.1 will exhibit the linear phase property discussed in Sec. 10.3, provided that the target frequency response $H_d(\lambda)$ is either symmetric or antisymmetric.

TABLE 11.1   Impulse Response Coefficients for the 21-tap Lowpass Filter of Example 11.1

$h[0] = h[20] =$	0.000000
$h[1] = h[19] =$	-0.033637
$h[2] = h[18] =$	-0.023387
$h[3] = h[17] =$	0.026728
$h[4] = h[16] =$	0.050455
$h[5] = h[15] =$	0.000000
$h[6] = h[14] =$	-0.075683
$h[7] = h[13] =$	-0.062366
$h[8] = h[12] =$	0.093549
$h[9] = h[11] =$	0.302731
$h[10] =$	0.400000

2. As a consequence of the Gibbs phenomenon, the frequency response of filters designed with Algorithm 11.1 will contain undershoots and overshoots at the band edges as exhibited by the responses shown in Figs. 11.2 and 11.3. As long as the number of filter taps remains finite, these disturbances cannot be eliminated by increasing the number of taps.

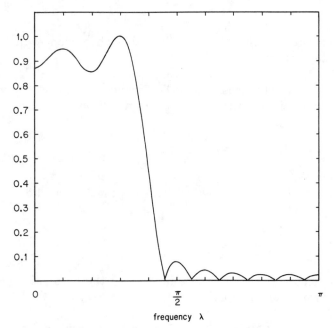

frequency λ

Figure 11.2 Magnitude response (as a percentage of peak) obtained from the 21-tap lowpass filter of Example 11.1.

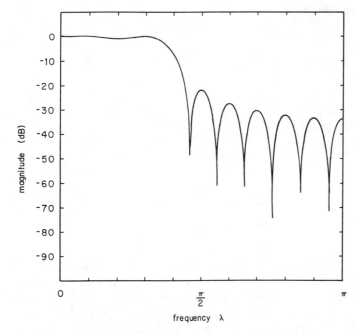

Figure 11.3 Magnitude response (in decibels) obtained from the 21-tap lowpass filter of Example 11.1.

Windowing techniques to reduce the effects of the Gibbs phenomena will be presented later in this chapter.

Result 11.1 FIR approximation for ideal lowpass filter. The impulse response coefficients for an FIR approximation to the ideal lowpass amplitude response shown in Fig. 11.4 are given by

$$h[n] = \frac{\sin(m\lambda_U)}{n\pi} \qquad \begin{aligned} n &= 0, 1, \ldots, N-1 \\ m &= n - (N-1)/2 \end{aligned}$$

For odd-length filters, the coefficient at $n = (N-1)/2$ is obtained by application of L'Hospital's rule to yield

$$h\left[\frac{N-1}{2}\right] = \frac{\lambda_U}{\pi}$$

The coefficients given by Result 11.1 can be computed using the C function **idealLowpass( )**, which is provided in Listing 11.1.

Result 11.2 FIR approximation for ideal highpass filter. The impulse response coefficients for an FIR approximation to the ideal highpass amplitude response

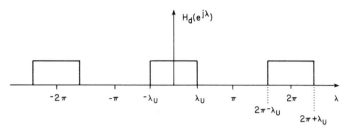

Figure 11.4 Frequency response of ideal lowpass digital filter.

shown in Fig. 11.5 are given by

$$h[n] = \begin{cases} 1 - \dfrac{\lambda_L}{\pi} & m = 0 \\[2ex] \dfrac{-\sin(m\lambda_L)}{m\pi} & m \neq 0 \end{cases}$$

where $m = n - (N-1)/2$.

The coefficients given by Result 11.2 can be computed using the C function **idealHighpass( )**, which is provided in Listing 11.2.

Example 11.2 Use Result 11.2 to design a 21-tap FIR filter that approximates the amplitude response of an ideal highpass filter with a normalized cutoff frequency of $\lambda_U = 3\pi/5$.

solution The coefficients $h(n)$ are listed in Table 11.2, and the resulting frequency response is shown in Figs. 11.6 and 11.7.

Result 11.3 FIR approximation for ideal bandpass filter. The impulse response coefficients for an FIR approximation to the ideal bandpass amplitude response shown in Fig. 11.8 are given by

$$h[n] = \begin{cases} \dfrac{\lambda_U - \lambda_L}{\pi} & m = 0 \\[2ex] \dfrac{1}{n\pi}[\sin(m\lambda_U) - \sin(m\lambda_L)] & m \neq 0 \end{cases}$$

where $m = n - (N-1)/2$.

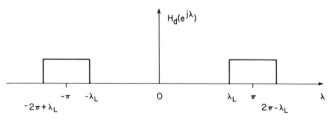

Figure 11.5 Frequency response of ideal highpass digital filter.

TABLE 11.2 Impulse Response Coefficients for the 21-tap Highpass Filter of Example 11.2

$h[0] = h[20] =$	0.000000
$h[1] = h[19] =$	0.033637
$h[2] = h[18] =$	-0.023387
$h[3] = h[17] =$	-0.026728
$h[4] = h[16] =$	0.050455
$h[5] = h[15] =$	0.000000
$h[6] = h[14] =$	-0.075683
$h[7] = h[13] =$	0.062366
$h[8] = h[12] =$	0.093549
$h[9] = h[11] =$	-0.302731
$h[10] =$	0.400000

The coefficients given by Result 11.3 can be computed using the C function **idealBandpass( )**, which is provided in Listing 11.3.

Example 11.3 Use Result 11.3 to design a 21-tap FIR filter that approximates the amplitude response of an ideal bandpass filter with a pass band that extends from $\lambda_L = 2\pi/5$ to $\lambda_U = 3\pi/5$.

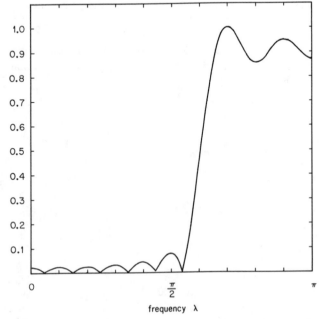

frequency λ

Figure 11.6 Magnitude response (as a percentage of peak) obtained from the 21-tap highpass filter of Example 11.2.

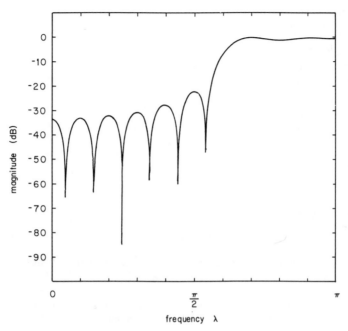

Figure 11.7 Magnitude response (in decibels) obtained from 21-tap highpass filter of Example 11.2.

solution The coefficients $h(n)$ are listed in Table 11.3, and the resulting frequency response is shown in Fig. 11.9.

Result 11.4 FIR approximation for ideal bandstop filter. The impulse response coefficients for an FIR approximation to the ideal bandstop amplitude response shown in Fig. 11.10 are given by

$$h[n] = \begin{cases} 1 + \dfrac{\lambda_L - \lambda_U}{\pi} & m = 0 \\[2ex] \dfrac{1}{n\pi}\left[\sin(m\lambda_L) - \sin(m\lambda_U)\right] & m \neq 0 \end{cases}$$

where $m = n - (N-1)/2$.

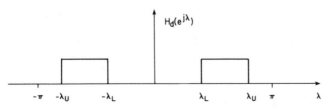

Figure 11.8 Frequency response of ideal bandpass digital filter.

TABLE 11.3 Impulse Response Coefficients for the 21-tap Bandpass Filter of Example 11.3

$$h[0] = h[20] = \quad 0.000000$$
$$h[1] = h[19] = \quad 0.000000$$
$$h[2] = h[18] = \quad 0.046774$$
$$h[3] = h[17] = \quad 0.000000$$
$$h[4] = h[16] = -0.100910$$
$$h[5] = h[15] = \quad 0.000000$$
$$h[6] = h[14] = \quad 0.151365$$
$$h[7] = h[13] = \quad 0.000000$$
$$h[8] = h[12] = -0.187098$$
$$h[9] = h[11] = \quad 0.000000$$
$$h[10] = \quad 0.200000$$

The coefficients given by Result 11.4 can be computed using the C function **idealBandstop( )**, which is provided in Listing 11.4.

Example 11.4 Use Result 11.4 to design a 31-tap FIR filter that approximates the amplitude response of an ideal bandstop filter with a stop band that extends from $\lambda_L = 2\pi/5$ to $\lambda_U = 3\pi/5$.

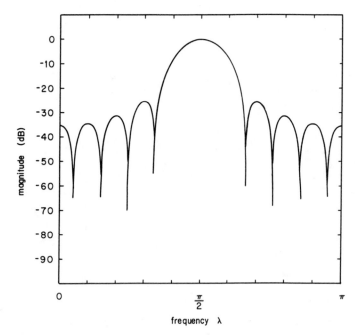

Figure 11.9 Magnitude response (in decibels) obtained from the 21-tap bandpass filter of Example 11.3.

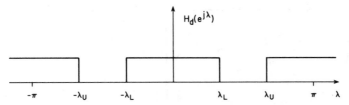

Figure 11.10 Frequency response of ideal bandstop digital filter.

TABLE 11.4 Impulse Response Coefficients for the 31-tap Bandstop Filter of Example 11.4

$$h[0] = h[30] = 0.000000$$
$$h[1] = h[29] = -0.043247$$
$$h[2] = h[28] = 0.000000$$
$$h[3] = h[27] = 0.031183$$
$$h[4] = h[26] = 0.000000$$
$$h[5] = h[25] = 0.000000$$
$$h[6] = h[24] = 0.000000$$
$$h[7] = h[23] = -0.046774$$
$$h[8] = h[22] = 0.000000$$
$$h[9] = h[21] = 0.100910$$
$$h[10] = h[20] = 0.000000$$
$$h[11] = h[19] = -0.151365$$
$$h[12] = h[18] = 0.000000$$
$$h[13] = h[17] = 0.187098$$
$$h[14] = h[16] = 0.000000$$
$$h[15] = 0.800000$$

solution The coefficients $h(n)$ are listed in Table 11.4, and the resulting frequency response is shown in Figs. 11.11 and 11.12.

11.2 Rectangular Window

As shown in the previous section, filters designed via the Fourier series method will, as a consequence of the Gibbs phenomenon, have frequency responses that contain overshoots and ripple. One way to reduce these effects involves multiplying the filter's impulse response by a *window* that "tapers off" the impulse response instead of abruptly truncating it to a finite number of terms. The basic idea of windowing is very straightforward, and most of the effort in this area is directed toward finding "good" window functions. A discussion of just what constitutes a good window function will be easier if we first develop a windowing viewpoint of truncation.

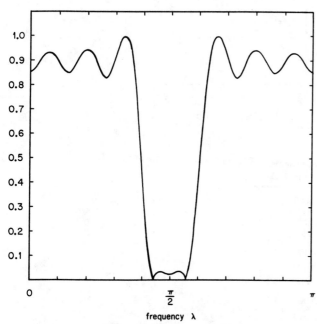

Figure 11.11 Magnitude response (as a percentage of peak) obtained from 31-tap bandstop filter of Example 11.4.

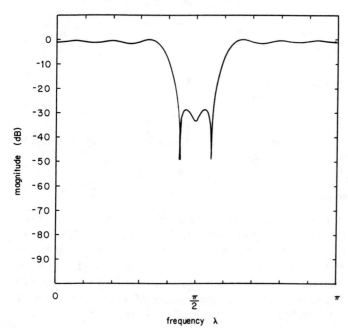

Figure 11.12 Magnitude response (in decibels) obtained from 31-tap bandstop filter of Example 11.4.

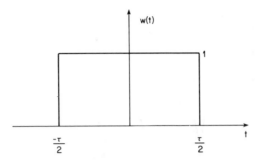

Figure 11.13 Rectangular window.

Truncating a filter's impulse response can be thought of as multiplying the infinite-length impulse response by a rectangular window such as the one shown in Fig. 11.13. This window has a value of unity for all values of t at which the impulse response is to be preserved, and a value of zero for all values of t at which the impulse response is to be eliminated:

$$w(t) = \begin{cases} 1 & |t| < \dfrac{\tau}{2} \\ 0 & \text{otherwise} \end{cases} \tag{11.3}$$

The rectangular window's Fourier transform is given by

$$W(f) = \frac{\tau \sin \pi f \tau}{\pi f \tau} \tag{11.4}$$

The magnitude of (11.4) is plotted in Fig. 11.14. The peaks of the first through ninth sidelobes are attenuated by 13.3, 17.8, 20.8, 23.0, 24.7, 26.2, 27.4, 28.5, and 29.5 dB, respectively. The data for Fig. 11.14 was generated using the C function **contRectangularResponse( )** provided in Listing 11.5.

The rectangular window's response will serve primarily as a benchmark to which the responses of other windows can be compared [*Note*: By omitting further explanation, some texts such as Stanley (1975) imply that Eq. (11.4) also applies to the discrete-time version of the rectangular window. However, as we will discover below, the Fourier transforms of the continuous-time and discrete-time windows differ significantly. A similar situation exists with respect to the triangular window.]

Discrete-time window

Since FIR filter coefficients exist only for integer values of n or discrete values of $t = nT$, it is convenient to work with a window function that is defined in terms of n rather than t. If the function defined by (11.3) is sampled using $N = 2M + 1$ samples with one sample at $t = 0$ and samples at nT for $n = \pm 1, \pm 2, \ldots, \pm M$; the sampled window function becomes

$$w[n] = \begin{cases} 1 & -M \leq n \leq M \\ 0 & \text{otherwise} \end{cases} \tag{11.5}$$

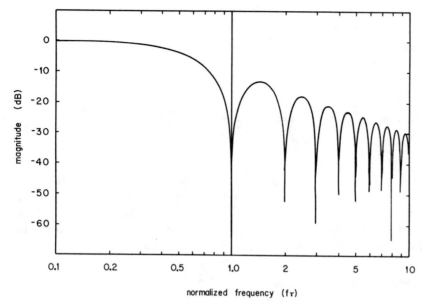

Figure 11.14 Magnitude spectrum for a continuous-time rectangular window.

For an even number of samples, the rectangular window can be defined as either

$$w[n] = 1 \qquad -(M-1) \leq n \leq M \qquad\qquad (11.6)$$

or $\qquad\qquad w[n] = 1 \qquad -M \leq n \leq (M-1) \qquad\qquad (11.7)$

The window specified by (11.6) will be centered around a point midway between $n = 0$ and $n = 1$, and the window specified by (11.7) will be centered around a point midway between $n = -1$ and $n = 0$. In many applications (especially in languages like C that use zero-origin indexing), it is convenient to have $w[n]$ defined for $0 \leq n \leq (N-1)$:

$$w[n] = 1 \qquad 0 \leq n \leq (N-1) \qquad\qquad (11.8)$$

In order to emphasize the difference between windows such as (11.5), which are defined over positive and negative frequencies, and windows such as (11.8) which are defined over nonnegative frequencies, digital-signal processing "borrows" terminology from the closely related field of time-series analysis. Using this borrowed terminology, windows such as (11.5) are called *lag windows*, and windows such as (11.8) are called *data windows*. Data windows are also referred to as *tapering windows* and occasionally *tapers* or *faders*. To avoid having to deal with windows centered around $\frac{1}{2}$ or $-\frac{1}{2}$, many authors state that N must be odd for lag windows. However, even-length *data* windows are widely used for leakage reduction in FFT applications.

Frequency windows and spectral windows

The discrete-time Fourier transform (DTFT) of the lag window (11.5) is given by

$$W(f) = \frac{\sin[\pi f(2M+1)]}{\sin(\pi f)} \tag{11.9}$$

The form of (11.9) is closely related to the so-called Dirichlet kernel $D_n(\cdot)$ which is variously defined as

$$D_n(\theta) \triangleq \frac{1}{2\pi} \sum_{k=-n}^{n} \cos k\theta = \frac{\sin\{[n+(1/2)]\theta\}}{\sin(\theta/2)}$$

(Priestley 1981)

$$D_n(x) \triangleq \sum_{k=-n}^{n} \exp(2\pi jkx) = \frac{\sin[(2n+1)\pi x]}{\sin(\pi x)}$$

(Dym and McKean 1972)

$$D_n(x) \triangleq \frac{1}{2} \sum_{k=-n}^{n} \cos(kx) = \frac{\sin\{[n+(1/2)]x\}}{2\sin(x/2)}$$

(Weaver 1989)

The magnitude of (11.9) is plotted in Fig. 11.15 for $N = 11$ and Fig. 11.16 for $N = 21$. As indicated by these two cases, when the number of points in the

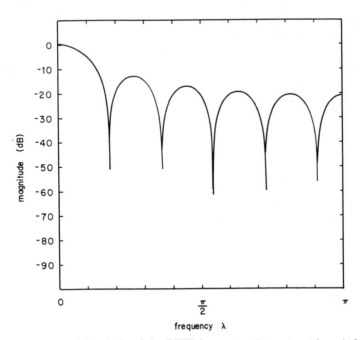

Figure 11.15 Magnitude of the DTFT for an 11-point rectangular window.

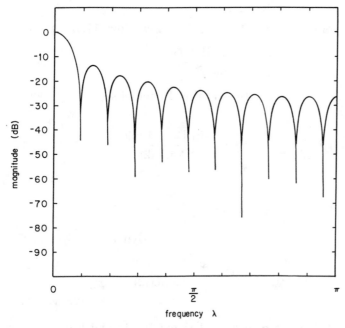

Figure 11.16 Magnitude of the DTFT for a 21-point rectangular window.

window increases, the width of the DTFT sidelobes decreases. The sidelobes in Fig. 11.15 are attenuated by 13.0, 17.1, 19.3, 20.5, and 20.8 dB; and the sidelobes in Fig. 11.16 are attenuated by 13.2, 17.6, 20.4, 22.3, 23.7, 24.8, 25.5, 26.1, and 26.3 dB. The data for these plots were generated using the C function **discRectangularResponse( )** provided in Listing 11.6.

The DTFT of the data window (11.8) is given by

$$W(f) = \exp[-j\pi f(N-1)] \frac{\sin(N\pi f)}{\sin(\pi f)} \qquad (11.10)$$

A function such as (11.9), which is the Fourier transform of a lag window, is called a *spectral window*. A function such as (11.10), which is the Fourier transform of a data window, is called a *frequency window*. The forms of (11.9) and (11.10) differ from the form of (11.4) due to the aliasing that occurs when the continuous-time window function is sampled to obtain a discrete-time window.

11.3 Triangular Window

A simple, but not particularly high-performance, window is the *triangular window* shown in Fig. 11.17 and is defined by

$$w(t) = 1 - \frac{2|t|}{\tau} \qquad |t| \le \frac{\tau}{2} \qquad (11.11)$$

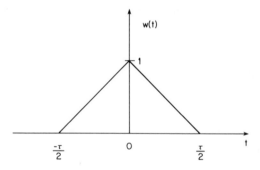

Figure 11.17   Triangular window.

Window functions are almost always even symmetric, and it is customary to show only the positive-time portion of the window as in Fig. 11.18. The triangular window is sometimes called the *Bartlett window* after M. S. Bartlett who described its use in a 1950 paper (Bartlett 1950). The Fourier transform of Eq. (11.11) is given by

$$W(f) = \frac{\tau}{2}\left[\frac{\sin(\pi f \tau/2)}{(\pi f \tau/2)}\right]^2 \qquad (11.12)$$

The magnitude of (11.12) is plotted in Fig. 11.19. The peaks of the first through fourth sidelobes are attenuated by 26.5, 35.7, 41.6, and 46.0 dB,

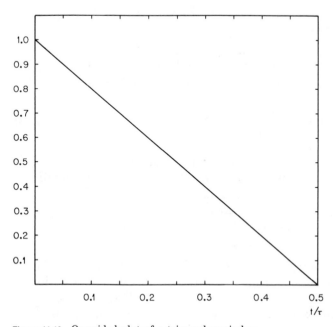

Figure 11.18   One-sided plot of a triangular window.

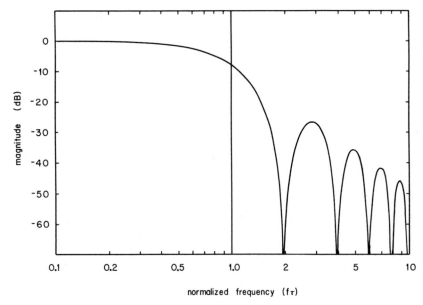

Figure 11.19 Magnitude response of a continuous-time triangular window.

respectively. The data for Fig. 11.19 was generated using the C function **contTriangularResponse( )** provided in Listing 11.7.

Discrete-time triangular window

If the function defined by (11.11) is sampled using $N = 2M + 1$ samples with $\tau = 2MT$, one sample at $t = 0$, and samples at nT for $n = \pm 1, \pm 2, \ldots, \pm M$, the sampled window function becomes the lag window defined by

$$w[n] = 1 - \frac{2|n|}{2M} \qquad -M \leq n \leq M \qquad (11.13)$$

for the normalized case of $T = 1$. This equation can be expressed in terms of the total number of samples N by substituting $(N-1)/2$ for M to obtain

$$w[n] = 1 - \frac{2|n|}{N-1} \qquad \frac{-(N-1)}{2} \leq n \leq \frac{N-1}{2} \qquad (11.14)$$

In some texts (such as Marple 1987 and Kay 1988), Eq. (11.14) is given as the definition of the discrete-time triangular window. However, evaluation of this equation reveals that $w[n] = 0$ for $n = \pm[(N-1)/2]$. This means that the two endpoints do not contribute to the window contents and that the window length is effectively reduced to $N - 2$ samples. In order to maintain a total of

N *nonzero* samples, many authors substitute $(N+2)$ for N in Eq. (11.14) to obtain

$$w[n] = 1 - \frac{|2n|}{N+1} \qquad \frac{-(N-1)}{2} \le n \le \frac{N-1}{2} \qquad (11.15)$$

$$N \text{ odd}$$

For an even number of samples, the window values can be obtained by substituting $(n + \frac{1}{2})$ for n in Eq. (11.15) to obtain a window that is symmetrical about a line midway between $n = -1$ and $n = 0$. (The equals sign in the box below is in quotes because n can assume only integer values; nevertheless, n "=" $-\frac{1}{2}$ is a convenient shorthand way of saying "midway between $n = -1$ and $n = 0$.")

$$w[n] = 1 - \frac{|2n+1|}{N+1} \qquad \frac{-N}{2} \le n \le \frac{N}{2} - 1 \qquad (11.16)$$

$$N \text{ even, center at } n \text{ "="} \frac{-1}{2}$$

Alternatively, we could substitute $(n - \frac{1}{2})$ for n in Eq. (11.15) to obtain a window symmetric about a line midway between $n = 0$ and $n = 1$:

$$w[n] = 1 - \frac{|2n-1|}{N+1} \qquad \frac{-N}{2} + 1 \le n \le \frac{N}{2} \qquad (11.17)$$

$$N \text{ even, center at } n \text{ "="} \frac{1}{2}$$

An expression for the triangular *data* window can be obtained by substituting $[n - (N-1)/2]$ for n in Eq. (11.15) or by substituting $(n - N/2)$ for n in Eq. (11.16) to yield

$$w[n] = 1 - \frac{|2n - N + 1|}{N+1} \qquad 0 \le n \le N - 1 \qquad (11.18)$$

Section 11.4 will present several C functions for generating various forms of the discrete-time triangular window.

Frequency and spectral windows

The spectral window obtained from the DTFT of the lag window (11.14) is given by

$$W(f) = \frac{1}{M} \left[\frac{\sin(M\pi f)}{\sin(\pi f)} \right]^2 \qquad (11.19a)$$

or
$$W(\theta) = \frac{2}{N} \left\{ \frac{\sin[(N/4)\theta]}{\sin[(1/2)\theta]} \right\}^2$$
(11.19b)

where $M = \dfrac{N-1}{2}$

$$\theta = \frac{2\pi f}{f_s}$$

The form of (11.19) is closely related to the Fejer kernel $F_n(\cdot)$, which, like the Dirichlet kernel presented in Sec. 11.3, has some variety in its definition:

$$F_n(x) \triangleq \frac{\sin^2(n\pi x)}{n \sin^2(\pi x)}$$

(Priestley 1981)

$$F_n(\theta) \triangleq \frac{\sin^2(n\theta/2)}{2\pi n \sin^2(\theta/2)}$$

(Dym and McKean 1972)

The magnitude of (11.19) for $N = 11$ and $N = 21$ is plotted in Fig. 11.20. The data for these plots were obtained using the C function **discTriangularResponse( )** provided in Listing 11.8.

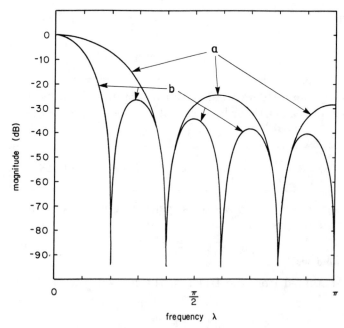

Figure 11.20 Magnitude of the DTFT for (a) an 11-point triangular window and (b) a 21-point triangular window.

11.4 Window Software

As we saw in the previous section, a window function can come in a number of different varieties—odd-length lag window, even-length lag window centered on $n = \frac{1}{2}$, and so on. As was done for the triangular window, an explicit function for each variety can be derived. However, the task of designing and coding computer programs to generate window coefficients can be simplified somewhat if we view the different varieties from a slightly different perspective. Despite the apparent variety of specific formats, there are really only two basic forms that need to be generated—one form for odd-length windows and one form for even-length windows. All of the specific varieties can be generated as simply horizontal translations of these two forms. Furthermore, since all the windows considered in this book are symmetric, we need to generate the coefficients for only half of each window. An odd-length lag window is probably the most "natural" of the discrete-time windows. Consider the triangular window shown in Fig. 11.21, which has sample values indicated at $t = \pm nT$ for $n = 0, 1, 2, \ldots$. Because of symmetry, we will require our program to generate the $(N+1)/2$ coefficients corresponding to $t = 0, T, 2T, 3T, \ldots, (N-1)T/2$ and place them in locations 0 through $(N-1)/2$ of an array called **window[ ]**. These coefficients can be obtained using Eq. (11.15). Next we consider the triangular window shown in Fig. 11.22. This window has been shifted so that its axis of symmetry lies at $t = -T/2$. The sample values indicated in the figure can be obtained from Eq. (11.16). The sample values for either the even-length case of Fig. 11.22 or the odd-length case of Fig. 11.21 can be obtained from the combined formula

$$w[n] = 1 - \frac{2|x|}{N+1}$$

where $x = \begin{cases} n & \text{for } N \text{ odd} \\ n + \frac{1}{2} & \text{for } N \text{ even} \end{cases}$

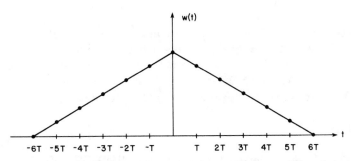

Figure 11.21 Triangular window sampled to produce an odd-length lag window.

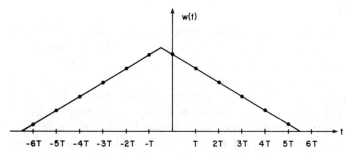

Figure 11.22 Triangular window shifted and sampled to produce an even-length lag window with axis of symmetry midway between $n = -1$ and $n = 0$.

The C function, **triangularWindow( )**, provided in Listing 11.9, uses this formula to generate coefficients for both odd- and even-length triangular windows. For N odd, the value returned in **window[0]** lies on the full window's axis of symmetry and is the value of the continuous-time window at $t = 0$. For N even, the value returned in **window[0]** lies one-half sample-time to the right of the full window's axis of symmetry and is the value of the continuous-time window at $t = T/2$.

Generating and storing a complete lag window would be conceptually straightforward if C allowed the use of negative indices for arrays. Although it is not possible to define an array that takes negative indices, it is possible to give the appearance of negative indices by using the special structure called **WWWW**, which is defined by the following code fragment:

```
typedef struct{
            real left[256];
            real right[256];
            } timeRecord;
union timeRec{
            real full[512];
            timeRecord half;
            } WWWW;
    # define LAG_WINDOW WWWW.half.right
    # define DATA_WINDOW WWWW.full
```

Use of this special structure is one way to permit negative index values for an array. The array **WWWW.half.right** can take a negative index because of the space reserved by the **left[ ]** array within the structure half of type **timeRecord**. The macro **LAG_WINDOW** is defined to facilitate easier reference to **WWWW.half.right**. For example, the C statement

```
LAG_WINDOW[5] = 0.735;
```

will place the value 0.735 into location 5 of the array **WWWW.half.right** (which, owing to the union, is also location 261 of the array **WWWW.full** or

DATA_WINDOW). The statements

```
LAG_WINDOW[-1] = 0.25;
LAG_WINDOW[-256] = 0.5;
```

will place the value 0.25 into location 255 and the value 0.5 into location 0 of the array **WWWW.half.left**.

The C function **makeLagWindow( )**, provided in Listing 11.10, takes a half window as generated by **triangularWindow( )** (or similar functions for other window shapes to be presented in subsequent sections) and converts it into a full lag window. For the output array, the call of this function should use the array **WWWW.half.right** or its defined alias **LAG_WINDOW**:

```
makeLagWindow( numbTaps, window, center, LAG_WINDOW);
```

If N is odd, the full window will be placed in locations $-(N-1)/2$ through $(N-1)/2$ of the "array" **LAG_WINDOW[ ]**. If N is even and **center** is negative, the full window will be placed in locations $-N/2$ through $(N/2)-1$ of **LAG_WINDOW[ ]**. If N is even and **center** is positive, the full window will be placed in locations $-(N/2)+1$ through $N/2$ of **LAG_WINDOW[ ]**.

The C function **makeDataWindow( )**, provided in Listing 11.11, takes a half window as generated by **triangularWindow( )** (or similar functions) and converts it into a full data window. For the output array, the call of this function should use the array **WWWW.full** or its defined alias **DATA_WINDOW—**

```
makeDataWindow( numbTaps, window, DATA_WINDOW);
```

If N is odd, the input value **window[0]** will lie on the axis of symmetry of the output in **DATA_WINDOW[ ]**. If N is even, the input value **window[0]** will appear in two consecutive locations in the center of the output window, and the axis of symmetry will lie between these two locations.

11.5 Applying Windows to Fourier Series Filters

Conceptually, a tapering window such as the triangular window is applied to the input of an FIR approximation to an ideal filter. However, since multiplication is associative, a much more computationally efficient implementation can be had by multiplying the window coefficients and the original filter coefficients to arrive at a modified set of filter coefficients. The impulse response coefficients produced by the C functions of Sec. 11.1 are generated in a data window format {that is, $h[n]$ is defined for $0 \le n \le N-1$}. Therefore the window coefficients should also be put into a data window format before multiplying them with the ideal filter coefficients of Sec. 11.1.

192   **Chapter Eleven**

TABLE 11.5   Coefficients for a 21-tap Lowpass Filter
{$h[n]$ are the original coefficients; $w[n]$ are triangular window coefficients}

n	$h[n]$	$w[n]$	$w[n] \cdot h[n]$
0, 20	0.000000	0.000000	0.000000
1, 19	−0.033637	0.090909	−0.006116
2, 18	−0.023387	0.181818	−0.006378
3, 17	0.026728	0.272727	0.009719
4, 16	0.050455	0.363636	0.022934
5, 15	0.000000	0.454545	0.000000
6, 14	−0.075683	0.545455	−0.048162
7, 13	−0.062366	0.636364	−0.045357
8, 12	0.093549	0.727273	0.076540
9, 11	0.302731	0.909091	0.275210
10	0.400000	1.00	0.400000

Example 11.5   Apply a triangular window to the 21-tap lowpass filter of Example 11.1.

solution   Table 11.5 lists the original values of the filter coefficients, the corresponding discrete-time window coefficients, and the final values of the filter coefficients after the windowing has been applied. The frequency response of the windowed filter is shown in Figs. 11.23 and 11.24. The response looks pretty good when plotted against a linear axis

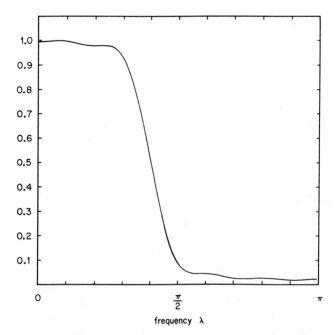

Figure 11.23   Magnitude response (as a percentage of peak) for a triangular-windowed 21-tap lowpass filter.

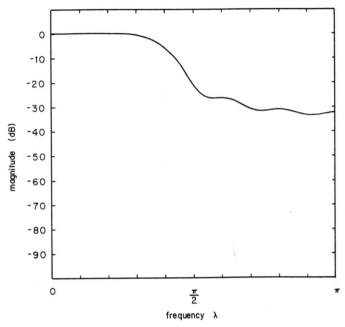

Figure 11.24 Magnitude response (in decibels) for a triangular-windowed 21-tap lowpass filter.

as in Fig. 11.23, but the poor stop-band performance is readily apparent when the response is plotted on a decibel scale as in Fig. 11.24.

11.6 von Hann Window

The continuous-time von Hann window function shown in Fig. 11.25 is defined by

$$w(t) = 0.5 + 0.5 \cos \frac{2\pi t}{\tau} \qquad |t| \le \frac{\tau}{2} \tag{11.20}$$

The corresponding frequency response, shown in Fig. 11.26, is given by

$$W(f) = 0.54\tau \ \text{sinc}(\pi f \tau) + 0.23\tau \ \text{sinc}[\pi\tau(f - \tau)] + 0.23\tau \ \text{sinc}[\pi\tau(f + \tau)] \tag{11.21}$$

The first sidelobe of this response is 31.4 dB below the main lobe, and the main lobe is twice as wide as the main lobe of the rectangular window. References to the von Hann window as the "hanning" window are widespread throughout the signal processing literature. This is unfortunate for two reasons. First, the window gets its name from Julius von Hann, *not* some nondescript Mr. Hanning. Second, the term *hanning* is easily (and often) confused with *Hamming*. Oppenheim and Schafer (1975) insinuate that the

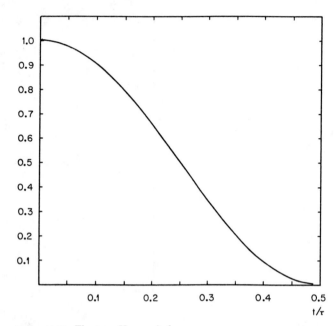

Figure 11.25 The von Hann window.

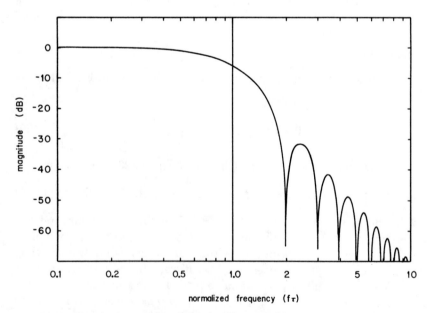

Figure 11.26 Magnitude response of the von Hann window.

incorrect use of *hanning* is due to Blackman and Tukey (1958). This window is ocassionally called a *raised-cosine window*.

Discrete-time von Hann window

If the function defined by Eq. (11.20) is sampled using $N = 2M + 1$ samples with one sample at $t = 0$ and samples at nT for $n = \pm 1, \pm 2, \ldots, \pm M$, the sampled window function becomes

$$w[n] = 0.5 + 0.5 \cos \frac{\pi n}{M} \qquad -M \le n \le M \qquad (11.22)$$

for the normalized case of $T = 1$. Evaluation of (11.22) reveals that $w(n) = 0$ for $n = \pm M$. This means that the two endpoints do not contribute to the window contents and that the window length is effectively reduced to $N - 2$ samples. In order to mantain a total of N *nonzero* samples, we must substitute $M + 1$ for M in Eq. (11.22) to yield

$$w[n] = 0.5 + 0.5 \cos \frac{2\pi n}{2(M + 1)} \qquad -M \le n \le M \qquad (11.23)$$

Equation (11.23) can now be recast in terms of N by substituting $(N - 1)/2$ for M to obtain

$$w[n] = 0.5 + 0.5 \cos \frac{2\pi n}{N - 1} \qquad \frac{-(N - 1)}{2} \le n \le \frac{N - 1}{2} \qquad (11.24)$$

$$n \text{ odd}$$

For an even number of samples, the window values can be obtained by substituting either $(n + \frac{1}{2})$ or $n(-\frac{1}{2})$ for n in Eq. (11.24) to obtain

$$w[n] = 0.5 + 0.5 \cos \frac{\pi(2n + 1)}{N - 1} \qquad \frac{-N}{2} \le n \le \frac{N}{2} - 1 \qquad (11.25)$$

$$N \text{ even, center at } n \text{ "=" } \frac{-1}{2}$$

$$w[n] = 0.5 + 0.5 \cos \frac{\pi(2n - 1)}{N - 1} \qquad \frac{-N}{2} + 1 \le n \le \frac{N}{2} \qquad (11.26)$$

$$N \text{ even, center at } n \text{ "=" } \frac{1}{2}$$

The C function, **hannWindow( )**, provided in Listing 11.12, generates coefficients for the von Hann window.

TABLE 11.6 Coefficients for a 21-tap Lowpass Filter

{$h[n]$ are the original coefficients; $w[n]$ are von Hann window coefficients}

n	$h[n]$	$w[n]$	$w[n] \cdot h[n]$
0, 20	0.000000	0.000000	0.000000
1, 19	−0.033637	0.024472	−0.000823
2, 18	−0.023387	0.095492	−0.002233
3, 17	0.026728	0.206107	0.005509
4, 16	0.050455	0.345492	0.017432
5, 15	0.000000	0.500000	0.000000
6, 14	−0.075683	0.654508	−0.049535
7, 13	−0.062366	0.793893	−0.049512
8, 12	0.093549	0.904508	0.084616
9, 11	0.302731	0.975528	0.295323
10	0.400000	1.00	0.400000

Example 11.6 Apply a von Hann window to the 21-tap lowpass filter of Example 11.1.

solution Table 11.6 lists the original values of the filter coefficients, the corresponding discrete-time window coefficients, and the final values of the filter coefficients after the windowing has been applied. The frequency response of the windowed filter is shown in Fig. 11.27.

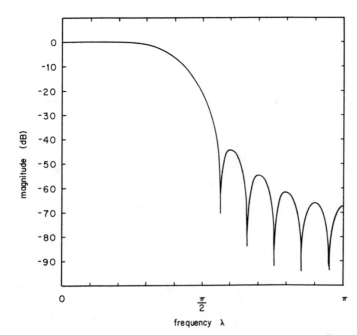

Figure 11.27 Magnitude response for a von Hann-windowed 21-tap lowpass filter.

11.7   Hamming Window

The continuous-time Hamming window function shown in Fig. 11.28 is defined by

$$w(t) = 0.54 + 0.46 \cos \frac{2\pi t}{\tau} \qquad |t| \le \frac{\tau}{2} \qquad (11.27)$$

The Fourier transform of Eq. (11.27) is given by

$$W(f) = 0.54\tau \ \mathrm{sinc}(\pi f\tau) + 0.23\tau \ \mathrm{sinc}[\pi\tau(f-\tau)] + 0.23\tau \ \mathrm{sinc}[\pi\tau(f+\tau)] \qquad (11.28)$$

The magnitude of (11.28) is plotted in Fig. 11.29. The highest sidelobe of this response is 42.6 dB below the main lobe, and the main lobe is twice as wide as the main lobe of the rectangular window's response. This window gets its name from R. W. Hamming, a pioneer in the areas of numerical analysis and signal processing, who opened his numerical analysis text (Hamming 1972) with the now famous and oft-quoted pearl, "The purpose of computing is insight, not numbers."

Discrete-time Hamming windows

If the function defined by Eq. (11.27) is sampled using $N = 2M + 1$ samples with one sample at $t = 0$ and samples at nT for $n = \pm 1, \pm 2, \dots, \pm M$, the

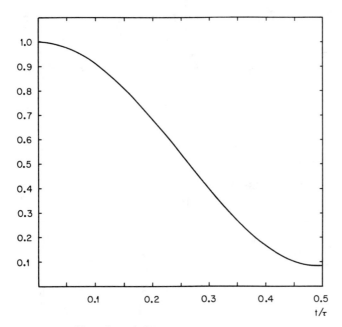

Figure 11.28   Hamming window.

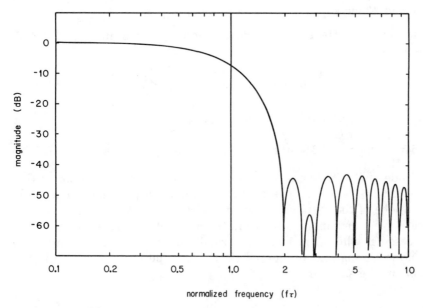

Figure 11.29 Magnitude response of the Hamming window.

sampled window function becomes the lag window defined by

$$w[n] = 0.54 + 0.46 \cos \frac{2\pi n}{2M} \qquad -M \leq n \leq M \qquad (11.29)$$

for the normalized case of $T = 1$. Equation (11.29) can be expressed in terms of the total number of samples N by substituting $(N-1)/2$ for M to obtain

$$w[n] = 0.54 + 0.46 \cos \frac{2\pi n}{N-1} \qquad \frac{-(N-1)}{2} \leq n \leq \frac{N-1}{2} \qquad (11.30)$$

$$n \text{ odd}$$

For an even number of samples, the window values can be obtained by substituting $n + \frac{1}{2}$ for n in Eq. (11.30) to obtain

$$w[n] = 0.54 + 0.46 \cos \frac{\pi(2n+1)}{N-1} \qquad \frac{-N}{2} \leq n \leq \frac{N}{2} - 1 \qquad (11.31)$$

$$N \text{ even, center at } n \text{ ``='' } \frac{-1}{2}$$

The data window form can be obtained by substituting $[n - (N-1)/2]$ for n in

Eq. (11.30) or by substituting $(n - N/2)$ for n in Eq. (11.31) to yield

$$w[n] = 0.54 - 0.46 \cos \frac{2\pi n}{N - 1} \qquad 0 \le n \le N - 1 \qquad (11.32)$$

(Note the change in sign for the cosine term—this is *not* a typographical error.)

Example 11.7 Apply a Hamming window to the 21-tap lowpass filter of Example 11.1.

solution The windowed values of $h[k]$ are listed in Table 11.7, and the corresponding frequency response is shown in Fig. 11.30.

Computer generation of window coefficients

The C function **hammingWindow( )**, provided in Listing 11.13, generates ordinates for the Hamming window. The output conventions for even and odd N are as described in Sec. 11.4.

11.8 Dolph-Chebyshev Window

The Dolph-Chebyshev window is somewhat different from the other windows in this chapter in that a closed-form expression for the time domain window is not known. Instead, this window is defined as the inverse Fourier transform of the sampled-frequency response which is given by

$$W[k] = (-1)^k \frac{\cos\{N \cos^{-1}[\beta \cos(\pi k/N)]\}}{\cosh(N \cosh^{-1} \beta)} \qquad -(N-1) \le k \le N-1 \qquad (11.33)$$

A sidelobe level of -80 dB is often claimed for this response, but in fact, Eq. (11.33) defines a family of windows in which the minimum stop-band attenuation is a factor of β. A stop-band attenuation of 20α dB is obtained for a value

TABLE 11.7 Coefficients for a 21-tap Hamming-Windowed Lowpass Filter

k	$h[k]$
0, 20	0.000000
1, 19	-0.003448
2, 18	-0.003926
3, 17	0.007206
4, 16	0.020074
5, 15	0.000000
6, 14	-0.051627
7, 13	-0.050540
8, 12	0.085330
9, 11	0.295915
10	0.400000

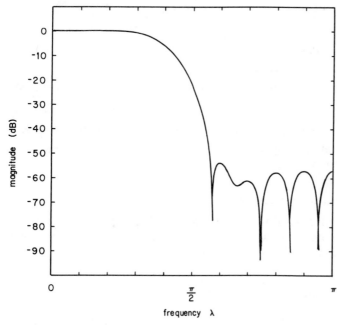

Figure 11.30 Magnitude response for a Hamming-windowed 21-tap lowpass filter.

of β given by

$$\beta = \cosh\left[\frac{1}{N}\cosh^{-1}(10^{\alpha})\right] \tag{11.34}$$

Often, $\beta > 1$ and consequently, evaluation of (11.32) may entail taking the inverse cosine of values with magnitudes greater than unity. In such cases, the following formula can be used:

$$\cos^{-1} x = \begin{cases} \dfrac{\pi}{2} - \tan^{-1}\left(\dfrac{x}{\sqrt{1-x^2}}\right) & |x| < 1 \\ \ln(x + \sqrt{x^2 - 1}) & |x| \geq 1 \end{cases} \tag{11.35}$$

The Dolph-Chebyshev window takes its name from C. L. Dolph and Pafnuti Chebyshev. The function $W(k)$ is a normalized form of the function developed by Dolph (1946) for specifying an antenna pattern optimized to achieve a narrow main lobe while simultaneously restricting the sidelobe response. Helms (1968) applied Dolph's result to the analogous problem of optimizing a filter response for a narrow transition band while simultaneously restricting sidelobe response. The name of Chebyshev is associated with this window because for integer values of z, the numerator of Eq. (11.33) is the zth order Chebyshev polynomial:

$$T_z(x) \equiv \cos(z \cos^{-1} x)$$

Listing 11.1   idealLowpass( )

```
/**********************************/
/*                                */
/*    Listing 11.1                */
/*                                */
/*    idealLowpass()              */
/*                                */
/**********************************/

void idealLowpass(    int numbTaps,
                      real lambdaU,
                      real hh[])
{
int n,nMax;
real mm;
printf("in idealLowpass\n");

for( n=0; n<numbTaps; n++)
    {
    mm = n - (real)(numbTaps-1)/2.0;
    if(mm==0)
        {hh[n] = lambdaU/PI;}
    else
        {hh[n] = sin(mm * lambdaU)/(mm * PI);}
    }
return;
}
```

Listing 11.2   idealHighpass( )

```
/**********************************/
/*                                */
/*    Listing 11.2                */
/*                                */
/*    idealHighpass()             */
/*                                */
/**********************************/

void idealHighpass( int numbTaps,
                    real lambdaL,
                    real hh[])
{
int n,nMax;
real mm;
printf("in idealHighpass\n");
```

```
for( n=0; n<numbTaps; n++)
    {
    mm = n - (real)(numbTaps-1)/2.0;
    if(mm==0)
        {hh[n] = 1.0 - lambdaL/PI;}
    else
        {hh[n] = -sin(mm * lambdaL)/(mm * PI);}
    }
return;
}
```

Listing 11.3   idealBandpass( )

```
/**********************************/
/*                                */
/*    Listing 11.3                */
/*                                */
/*    idealBandpass()             */
/*                                */
/**********************************/

void idealBandpass( int numbTaps,
                    real lambdaL,
                    real lambdaU,
                    real hh[])
{
int n,nMax;
real mm;
printf("in idealBandpass\n");

for( n=0; n<numbTaps; n++)
    {
    mm = n - (real)(numbTaps-1)/2.0;
    if(mm==0)
        {hh[n] = (lambdaU - lambdaL)/PI;}
    else
        {hh[n] = (sin(mm * lambdaU) - sin(mm * lambdaL))/(mm * PI);}
    }
return;
}
```

Listing 11.4   idealBandstop( )

```
/**********************************/
/*                                */
/*    Listing 11.4                */
/*                                */
/*    idealBandstop()             */
/*                                */
/**********************************/

void idealBandstop( int numbTaps,
                    real lambdaL,
                    real lambdaU,
                    real hh[])
{
int n,nMax;
real mm;
printf("in idealBandstop\n");

for( n=0; n<numbTaps; n++)
    {
    mm = n - (real)(numbTaps-1)/2.0;
    if(mm==0)
        {hh[n] = 1.0 + (lambdaL - lambdaU)/PI;}
    else
        {hh[n] = (sin(n * lambdaL) - sin(mm * lambdaU))/(mm * PI);}
    }
return;
}
```

Listing 11.5   contRectangularResponse( )

```
/**********************************/
/*                                */
/*    Listing 11.5                */
/*                                */
/*    contRectangularResponse()   */
/*                                */
/**********************************/

#define TINY 3.16e-5

real contRectangularResponse( real freq, real tau, logical dbScale)
{
real x;
```

```
x = sinc(PI * freq * tau);
if(dbScale)
    {
    if(fabs(x) < TINY)
        {x = -90.0;}
    else
        {x = 20.0*log10(fabs(x));}
    }
return(x);
}
```

Listing 11.6   discRectangularResponse( )

```
/************************************/
/*                                  */
/*    Listing 11.6                  */
/*                                  */
/*    discRectangularResponse()     */
/*                                  */
/************************************/


real discRectangularResponse( real freq,
                              int M,
                              logical normalizedAmplitude)
{
real result;

if(freq == 0.0)
    { result = (real) (2*M+1);}
else
    { result = fabs(sin(PI * freq * (2*M+1))/ sin( PI * freq));}

if( normalizedAmplitude ) result = result / (real) (2*M+1);
return(result);
}
```

Listing 11.7   contTriangularResponse( )

```
/***********************************/
/*                                 */
/*    Listing 11.7                 */
/*                                 */
/*    contTriangularResponse()     */
/*                                 */
/***********************************/


real contTriangularResponse(  real freq,
                              real tau,
                              logical dbScale)
{
real amp0, x;
amp0 = 0.5 * tau;
x = PI * freq * tau / 2.0;
x = 0.5 * tau * sincSqrd(x);
if(dbScale)
    {
    if(fabs(x/amp0) < TINY)
        {x = -90.0;}
    else
        {x = 20.0*log10(fabs(x/amp0));}
    }
return(x);
}
```

Listing 11.8   discTriangularResponse( )

```
/***********************************/
/*                                 */
/*    Listing 11.8                 */
/*                                 */
/*    discTriangularResponse()     */
/*                                 */
/***********************************/


real discTriangularResponse(  real freq,
                              int M,
                              logical normalizedAmplitude)
{
real result;
```

```
if(freq == 0.0)
    { result = (real) M;}
else
    { result = (sin(PI * freq * M) * sin(PI * freq * M)) /
                (M * sin( PI * freq) * sin( PI * freq));
    }

if( normalizedAmplitude ) result = result / (real) M;
return(result);
}
```

Listing 11.9   triangularWindow( )

```
/**********************************/
/*                                */
/*    Listing 11.9                */
/*                                */
/*    triangularWindow()          */
/*                                */
/**********************************/

void triangularWindow( int N, real window[])
{
real offset;
int n;
offset = (real) (1-(N%2));

for(n=0; n<(N/2.0); n++)
    {
    window[n] = 1.0 - (2.0*n + offset)/(N+1.0);
    }
return;
}
```

Listing 11.10   makeLagWindow( )

```
/**********************************/
/*                                */
/*    Listing 11.10               */
/*                                */
/*    makeLagWindow()             */
/*                                */
/**********************************/

void makeLagWindow(    int N,
                       real window[],
                       int center,
                       real outWindow[])
```

```
{
int n,M;

if(N%2) {
    M=(N-1)/2;
    for(n=0; n<=M; n++) {
        outWindow[n] = window[n];
        outWindow[-n] = outWindow[n];
        }
    }
else {
    M=(N-2)/2;
    if(center == negative) {
        for( n=0; n<=M; n++) {
            outWindow[n] = window[n];
            outWindow[-(1+n)] = window[n];
            }
        }
    else {
        for( n=0; n<=M; n++) {
            outWindow[n+1] = window[n];
            outWindow[-n] = window[n];
            }
        }
    }
return;
}
```

Listing 11.11   makeDataWindow( )

```
/*********************************/
/*                               */
/*    Listing 11.11              */
/*                               */
/*    makeDataWindow()           */
/*                               */
/*********************************/


void makeDataWindow( int N,
                     real window[],
                     real outWindow[])
{
int n,M;
```

```
if(N%2) {
    M=(N-1)/2;
    for(n=0; n<=M; n++) {
        outWindow[n] = window[M-n];
        outWindow[M+n] = window[n];
        }
    }
else {
    M=(N-2)/2;
    for(n=0; n<=M; n++) {
        outWindow[n] = window[M-n];
        outWindow[M+n+1] = window[n];
        }
    }
return;
}
```

Listing 11.12   hannWindow( )

```
/***********************************/
/*                                 */
/*    Listing 11.12                */
/*                                 */
/*    hannWindow()                 */
/*                                 */
/***********************************/
void hannWindow( int N, real window[])
{
logical odd;
int n;
odd = N%2;

for(n=0; n<(N/2.0); n++)
    {
    if( odd)
        {window[n] = 0.5 + 0.5 * cos(TWO_PI*n/(N-1));}
    else
        {window[n] = 0.5 + 0.5 * cos(TWO_PI * (2*n+1)/(2.0*(N-1)));}
    }
return;
}
```

Listing 11.13   hammingWindow( )

```
/***********************************/
/*                                 */
/*    Listing 11.13                */
/*                                 */
/*    hammingWindow()              */
/*                                 */
/***********************************/


void hammingWindow( int N, real window[])
{
logical odd;
int n;
odd = N%2;

for(n=0; n<(N/2.0); n++)
    {
    if( odd)
        {window[n] = 0.54 + 0.46 * cos(TWO_PI*n/(N-1));}
    else
        {window[n] = 0.54 + 0.46 *
                    cos(TWO_PI * (2*n+1)/(2.0*(N-1)));}
    }
return;
}
```

FIR Filter Design: Frequency Sampling Method

12.1 Introduction

In Chap. 11, the desired frequency response for an FIR filter was specified in the continuous-frequency domain, and the discrete-time impulse response coefficients were obtained via the Fourier series. We can modify this procedure so that the desired frequency response is specified in the discrete-frequency domain and then use the inverse discrete Fourier transform (DFT) to obtain the corresponding discrete-time impulse response.

Example 12.1 Consider the case of a 21-tap lowpass filter with a normalized cutoff frequency of $\lambda_U = 3\pi/7$. The sampled magnitude response for positive frequencies is shown in Fig. 12.1. The normalized cutoff frequency λ_U falls midway between $n = 4$ and $n = 5$, and the normalized folding frequency of $\lambda = \pi$ falls midway between $n = 10$ and $n = 11$. (Note that $45/10.5 = 3/7$.) We assume that $H_d(-n) = H_d(n)$ and use the inverse DFT to obtain the filter coefficients listed in Table 12.1. The actual continuous-frequency

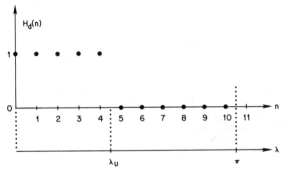

Figure 12.1 Desired discrete-frequency magnitude response for a lowpass filter with $\lambda_U = 3\pi/7$.

TABLE 12.1   Coefficients for the 21-tap Filter of Example 12.1

$$h[0] = h[20] = 0.037334$$
$$h[1] = h[19] = -0.021192$$
$$h[2] = h[18] = -0.049873$$
$$h[3] = h[17] = 0.000000$$
$$h[4] = h[16] = 0.059380$$
$$h[5] = h[15] = 0.030376$$
$$h[6] = h[14] = -0.066090$$
$$h[7] = h[13] = -0.085807$$
$$h[8] = h[12] = 0.070096$$
$$h[9] = h[11] = 0.311490$$
$$h[10] = 0.428571$$

response of an FIR filter having these coefficients is shown in Figs. 12.2 and 12.3. Figure 12.2 is plotted against a linear ordinate, and dots are placed at points corresponding to the discrete-frequencies specified in Fig. 12.1. Figure 12.3 is included to provide a convenient baseline for comparison of subsequent plots that will have to be plotted against decibel ordinates in order to show low stop-band levels.

The ripple performance in both the pass-band and stop-band responses can be improved by specifying one or more transition-band samples at values somewhere between the pass-band value of $H_d(m) = 1$ and the stop-band

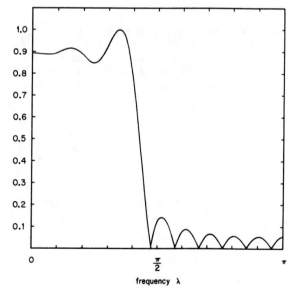

Figure 12.2 Magnitude response for filter of Example 12.1.

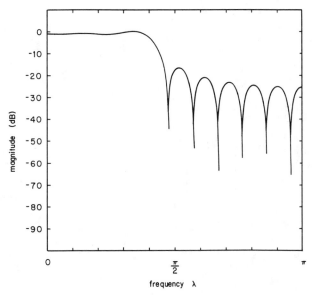

Figure 12.3 Filter response for Example 12.1 plotted on decibel scale.

value of $H_d(m) = 0$. Consider the case depicted in Fig. 12.4 where we have modified the response of Fig. 12.1 by introducing a one-sample transition band by setting $H_d(5) = 0.5$. The continuous-frequency response of this modified filter is shown in Fig. 12.5, and the coefficients are listed in Table 12.2.

The peak stop-band ripple has been reduced by 13.3 dB. An even greater reduction can be obtained if the transition-band value is optimized rather than just arbitrarily set halfway between the pass-band and the stop-band levels. It is also possible to have more than one sample in the transition band. The methods for optimizing transition-band values are iterative and involve repeatedly computing sets of impulse response coefficients and the corresponding frequency responses. Therefore, before moving on to specific optimization approaches, we will examine some of the mathematical details and

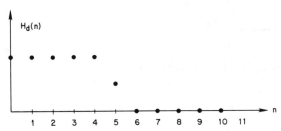

Figure 12.4 Discrete-frequency magnitude response with one transition-band sample midway between the ideal pass-band and stop-band levels.

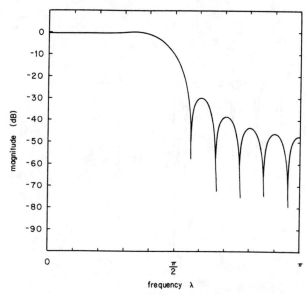

Figure 12.5 Continuous-frequency magnitude response corresponding to the discrete-frequency response of Fig. 12.3.

**TABLE 12.2 Coefficients for the 21-tap
Filter with a Single Transition-Band
Sample Value of 0.5**

$h[0] = h[20] = \quad 0.002427$
$h[1] = h[19] = \quad 0.008498$
$h[2] = h[18] = -0.010528$
$h[3] = h[17] = -0.023810$
$h[4] = h[16] = \quad 0.016477$
$h[5] = h[15] = \quad 0.047773$
$h[6] = h[14] = -0.020587$
$h[7] = h[13] = -0.096403$
$h[8] = h[12] = \quad 0.023009$
$h[9] = h[11] = \quad 0.315048$
$h[10] = 0.476190$

explore some ways for introducing some computational efficiency into the process.

12.2 Odd *N* versus Even *N*

Consider the desired response shown in Fig. 12.6 for the case of an odd-length filter with no transition band. If we assume that the cutoff lies midway

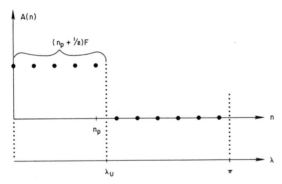

Figure 12.6 Desired frequency-sampled response for an odd-length filter with no transition-band samples.

between $n = n_p$ and $n = n_p + 1$ as shown, the cutoff frequency is $2\pi F(n_p + \frac{1}{2})$, where F is the interval between frequency domain samples. For the normalized case where $T = 1$, we find $F = 1/N$, so the normalized cutoff is given by

$$\lambda_U = \frac{\pi(2n_p + 1)}{N} \qquad (12.1)$$

This equation allows us to compute the cutoff frequency when n_p and N are given. However, in most design situations we will need to start with known (desired) values of N and λ_U and then determine n_p. We can solve (12.1) for n_p, but for an arbitrary value λ_U, the resulting value of n_p might not be an integer. Therefore, we write

$$n_p = \left\lfloor \frac{N\lambda_{UD}}{2\pi} - \frac{1}{2} \right\rfloor \qquad (12.2)$$

where λ_{UD} denotes desired λ_U and $\lfloor \cdot \rfloor$ denotes the "floor" function that truncates the fractional part from its argument. Equation (12.2) yields a value for n_p that guarantees that the cutoff will lie *somewhere* between n_p and $n_p + 1$, but not necessarily at the midpoint. The difference $\Delta\lambda = |\lambda_U - \lambda_{UD}|$ is an indication of how "good" the choices of n_p and N are—the smaller $\Delta\lambda$ is, the better the choices are.

It is a common practice to assume that the cutoff frequency lies midway between $n = n_p$ and $n = n_p + 1$ as in the preceding analysis. If the continuous-frequency amplitude response is a straight line between $A(n) = 1$ at $n = n_p$ and $A(n) = 0$ at $n = n_p + 1$, the value of the response midway between these points will be 0.5. However, since $A(n)$ is the *amplitude* response, the attenuation at the assumed cutoff is 6 dB. For an attenuation of 3 dB, the cutoff should be assigned to lie at a point which is 0.293 to the right of n_p and 0.707 to the left of $n_p + 1$.

If we assume that the cutoff lies at $n_p + 0.293$, the cutoff frequency is $2\pi F(n_p + 0.293)$ and the normalized cutoff is given by

$$\lambda_U = \frac{2\pi(n_p + 0.293)}{N} \qquad (12.3)$$

The required number of samples in the (two-sided) pass band is $2n_p + 1$ where

$$n_p = \left\lfloor \frac{N\lambda_{UD}}{2\pi} - 0.293 \right\rfloor$$

For convenience we will denote the λ_U given by (12.1) as λ_6 and the λ_U given by (12.3) as λ_3.

Even N

Now let's consider the response shown in Fig. 12.7 for the case of an even-length filter with no transition band. If we assume that the cutoff lies midway between $n = n_p$ and $n = n_p + 1$, the cutoff frequency is $2\pi F n_p$ and the normalized cutoff is

$$\lambda_6 = \frac{2\pi n_p}{N}$$

Solving for n_p and using the floor function to ensure integer values, we obtain

$$n_p = \left\lfloor \frac{N\lambda_{6D}}{2\pi} \right\rfloor$$

If we assume that the cutoff lies at $n_p + 0.293$, the cutoff frequency is $2\pi F(n_p - 0.207)$ and the normalized cutoff is

$$\lambda_3 = \frac{2\pi(n_p - 0.207)}{N}$$

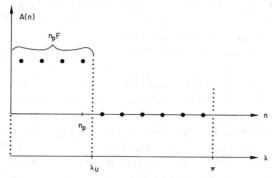

Figure 12.7 Desired frequency-sampled response for an even-length filter with no transition-band samples.

The required number of samples in the (two-sided) pass band $2n_p$ where

$$n_p = \left\lfloor \frac{N\lambda_{3D}}{2\pi} + 0.207 \right\rfloor$$

If processing constraints or other implementation considerations place an upper limit N_{max} on the total number of taps that can be used in a particular situation, it might be smart to choose between $N = N_{max}$ and $N = (N_{max} - 1)$ based upon which value of N yields λ_U that is closer to λ_{UD}.

Example 12.2   For $N_{max} = 21$ and $\lambda_{6D} = {}^{3\pi}/_7$, determine whether $N = 21$ or $N = 20$ would be the better choice based on values of $\Delta\lambda$.

solution   For $N = 20$,

$$n_p = \left\lfloor \frac{20[(3\pi/7)]}{2\pi} \right\rfloor = \left\lfloor \frac{30}{7} \right\rfloor = 4$$

$$\lambda_6 = \frac{2\pi(4)}{20} = \frac{2\pi}{5}$$

$$\Delta\lambda = \left| \frac{3\pi}{7} - \frac{2\pi}{5} \right| = \frac{\pi}{35}$$

For $N = 21$,

$$n_p = \left\lfloor \frac{21[(3\pi/7)]}{2\pi} - \frac{1}{2} \right\rfloor = \lfloor 4 \rfloor = 4$$

$$\lambda_6 = \frac{9\pi}{21} = \frac{3\pi}{7}$$

$$\Delta\lambda = \left| \frac{3\pi}{7} - \frac{3\pi}{7} \right| = 0$$

For this contrived case, $N = 21$ is not only the better choice—it is the best choice, yielding $\Delta\lambda = 0$.

Example 12.3   For $N_{max} = 21$ and $\lambda_{3D} = {}^{2\pi}/_5$, determine whether $N = 21$ or $N = 20$ would be the better choice based on values of $\Delta\lambda$.

solution   For $N = 20$,

$$n_p = \left\lfloor \frac{20[(2\pi/5)]}{2\pi} + 0.207 \right\rfloor = \lfloor 4.209 \rfloor = 4$$

$$\lambda_3 = \frac{2\pi(4 - 0.207)}{20} = 1.1916$$

$$\Delta\lambda = \left| \frac{2\pi}{5} - 1.1916 \right| = 0.065$$

For $N = 21$,

$$n_p = \left\lfloor \left| \frac{21[(2\pi/5)]}{2\pi} - 0.293 \right| \right\rfloor = \lfloor 3.907 \rfloor = 3$$

$$\lambda_3 = \frac{2\pi(3.293)}{21} = 0.9853$$

$$\Delta\lambda = \left| \frac{2\pi}{5} - 0.9853 \right| = 0.2714$$

Since $0.065 < 0.2714$, the better choice appears to be $N = 20$.

12.3 Design Formulas

The inverse DFT can be used as it was in Example 12.1 to obtain the impulse response coefficients $h(n)$ from a desired frequency response that has been specified at uniformly spaced discrete frequencies. However, for the special case of FIR filters with constant group delay, the inverse DFT can be modified to take advantage of symmetry conditions. Back in Sec. 8.2, the DTFT was adapted to the four specific types of constant-group-delay FIR filters to obtain the dedicated formulas for $H(\omega)$ and $A(\omega)$ that were summarized in Table 10.1. For the discrete-frequency case, the DFT can be similarly adapted to obtain the explicit formulas for $A(k)$ given in Table 12.3. (The entries in the table are for the normalized case where $T = 1$.) After some trigonometric manipulation, we can arrive at the corresponding inverse relations or *design formulas* listed in Table 12.4. These formulas are implemented by the C function **fsDesign( )** provided in Listing 12.1.

TABLE 12.3 Discrete-Frequency Amplitude Response of FIR Filters with Constant Group Delay

Type	
1 $h[n]$ symmetric N odd	$h[M] + \displaystyle\sum_{n=0}^{M-1} 2h[n] \cos\left[\frac{2\pi(M-n)k}{N}\right] = h[M] + \displaystyle\sum_{n=1}^{M} 2h[M-n] \cos\left(\frac{2\pi kn}{N}\right)$
2 $h[n]$ symmetric N even	$\displaystyle\sum_{h=0}^{(N/2)-1} 2h[n] \cos\left[\frac{2\pi(M-n)k}{N}\right] = \displaystyle\sum_{n=1}^{N/2} 2h\left[\frac{N}{2}-n\right] \cos\left\{\frac{2\pi k[n-(1/2)]}{N}\right\}$
3 $h[n]$ antisymmetric N odd	$\displaystyle\sum_{n=0}^{M-1} 2h[n] \sin\left[\frac{2\pi(M-n)k}{N}\right] = \displaystyle\sum_{n=1}^{M} 2h[M-n] \sin\left(\frac{2\pi kn}{N}\right)$
4 $h[n]$ antisymmetric N even	$\displaystyle\sum_{n=0}^{(N/2)-1} 2h[n] \sin\left[\frac{2\pi(M-n)k}{N}\right] = \displaystyle\sum_{n=1}^{N/2} 2h\left[\frac{N}{2}-n\right] \sin\left\{\frac{2\pi k[n-(1/2)]}{N}\right\}$

TABLE 12.4 Formulas for Frequency Sampling Design of FIR Filters with Constant Group Delay

Type	$h[n]$ $n = 0, 1, 2, \ldots, N-1$
1 $h[n]$ symmetric N odd	$\dfrac{1}{N}\left\{A(0) + \displaystyle\sum_{k=1}^{M} 2A(k)\cos\left[\dfrac{2\pi(n-M)k}{N}\right]\right\}$
2 $h[n]$ symmetric N even	$\dfrac{1}{N}\left\{A(0) + \displaystyle\sum_{k=1}^{(N/2)-1} 2A(k)\cos\left[\dfrac{2\pi(n-M)k}{N}\right]\right\}$
3 $h[n]$ antisymmetric N odd	$\dfrac{1}{N}\left\{\displaystyle\sum_{k=1}^{M} 2A(k)\sin\left[\dfrac{2\pi(M-n)k}{N}\right]\right\}$
4 $h[n]$ antisymmetric N even	$\dfrac{1}{N}\left\{A\left(\dfrac{N}{2}\right)\sin[\pi(M-n)] + \displaystyle\sum_{k=1}^{(N/2)-1} 2A(k)\sin\left[\dfrac{2\pi(M-n)k}{N}\right]\right\}$

12.4 Frequency Sampling Design with Transition-Band Samples

As mentioned in the introduction to this chapter, the inclusion of one or more samples in a transition band can greatly improve the performance of filters designed via the frequency sampling method. In Sec. 12.1, some improvement was obtained by simply placing one transition-band sample halfway between the pass band's unity amplitude and the stop band's zero value. However, even more improvement can be obtained if the value of this single transition-band sample is "optimized." Before proceeding, we need to first decide just what constitutes an "optimal" value for this sample—we could seek the sample that minimizes pass-band ripple, minimizes stop-band ripple, or minimizes some function that depends upon both stop-band and pass-band ripple. The most commonly used approach is to optimize the transition-band value so as to minimize the peak stop-band ripple.

For any given set of desired amplitude response samples, determination of the peak stop-band ripple entails the following steps:

1. From the specified set of desired amplitude response samples H_d, compute the corresponding set of impulse response coefficients h using the C function **fsDesign( )** presented in Sec. 12.3.

2. From the impulse response coefficients generated in step 1, compute a fine-grained discrete-frequency approximation to the continuous-frequency amplitude response using the C function **cgdFirResponse( )** presented in Sec. 10.3.

3. Search the amplitude response generated in step 2 to find the peak value in the stop band. This search can be accomplished using the C function **findSbPeak( )** given in Listing 12.2.

In general, we will need five parameters to specify the location of the stop band(s) so that **findSbPeak( )** "knows" where to search. The first parameter specifies the band configuration—lowpass, highpass, bandpass, or bandstop. The other parameters are indices of the first and last samples in the filter's pass bands and stop bands. Lowpass and highpass filters need only two parameters n_1 and n_2, but bandpass and bandstop filters need four: n_1, n_2, n_3, and n_4. The specific meaning of these parameters for each of the basic filter configurations is shown in Fig. 12.8. For easier argument passing, **find-SbPeak( )** has been designed to expect the filter configuration specified in a single input array **bandConfig[ ]** as follows:

> **bandConfig[0]** = 1 for lowpass, 2 for highpass,
>   3 for bandpass, 4 for bandstop
>
> **bandConfig[1]** = n_1
>
> **bandConfig[2]** = n_2
>
> **bandConfig[3]** = n_3
>
> **bandConfig[4]** = n_4
>
> **bandConfig[5]** = number of taps in filter

To see how this information is used, consider the lowpass case where n_2 is the index of the first stop-band sample in the desired response $H_d[n]$. The goal is to find the peak stop-band value in the filter's *continuous-frequency* magnitude response. The computer must compute samples of a discrete-frequency approximation to this continuous-frequency response. This approximation should not be confused with the desired response $H_d[n]$, which is also a discrete-frequency magnitude response. The latter contains only N samples, where N is the number of taps in the filter. The approximation to the continuous-frequency response must contain a much larger number of points. The number of samples in the (one-sided) approximation to the continuous response is supplied to **findSbPeak( )** as the integer argument **numPts**. For the examples in this chapter, values for **numPts** ranging from 120 to 480 have been used. In searching for the peak of a lowpass response, **findSbPeak( )** directs its attention to samples n_s and beyond in the discrete-frequency approximation to the continuous-frequency amplitude response where

$$n_s = \frac{2Ln_2}{N}$$

and L = number of samples in the (one-sided) approximation to the continuous response (that is, **numPts**)
    N = number of taps in the filter
    n_2 = index of first sample in the desired (positive-frequency) stop band

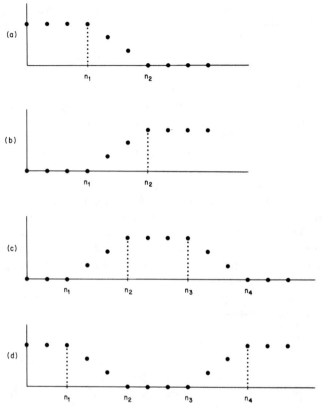

Figure 12.8 Parameters for specifying band configurations: (a) lowpass, (b) highpass, (c) bandpass, and (d) bandstop.

For highpass, bandpass, and bandstop filters, the search is limited to the stop band in a similar fashion.

The approach for finding the peak, as outlined in steps 1 through 3 above, contains some "fat" that could be eliminated to gain speed at the expense of clarity and modularity. For example, computing the entire amplitude response is not necessary, since only the stop-band values are of interest to the optimization procedure. Also, for any given filter, consecutive peaks in the response will be separated by a number of samples that remains more or less constant—this fact could be exploited to compute and examine only those portions of the response falling within areas where stop-band ripple peaks can be expected.

Optimization

In subsequent discussions, T_A will be used to denote the value of the single transition-band sample. One simple approach for optimizing the value of T_A

is to just start with $T_A = 1$ and keep decreasing by some fixed increment, evaluating the peak stop-band ripple after each decrease. At first, the ripple will decrease each time T_A is decreased, but once the optimal value is passed, the ripple will increase as we continue to decrease T_A. Therefore, once the peak ripple starts to increase, we should decrease the size of the increment and begin *increasing* instead of decreasing T_A. Once peak ripple again stops decreasing and starts increasing, we again decrease the increment and reverse the direction. Eventually, T_A should converge to the optimum value. A slightly more sophisticated strategy for finding the optimum value of T_A is provided by the so-called *golden section search* (Press et al. 1986). This method is based on the fact that the minimum of a function $f(x)$ is known to be "bracketed" by a triplet of points $a < b < c$ provided that $f(b) < f(a)$ and $f(b) < f(c)$. Once an initial bracket is established, the span of the bracket can be methodically decreased until the three points a, b, and c converge on the abscissa of the minimum. The name "golden section" comes from the fact that the most efficient search results when the middle point of the bracket is a fraction distance 0.61803 from one endpoint and 0.38197 from the other. A C function **goldenSearch( )**, provided in Listing 12.3, performs a golden section search for our specific application. This function calls **fsDesign( )**, **cgdFirResponse( )**, **normalizeResponse( )**, **findSbPeak( )**, and **set-Trans( )**. All of these have been discussed previously, with the exception of **setTrans( )**, which is provided in Listing 12.4. For the single-sample case this function is extremely simple, but we shall maintain it as a separate function to facilitate anticipated extensions for the case of multiple samples in the transition band that will be treated in Secs. 12.5 and 12.6. The inputs accepted by **goldenSearch** are as follows:

firType: 1 for N odd, $h[n]$ symmetric; 2 for N even, $h[n]$ symmetric; 3 for N odd, $h[n]$ antisymmetric; 4 for N even, $h[n]$ antisymmetric

numTaps: The number of taps in the desired FIR filter

Hd[ ]: The positive-frequency samples of the desired magnitude response

tol: The tolerance used to terminate the golden section search

numFreqPts: The number of samples in the (one-sided) discrete-frequency approximation to the filter's continuous-frequency response

bandConfig[ ]: An array containing filter configuration information as explained above for **findSbPeak( )**

The function provides two outputs—the peak stop-band value of the magnitude response is provided as the function's return value, and the corresponding abscissa (frequency) is written into ***fmin**.

Example 12.4 For a 21-tap lowpass filter, find the value for the transition-band sample $H_d[5]$ such that the peak stop-band ripple is minimized.

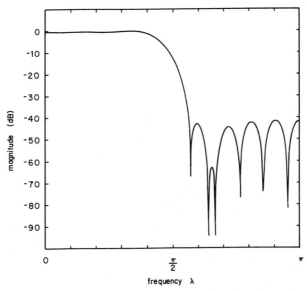

Figure 12.9 Magnitude response of 21-tap filter from Example 12.4.

solution The optimal value for $H_d[5]$ is 0.400147, and the corresponding amplitude response is shown in Fig. 12.9. The filter coefficients are listed in Table 12.5. Compared to the case where $H_d[5] = 0.5$, the peak stop-band ripple has been reduced by 11.2 dB.

12.5 Optimization with Two Transition-Band Samples

The optimization problem gets a bit more difficult when there are two or more samples in the transition band. Let's walk through the case of a type 1

TABLE 12.5 Coefficients for the Filter of Example 12.4

$$h[0] = h[20] = \quad 0.009532$$
$$h[1] = h[19] = \quad 0.002454$$
$$h[2] = h[18] = -0.018536$$
$$h[3] = h[17] = -0.018963$$
$$h[4] = h[16] = \quad 0.025209$$
$$h[5] = h[15] = \quad 0.044232$$
$$h[6] = h[14] = -0.029849$$
$$h[7] = h[13] = -0.094246$$
$$h[8] = h[12] = \quad 0.032593$$
$$h[9] = h[11] = \quad 0.314324$$
$$h[10] = 0.466498$$

lowpass filter with 21 taps having a desired response specified by

$$H_d[n] = \begin{cases} 1.0 & 0 \le |n| \le 4 \\ H_B & |n| = 5 \\ H_A & |n| = 6 \\ 0.0 & 7 \le |n| \le 10 \end{cases}$$

The values of H_A and H_B will be optimized to produce the filter having the smallest peak stop-band ripple.

1. Letting $H_B = 1$ and using a stopping tolerance of 0.01 in the single-sample **goldenSearch( )** function from Sec. 12.4, we find that the peak stop-band ripple is minimized for $H_A = 0.398227$. Thus we have defined one point in the H_A-H_B plane; specifically $(H_{A1} = 0.398227, H_{B1} = 1.0)$.

2. We define a second point in the plane by setting $H_B = 0.97$ and once again searching for the optimum H_A value that minimizes the peak stop-band ripple. This yields a second point at $(0.376941, 0.97)$.

3. The two points $(0.398227, 1)$ and $(0.376941, 0.97)$ can then be used to define a line in the H_A-H_B plane as shown in Fig. 12.10. Our ultimate goal is to determine the ordered pair (H_A, H_B) that minimizes the peak stop-band ripple of the filter. In the vicinity of $(H_{A1}, 1)$, the line shown in Fig. 12.10 is the "best" path along which to search and is therefore called the *line of steepest descent*. On the way to achieving our ultimate goal, a useful intermediate goal is to find the point along the line at which the filter's stop-band ripple is minimized. In order to use the single-sample search procedure from Sec. 12.4 to search along this line, we can define positions on the line in terms of their projections onto the H_A axis. To evaluate the filter response for a given value of H_A, we need to have H_B expressed as a function of H_A. The slope of the line is easily determined from points 1 and 2 as

$$m = \frac{1 - 0.97}{0.398227 - 0.376941} = 1.4093$$

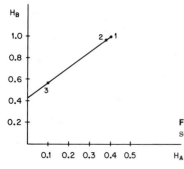

Figure 12.10 Line of steepest descent plotted in the H_A-H_B plane.

Thus we can write

$$H_B = 1.4093H_A + b \qquad (12.4)$$

where b is the H_B intercept. We can then solve for b by substituting the values for H_A, H_B at point 1 into (12.4) to obtain

$$b = H_B - 1.4093H_A$$

$$= 1 - 1.4093(0.398227) = 0.438779$$

Thus the line of steepest descent is defined in the H_A-H_B plane as

$$H_B = 1.4093H_A + 0.438779 \qquad (12.5)$$

The nature of the filter design problem requires that $0 \le H_A \le 1$ and $0 \le H_B \le 1$. Furthermore, examination of (12.5) indicates that $H_B < H_A$ for all values of H_A between zero and unity. Thus, the fact that H_B must not exceed unity can be used to further restrict the values of H_A. We find that $H_B = 1$ for $H_A = 0.39823$. Therefore, the search along the line is limited to values of H_A such that $0 \le H_A \le 0.39823$. The point along the line (12.5) at which the peak stop-band ripple is minimized is found to be (0.099248, 0.57863). The peak stop-band ripple at this point is -66.47 dB.

4. The ripple performance of -66.47 is respectable, but it is not the best that we can do. The straight line shown in Fig. 12.10 is in fact just an extrapolation from points 1 and 2. Generally, the actual *path* of steepest descent will not be a straight line and will diverge farther from the extrapolated line as the distance from point 1 increases. Thus when we find the optimum point (labeled as point 3) *lying along the straight line*, we really have not found the optimum point *in general*. One way to deal with this situation is to hold H_B constant at the value corresponding to point 3 and then find the optimal value of H_A—without constraining H_A to lie on the line. This results in point 4 as shown in Fig. 12.11. (Figure 12.11 uses a different scale than does Fig. 12.10 so that fine details can be more clearly shown.) The coordinates of point 4 are (0.98301, 0.57863).

5. We now perturb H_B by taking 97 percent of the value corresponding to point 4 [that is, $H_B = (0.97)(0.57863) = 0.561271$]. Searching for the value of H_A that minimizes the peak stop-band ripple, we obtain point 5 at (0.085145, 0.561271).

6. The two points (0.099248, 0.57863) and (0.085145, 0.561271) can then be used to define the new line of steepest descent shown in Fig. 12.11. Using the approach discussed above in 3, we then find the point along the line at which the peak stop-band ripple is minimized. This point is found to be (0.098592, 0.579014), and the corresponding peak ripple is -69.680885 dB.

7. We can continue this process of defining lines of steepest descent and optimizing along the line until the change in peak stop-band ripple from one iteration to the next is smaller than some preset limit. Typically, the opti-

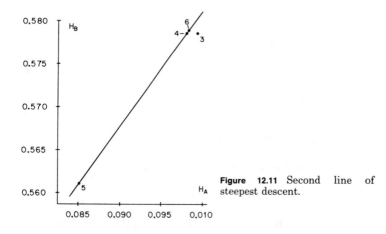

Figure 12.11 Second line of steepest descent.

mization is terminated when the peak ripple changes by less than 0.1 dB between iterations. Using this criterion, the present design converges after the fourth line of steepest descent is searched to find the point ($H_A =$ 0.098403, $H_B = 0.579376$) where the peak stop-band ripple is -71.08 dB.

Programming considerations

Optimizing the value of H_A, with H_B expressed as a function of H_A, requires some changes to the way in which the function **findSbPeak( )** interfaces to the function **goldenSearch( )**. In the single-sample-transition case, the search was conducted with H_A as the independent variable supplied (in the appropriate location of **Hd[ ]**) to **findSbPeak( )**. For the two-sample-transition case, the software has been designed to conduct the search in terms of the displacement ρ measured along an arbitrary line. (This approach is more general than it needs to be for the two-sample case, but doing things this way makes extension to three or more samples relatively easy—see Sec. 12.6 for details.) The function **findSbPeak( )** "expects" to have the H_A and H_B values "plugged into" the appropriate locations in the array **Hd[ ]**. The function **goldenSearch2( )** given in Listing 12.5 has been modified to include a call to **setTransition( )** before each call to **findSbPeak( )**. The function **setTransition( )**, shown in Listing 12.6, accepts ρ as an input and resolves it into the H_A and H_B components needed by **findSbPeak( )** for computation of the impulse response and the subsequent estimation of the continuous-frequency amplitude response. The line along which ρ is being measured is specified to **setTransition( )** via the **origins[ ]** and **slopes[ ]** arrays. The values of H_A and H_B corresponding to $\rho = 0$ are passed in **origins[1]** and **origins[2]**, respectively. The changes in H_A and H_B corresponding to $\Delta\rho = 1$ are passed in **slopes[1]** and **slopes[2]**, respectively. Setting **slopes[1]** $= 1$ and **origins[1]** $= 0$ is the correct way to specify $H_A = \rho$. (Note that if we set **slopes[1]** $= 1$, **origins[1]** $= 0$, **slopes[2]** $= 0$ and **origins[2]** $= 0$, the single-sample case can be handled as a special case of the two-sample case, since these values are equivalent to setting $H_A = \rho$ and $H_B = 0$.) The iterations of the optimization strategy are mechanized by the function **optimize2( )** given in Listing 12.7. After each call to **goldenSearch2( )**, the function **optimize2( )** uses the function **dumpRectComps( )** (shown in Listing 12.8) to print the H_A and H_B projections of the value returned by **goldenSearch2( )**.

Example 12.5   Complete the design of the 21-tap filter that was started at the beginning of this section.

solution   As mentioned previously, when **goldenSearch2( )** is used with a stopping tolerance of 0.01, the example design converges after four lines of steepest descent have been searched. Each line involves 3 points—2 points to define the line plus 1 point at which the ripple is minimized. The coordinates and peak stop-band ripple levels for the 12 points of the example design are listed in Table 12.6. Each of these points required 8 iterations of **goldenSearch2( )**. The impulse response coefficients for the filter corresponding to the transition-band values of $H_A = 0.098403$ and $H_B = 0.579376$ are listed in Table 12.7. The corresponding magnitude response is plotted in Fig. 12.12.

TABLE 12.6   Points Generated in the Optimization Procedure for Example 12.5

Iteration	H_A	H_B	Stop-band peak, dB
1	0.398227	1.0	−42.22
2	0.376941	0.97	−42.76
3	0.099248	0.578630	−66.47
4	0.098301	0.578630	−69.93
5	0.085145	0.561271	−65.87
6	0.098592	0.579014	−69.68
7	0.098301	0.579014	−71.05
8	0.085145	0.561643	−65.20
9	0.098473	0.579241	−70.89
10	0.098301	0.579241	−71.02
11	0.085145	0.561864	−64.61
12	0.098403	0.579376	−71.08

TABLE 12.7   Impulse Response Coefficients for the Filter of Example 12.5

$$h[0] = h[20] = 0.002798$$
$$h[1] = h[19] = 0.004783$$
$$h[2] = h[18] = -0.006541$$
$$h[3] = h[17] = -0.018285$$
$$h[4] = h[16] = 0.007862$$
$$h[5] = h[15] = 0.042175$$
$$h[6] = h[14] = -0.007896$$
$$h[7] = h[13] = -0.092308$$
$$h[8] = h[12] = 0.007530$$
$$h[9] = h[11] = 0.313553$$
$$h[10] = 0.492659$$

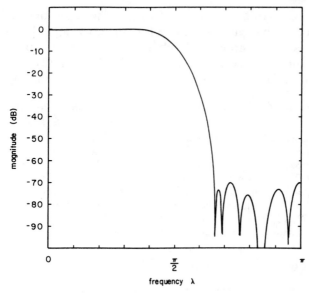

Figure 12.12   Magnitude response for Example 12.5.

Careful examination of the values in Table 12.6 reveals several anomalies. Points 1, 2, 4, 5, 7, 8, 10, and 11 define lines of steepest descent; and points 3, 6, 9, and 12 are the corresponding optimal points along these lines. The ripple performance of the "optimal" point 6 is −69.68 while the performance at point 4 is −69.93. These two points lie on the same line, and the performance at point 4 is better than the performance at point 6. A similar situation occurs with points 7 and 9. Such behavior indicates that the stopping criterion for **goldenSearch2( )** is not stringent enough, thereby allowing the search to stop before the best point on the line is found.

Example 12.6   Redesign the filter of Example 12.5 using **tol** = 0.001 instead of **tol** = 0.01.

solution   The number of iterations required for each point increases from 8 to 14, but the design procedure terminates after only two lines of steepest descent. The coordinates and peak stop-band ripple levels for the six points of this design are listed in Table 12.8. The impulse response coefficients are listed in Table 12.9.

TABLE 12.8   Points Generated in the Optimization Procedure for Example 12.6

Iteration	H_A	H_B	Stop-band peak, dB
1	0.399133	1.0	−42.24
2	0.377674	0.97	−42.73
3	0.100240	0.582148	−70.46
4	0.100220	0.582148	−70.34
5	0.087517	0.564683	−65.10
6	0.100425	0.582429	−70.39

TABLE 12.9 Impulse Response Coefficients for
the Filter of Example 12.6

$$
\begin{aligned}
h[0] = h[20] &= 0.002636 \\
h[1] = h[19] &= 0.004775 \\
h[2] = h[18] &= -0.006170 \\
h[3] = h[17] &= -0.018170 \\
h[4] = h[16] &= 0.007275 \\
h[5] = h[15] &= 0.042024 \\
h[6] = h[14] &= -0.007122 \\
h[7] = h[13] &= -0.092186 \\
h[8] = h[12] &= 0.006629 \\
h[9] = h[11] &= 0.313507 \\
h[10] &= 0.493605
\end{aligned}
$$

Comparison of Tables 12.6 and 12.8 reveals that performance obtained in Example 12.6 is 0.7 dB worse than the performance obtained in Example 12.5. Furthermore, within Example 12.6, the performance at point 3 is slightly better than the performance at point 6. Possible strategies for combatting these numeric effects would be to use a "tweaking factor" larger than 97 percent, or to have the tweaking factor approach unity with successive iterations.

12.6   Optimization with Three Transition-Band Samples

Just as the two-transition-sample case was more complicated than the single-sample case, the three-sample case is significantly more complicated than the two-sample case. Let's consider the case of a type 1 lowpass filter having a desired response as shown in Fig. 12.13. (The following discussion assumes that the three variables H_A, H_B, and H_C are each assigned to one of the axes in a three-dimensional rectilinear coordinate system.)

1. Consider points along the line defined by $H_C = 1$, $H_B = 1$. (Note: $H_C = 1$ defines a plane parallel to the H_A-H_B plane, and $H_B = 1$ defines a plane that intersects the $H_C = 1$ plane in a line which is parallel to the H_A axis.) Use a single-variable search strategy (such as the golden section search) to locate the point along this line for which the peak stop-band ripple is minimized. Denote the value of H_A at this point as H_{A1}.

2. Consider points along the line defined by $H_C = 1$, $H_B = 1 - \epsilon$. Use a single-variable search strategy to locate the point along this line for which the peak stop-band ripple is minimized. Denote the value of H_A at this point as H_{A2}.

3. The points $(H_{A1}, 1)$ and $(H_{A2}, 1 - \epsilon)$ define a line in the H_A-H_B plane as shown in Fig. 12.10 for the two-sample case. [Actually the points and the line

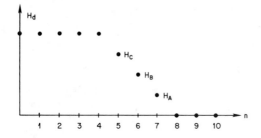

Figure 12.13 Desired response for a 21-tap type 1 filter with three samples in the transition band.

are in the plane defined by $H_C = 1$, and their *projections* onto the H_A-H_B plane are shown by Fig. 12.10. However, since the planes are parallel, everything looks the same regardless of whether we plot the points in the $H_C = 1$ plane or their projections in the H_A-H_B (that is, $H_C = 0$) plane.] In the vicinity of $(H_{A1}, 1)$, this line is the "best" path along which to search and is therefore called the *line of steepest descent*. Search along line to find the point at which the peak stop-band ripple is minimized. Denote the values of H_A and H_B at this point as H_{A3} and H_{B3}, respectively. As noted previously, the true path of steepest descent is in fact curved, and the straight line just searched is merely an extrapolation based on the two points $(H_{A1}, 1)$ and $(H_{A2}, 1 - \epsilon)$. Thus the point (H_{A3}, H_{B3}) is not a true minimum. However, this point can be taken as a starting point for a second round of steps 1, 2, and 3 which will yield a refined estimate of the minimum's location. This refined estimate can in turn be used as a starting point for a third round of steps 1, 2, and 3. This cycle of steps 1, 2, and 3 is repeated until the peak ripple at (H_{A3}, H_{B3}) changes by less than some predetermined amount (say, 0.1 dB).

Listing 12.1   fsDesign( )

```
/**********************************/
/*                                */
/*    Listing 12.1                */
/*                                */
/*    fsDesign()                  */
/*                                */
/**********************************/


int fsDesign(    int N,
                 int firType,
                 real A[],
                 real h[])
{
int n,k, status;
real x, M;

M = (N-1.0)/2.0;
status = 0;
switch (firType) {
    case 1:
        if(N%2) {
            for(n=0; n<N; n++) {
                h[n] = A[0];
                x = TWO_PI * (n-M)/N;
                for(k=1; k<=M; k++) {
                    h[n] = h[n] + 2.0*A[k]*cos(x*k);
                    }
                h[n] = h[n]/N;
                }
            }
        else
            {status = 1;}
        break;
    /*------------------------------------*/
    case 2:
        if(N%2)
            {status = 2;}
        else {
            for(n=0; n<N; n++) {
                h[n] = A[0];
                x = TWO_PI * (n-M)/N;

            for(k=1; k<=(N/2-1); k++) {
                h[n] = h[n] + 2.0*A[k]*cos(x*k);
                }
            h[n] = h[n]/N;
            }
```

```
            }
        break;
    /*-------------------------------------*/
    case 3:
        if(N%2) {
            for(n=0; n<N; n++) {
                h[n] = 0;
                x = TWO_PI * (M-n)/N;
                for(k=1; k<=M; k++) {
                    h[n] = h[n] + 2.0*A[k]*sin(x*k);
                    }
                h[n] = h[n]/N;
                }
            }
        else
            {status = 3;}
        break;
    /*-------------------------------------*/
    case 4:
        if(N%2)
            {status = 4;}
        else {
            for(n=0; n<N; n++) {
                h[n] = A[N/2]*sin(PI*(M-n));
                x = TWO_PI * (n-M)/N;
                for(k=1; k<=(N/2-1); k++) {
                    h[n] = h[n] + 2.0*A[k]*sin(x*k);
                    }
                h[n] = h[n]/N;
                }
            }
        break;
    }
return(status);
}
```

Listing 12.2   findSbPeak( )

```
/***********************************/
/*                                 */
/*    Listing 12.2                 */
/*                                 */
/*    findSbPeak()                 */
/*                                 */
/***********************************/


real findSbPeak( int bandConfig[],
                 int numPts,
                 real H[])
{
real peak;
int n, nBeg, nEnd, indexOfPeak;
int filterType;

filterType=bandConfig[0];

switch (filterType) {
    case 1:                /* lowpass */
        nBeg = 2*numPts*bandConfig[2]/bandConfig[5];
        nEnd = numPts-1;
        break;
    case 2:                /* highpass */
    case 3:                /* bandpass */
        nBeg = 0;
        nEnd = 2*numPts*bandConfig[1]/bandConfig[5];
        break;
    case 4:                /* bandstop */
        nBeg = 2*numPts*bandConfig[2]/bandConfig[5];
        nEnd = 2*numPts*bandConfig[3]/bandConfig[5];
        break;
    }
peak = -9999.0;
for(n=nBeg; n<nEnd; n++) {
    if(H[n]>peak) {
        peak=H[n];
        indexOfPeak = n;
        }
    }
if(filterType == 4) {      /* bandpass has second stopband */
    nBeg = 2*numPts*bandConfig[4]/bandConfig[5];
    nEnd = numPts;
    for(n=nBeg; n<nEnd; n++) {
        if(H[n]>peak) {
```

```
            peak=H[n];
            indexOfPeak = n;
            }
        }
    }
return(peak);
}
```

Listing 12.3   goldenSearch( )

```
/**********************************/
/*                                */
/*    Listing 12.3                */
/*                                */
/*    goldenSearch()              */
/*                                */
/**********************************/


real goldenSearch(    int firType,
                      int numbTaps,
                      real Hd[],
                      real tol,
                      int numFreqPts,
                      int bandConfig[],
                      real *fmin)
{
real x0, x1, x2, x3, xmin, f0, f1, f2, f3, oldXmin;
real leftOrd, rightOrd, midOrd, midAbsc, x, xb;
real delta;
static real hh[100], H[610];
int n;
logical dbScale;
FILE *logPtr;

printf("in goldenSearch\n");
logPtr = fopen("search.log","w");

dbScale = TRUE;
/*----------------------------------------------*/
setTrans( bandConfig, 0, Hd);
fsDesign( numbTaps, firType, Hd, hh);
cgdFirResponse(firType,numbTaps, hh, dbScale, numFreqPts,H);
normalizeResponse(dbScale,numFreqPts,H);
leftOrd = findSbPeak(bandConfig,numFreqPts,H);
printf("leftOrd = %f\n",leftOrd);
```

```
setTrans( bandConfig, 1.0, Hd);
fsDesign( numbTaps, firType, Hd, hh);
cgdFirResponse(firType,numbTaps, hh, dbScale, numFreqPts,H);
normalizeResponse(dbScale,numFreqPts,H);
rightOrd = findSbPeak(bandConfig,numFreqPts,H);
printf("rightOrd = %f\n",rightOrd);
pause(pauseEnabled);

if(leftOrd < rightOrd) {
    midAbsc=1.0;
    for(;;) {
        printf("checkpoint 3\n");
        midAbsc = GOLD3 * midAbsc;
        setTrans( bandConfig, midAbsc, Hd);
        fsDesign( numbTaps, firType, Hd, hh);
        cgdFirResponse(firType,numbTaps, hh, dbScale, numFreqPts,H);
        normalizeResponse(dbScale,numFreqPts,H);
        midOrd = findSbPeak(bandConfig,numFreqPts,H);
        printf("midOrd = %f\n",midOrd);
        if(midOrd < leftOrd) break;
        }
    }
else {
    x = 1.0;
    for(;;) {
        x = GOLD3 * x;
        midAbsc = 1.0 - x;
        printf("checkpoint 4\n");
        setTrans( bandConfig, midAbsc, Hd);
        fsDesign( numbTaps, firType, Hd, hh);
        cgdFirResponse(firType,numbTaps, hh, dbScale, numFreqPts,H);
        normalizeResponse(dbScale,numFreqPts,H);
        midOrd = findSbPeak(bandConfig,numFreqPts,H);
        printf("midOrd = %f\n",midOrd);
        if(midOrd < rightOrd) break;
        }
    }
xb = midAbsc:
/*-------------------------------------------*/
x0 = 0.0;
x3 = 1.0;
x1 = xb;
x2 = xb + GOLD3 * (1.0 - xb);
printf("x0= %f, x1= %f, x2= %f, x3= %f\n",x0,x1,x2,x3);

setTrans( bandConfig, x1, Hd);
fsDesign( numbTaps, firType, Hd, hh);
cgdFirResponse(firType,numbTaps, hh, dbScale, numFreqPts,H);
```

```
normalizeResponse(dbScale,numFreqPts,H);
f1 = findSbPeak(bandConfig,numFreqPts,H);


setTrans( bandConfig, x2, Hd);
fsDesign( numbTaps, firType, Hd, hh);
cgdFirResponse(firType,numbTaps, hh, dbScale, numFreqPts,H);
normalizeResponse(dbScale,numFreqPts,H);
f2 = findSbPeak(bandConfig,numFreqPts,H);


oldXmin = 0.0;

for(n=1; n<=100; n++) {
    if(f1<=f2) {
        x3 = x2;
        x2 = x1;
        x1 = GOLD6 * x2 + GOLD3 * x0;
        f3 = f2;
        f2 = f1;
        setTrans( bandConfig, x1, Hd);
        fsDesign( numbTaps, firType, Hd, hh);
        cgdFirResponse(firType,numbTaps, hh, dbScale, numFreqPts,H);
        normalizeResponse(dbScale,numFreqPts,H);
        f1 = findSbPeak(bandConfig,numFreqPts,H);
        printf("x0= %f, x1= %f, x2= %f, x3= %f\n",x0,x1,x2,x3);
        }
    else {
        x0 = x1;
        x1 = x2;
        x2 = GOLD6 * x1 + GOLD3 * x3;
        f0 = f1;
        f1 = f2;
        setTrans( bandConfig, x2, Hd);
        fsDesign( numbTaps, firType, Hd, hh);
        cgdFirResponse(firType,numbTaps, hh, dbScale, numFreqPts,H);
        normalizeResponse(dbScale,numFreqPts,H);
        f2 = findSbPeak(bandConfig,numFreqPts,H);
        printf("x0= %f, x1= %f, x2= %f, x3= %f\n",x0,x1,x2,x3);
        }

    delta = fabs(x3 - x0);
    oldXmin = xmin;
    printf("at iter %d, delta = %f\n",n,delta);
    printf("tol = %f\n",tol);
    if(delta <= tol) break;
    }
if(f1<f2)
    {xmin = x1;
    *fmin=f1;}
```

```
else
    {xmin = x2;
    *fmin=f2;}
printf("minimum of %f at x = %f\n", *fmin, xmin);
fprintf(logFptr,"minimum of %f at x = %f\n", *fmin, xmin);
return(xmin);
}
```

Listing 12.4   setTrans( )

```
/**********************************/
/*                                */
/*    Listing 12.4                */
/*                                */
/*    setTrans()                  */
/*                                */
/**********************************/


void setTrans(    int bandConfig[],
                  real x,
                  real Hd[])
{
int n1, n2, n3, n4;

n1 = bandConfig[1];
n2 = bandConfig[2];
n3 = bandConfig[3];
n4 = bandConfig[4];

switch (bandConfig[0]) {
    case 1:                    /* lowpass */
            Hd[n2-1] = x;
        break;
    case 2:                    /* highpass */
            Hd[n1+1] = x;
        break;
    case 3:                    /* bandpass */
            Hd[n1+1] = x;
            Hd[n4-1] = Hd[n1+1];
        break;
    case 4:                    /* bandstop */
            Hd[n2-1] = x;
            Hd[n3+1] = Hd[n2-1];
        break;
    }
return;
}
```

Listing 12.5   goldenSearch2( )

```
/*********************************/
/*                              */
/*    Listing 12.5              */
/*                              */
/*    goldenSearch2()           */
/*                              */
/*********************************/


real goldenSearch2(   real rhoMin,
                      real rhoMax,
                      int firType,
                      int numbTaps,
                      real Hd[],
                      real tol,
                      int numFreqPts,
                      real origins[],
                      real slopes[],
                      int bandConfig[],
                      real *fmin)
{
real x0, x1, x2, x3, xmin, f0, f1, f2, f3, oldXmin;
real leftOrd, rightOrd, midOrd, midAbsc, x, xb;
real delta;
static real hh[100], H[610];
int n;
logical dbScale;

dbScale = TRUE;

/*---------------------------------------------*/
setTransition( origins, slopes, bandConfig, 0, Hd);
fsDesign( numbTaps, firType, Hd, hh);
cgdFirResponse(firType,numbTaps, hh, dbScale, numFreqPts,H);
normalizeResponse(dbScale,numFreqPts,H);
leftOrd = findSbPeak(bandConfig,numFreqPts,H);

setTransition( origins, slopes, bandConfig, rhoMax, Hd);
fsDesign( numbTaps, firType, Hd, hh);
cgdFirResponse(firType,numbTaps, hh, dbScale, numFreqPts,H);
normalizeResponse(dbScale,numFreqPts,H);
rightOrd = findSbPeak(bandConfig,numFreqPts,H);

if(leftOrd < rightOrd) {
    midAbsc=rhoMax;
    for(;;) {
        midAbsc = GOLD3 * midAbsc;
```

```
                    setTransition( origins, slopes, bandConfig, midAbsc, Hd);
                    fsDesign( numbTaps, firType, Hd, hh);
                    cgdFirResponse(firType,numbTaps, hh, dbScale, numFreqPts,H);
                    normalizeResponse(dbScale,numFreqPts,H);
                    midOrd = findSbPeak(bandConfig,numFreqPts,H);
                    if(midOrd < leftOrd) break;
                    }
            }
    else {
        x = rhoMax;
        for(;;) {
            x = GOLD3 * x;
            midAbsc = rhoMax - x;
            setTransition( origins, slopes, bandConfig, midAbsc, Hd);
            fsDesign( numbTaps, firType, Hd, hh);
            cgdFirResponse(firType,numbTaps, hh, dbScale, numFreqPts,H);
            normalizeResponse(dbScale,numFreqPts,H);
            midOrd = findSbPeak(bandConfig,numFreqPts,H);
            if(midOrd < rightOrd) break;
            }
        }
    xb = midAbsc;

    /*-------------------------------------------*/
    x0 = rhoMin;
    x3 = rhoMax;
    x1 = xb;
    x2 = xb + GOLD3 * (rhoMax - xb);

    setTransition( origins, slopes, bandConfig, x1, Hd);
    fsDesign( numbTaps, firType, Hd, hh);
    cgdFirResponse(firType,numbTaps, hh, dbScale, numFreqPts,H);
    normalizeResponse(dbScale,numFreqPts,H);
    f1 = findSbPeak(bandConfig,numFreqPts,H);

    setTransition( origins, slopes, bandConfig, x2, Hd);
    fsDesign( numbTaps, firType, Hd, hh);
    cgdFirResponse(firType,numbTaps, hh, dbScale, numFreqPts,H);
    normalizeResponse(dbScale,numFreqPts,H);
    f2 = findSbPeak(bandConfig,numFreqPts,H);

    oldXmin = 0.0;

    for(n=1; n<=100; n++) {
        if(f1<=f2) {
            x3 = x2;
            x2 = x1;
            x1 = GOLD6 * x2 + GOLD3 * x0;
```

```
        f3 = f2;
        f2 = f1;
        setTransition( origins, slopes, bandConfig, x1, Hd);
        fsDesign( numbTaps, firType, Hd, hh);
        cgdFirResponse(firType,numbTaps, hh, dbScale, numFreqPts,H);
        normalizeResponse(dbScale,numFreqPts,H);
        f1 = findSbPeak(bandConfig,numFreqPts,H);
        }
            else {
                x0 = x1;
                x1 = x2;
                x2 = GOLD6 * x1 + GOLD3 * x3;
                f0 = f1;
                f1 = f2;
                setTransition( origins, slopes, bandConfig, x2, Hd);
                fsDesign( numbTaps, firType, Hd, hh);
                cgdFirResponse(firType,numbTaps, hh, dbScale, numFreqPts,H);
                normalizeResponse(dbScale,numFreqPts,H);
                f2 = findSbPeak(bandConfig,numFreqPts,H);
                }

        delta = fabs(x3 - x0);
        oldXmin = xmin;
        if(delta <= tol) break;
        }
if(f1<f2)
    {xmin = x1;
    *fmin=f1;}
else
    {xmin = x2;
    *fmin=f2;}
return(xmin);
}
```

Listing 12.6   setTransition( )

```
/**********************************/
/*                                */
/*    Listing 12.6                */
/*                                */
/*    setTransition()             */
/*                                */
/**********************************/


void setTransition(   real origins[],
                      real slopes[],
                      int bandConfig[],
```

```
                real x,
                real Hd[])
{
int n, nnn, n1, n2, n3, n4;

nnn = bandConfig[2] - bandConfig[1] - 1;
n1 = bandConfig[1];
n2 = bandConfig[2];
n3 = bandConfig[3];
n4 = bandConfig[4];

switch (bandConfig[0]) {
    case 1:                   /* lowpass */
        for( n=1; n<=nnn; n++) {
            Hd[n2-n] = origins[n] + x * slopes[n];
            }
        break;
    case 2:                   /* highpass */
        for( n=1; n<=nnn; n++){
            Hd[n1+n] = origins[n] + x * slopes[n];
            }
        break;
    case 3:                   /* bandpass */
        for( n=1; n<=nnn; n++) {
            Hd[n1+n] = origins[n] + x * slopes[n];
            Hd[n4-n] = Hd[n1+n];
            }
        break;
    case 4:                   /* bandstop */
        for( n=1; n<=nnn; n++) {
            Hd[n2-n] = origins[n] + x * slopes[n];
            Hd[n3+n] = Hd[n2-n];
            }
        break;
    }
return;
}
```

Listing 12.7   optimize2( )

```
/*********************************/
/*                               */
/*    Listing 12.7               */
/*                               */
/*    optimize2()                */
/*                               */
/*********************************/


void optimize2(  real yBase,
                 int firType,
                 int numbTaps,
                 real Hd[],
                 real gsTol,
                 int numFreqPts,
                 int bandConfig[],
                 real tweakFactor,
                 real rectComps[])
{
real r1, r2, r3, x1, x2, x3, y3, minFuncVal;
real slopes[5], origins[5];
real oldMin, xMax;
for(;;)
    {
    /*------------------------------------------------*/
    /*  do starting point for new steepest descent line  */
    slopes[1] = 1.0;
    slopes[2] = 0.0;
    origins[1] = 0.0;
    origins[2] = yBase;

    x1 = goldenSearch2(  0.0, 1.0,
                         firType,numbTaps,Hd,gsTol,numFreqPts,
                         origins,slopes,bandConfig,&minFuncVal);
/*------------------------------------*/
/*  do perturbed point to get         */
/*     slope for steepest descent line  */

origins[2]=yBase * tweakFactor;

x2 = goldenSearch2(  0.0, 1.0, firType,numbTaps,Hd,
                     gsTol,numFreqPts,origins,slopes,
                     bandConfig,&minFuncVal);


/*------------------------------------*/
/* define line of steepest descent     */
```

```
    /*  and find optimal point along line  */

    slopes[2] = yBase*(1-tweakFactor)/(x1-x2);
    origins[2] = yBase - slopes[2] * x1;
    xMax = (1.0 - origins[2])/slopes[2];

    x3 = goldenSearch2(  0.0, xMax, firType,numbTaps,Hd,
                         gsTol,numFreqPts,
                         origins,slopes,bandConfig,&minFuncVal);
    y3=origins[2] + x3 * slopes[2];
    /*----------------------------------------------------------------*/
    /*  if ripple at best point on current line is within specified  */
    /*     tolerance of ripple at best point on previous line,       */
    /*     then stop; otherwise stay in loop and define a new line   */
    /*     starting at the best point on line just completed.        */

    if(abs(oldMin-minFuncVal)<0.01) break;
    oldMin = minFuncVal;
    yBase = y3;
    }
rectComps[0] = x3;
rectComps[1] = origins[2] + x3 * slopes[2];
return;
}
```

Listing 12.8   dumpRectComps( )

```
/***********************************/
/*                                 */
/*    Listing 12.8                 */
/*                                 */
/*    dumpRectComps()              */
/*                                 */
/***********************************/


void dumpRectComps(  real origins[],
                     real slopes[],
                     int numTransSamps,
                     real x)
{
real rectComp;
int n;

for(n=0; n<numTransSamps; n++)
    {
    rectComp = origins[n+1] + x * slopes[n+1];
    printf("rectComp[%d] = %f\n",n,rectComp);
    }
return;
}
```

FIR Filter Design:
Remez Exchange Method

In general, an FIR approximation to an ideal lowpass filter will have an amplitude response of the form shown in Fig. 13.1. This response differs from the ideal lowpass response in three quantifiable ways:

1. The pass band has ripples that deviate from unity by $\pm \delta_p$.

2. The stop band has ripples that deviate from zero by $\pm \delta_s$. (Note that Fig. 13.1 shows an *amplitude* response rather than the usual magnitude response, and therefore negative ordinates are possible.)

3. There is a transition band of finite nonzero width ΔF between the pass band and stop band.

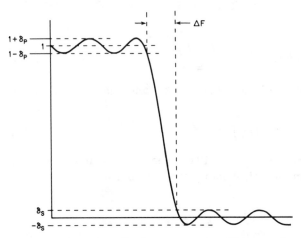

Figure 13.1 Typical amplitude response of an FIR approximation to an ideal lowpass filter.

The usual design goals are to, in some sense, minimize δ_p, δ_s, and ΔF. As it is generally not possible to simultaneously minimize for three different variables, some compromise is unavoidable. Chebyshev approximation is one approach to this design problem.

13.1   Chebyshev Approximation

In the Chebyshev approximation approach, the amplitude response of a type 1 (that is, odd-length, even-symmetric) linear phase lowpass N-tap FIR filter is formulated as a sum of r cosines:

$$A(f) = \sum_{k=0}^{r-1} c_k \cos(2\pi k f) \tag{13.1}$$

where $r = (N+1)/2$, and the coefficients c_k are chosen so as to yield an $A(f)$ which is optimal in a sense that will be defined shortly.

For a lowpass filter the pass band B_p and stop band B_s are defined as

$$B_p = \{F : 0 \le F \le F_p\} \tag{13.2}$$

$$B_s = \{F : F_s \le F \le 0.5\} \tag{13.3}$$

where F_p and F_s are, respectively, the edge frequencies for the pass band and stop band. [Equation (13.2) is read as "B_p is the set of all F such that F is greater than or equal to zero and less than or equal to F_p.] We can then define a set $\mathscr{F}$ as the union of B_p and B_s:

$$\mathscr{F} = B_p \cup B_s \tag{13.4}$$

In other words, $\mathscr{F}$ is the set of all frequencies between 0 and 0.5 not including the transition frequencies $F : F_p < F < F_s$. In mathematical terms, $\mathscr{F}$ is described as a *compact subset* of $[0, 0.5]$. The desired response $D(f)$ is the ideal lowpass response given by

$$D(f) = \begin{cases} 1 & F \in B_p \\ 0 & F \in B_s \end{cases} \tag{13.5}$$

Thus we could define the optimal approach as the one that minimizes the maximum error given by

$$\max_{F \in \mathscr{F}} |D(f) - A(f)| \tag{13.6}$$

However, the maximum error given by (13.6) treats pass-band error and stop-band error as equally important. A more general approach is to include a weighting function:

$$W(f) = \begin{cases} \dfrac{1}{K} & F \in B_p \\ 1 & F \in B_s \end{cases} \tag{13.7}$$

which allows stop-band errors to be given more importance than pass-band errors or vice versa. Thus we define the maximum approximation error as

$$\|E(f)\| = \max_{F \in \mathscr{F}} W(f) \cdot |D(f) - A(f)| \tag{13.8}$$

The crux of the Chebyshev approximation design approach is to identify the coefficients c_k for (13.1) that minimize $\|E(f)\|$.

Several examples of FIR design via Chebyshev approximation appear in the early literature (Martin 1962; Tufts, Rorabacher, and Moses 1970; Tufts and Francis 1970; Helms 1972; Herrman 1970; Hofstetter, Oppenheim, and Siegel 1971). However, the Chebyshev approximation method did not begin to enjoy widespread use until it was shown that the Remez exchange algorithm could be used to design linear phase FIR filters with the Chebyshev error criterion (Parks and McClellan 1972). Use of the Remez exchange algorithm depends upon an important mathematical result known as the *alternation theorem*.

Alternation theorem

The response $A(f)$ given by Eq. (13.1) will be the unique, best-weighted Chebyshev approximation to the desired response $D(f)$ if and only if the error function $E(f) = W(f)[D(f) - A(f)]$ exhibits at least $r + 1$ extrema at frequencies in $\mathscr{F}$. (Note: *Extrema* is a generic term that includes both maxima and minima.) The frequencies at which extrema occur are called *extremal frequencies*. Let f_n denote the nth extremal frequency such that

$$f_1 < f_2 < \cdots < f_{n-1} < f_n < f_{n+1} < \cdots < f_r < f_{r+1}$$

Then it can be proven (Cheyney 1966) that

$$E(f_n) = -E(f_{n+1}) \qquad n = 1, 2, \ldots, r \tag{13.9}$$

and
$$|E(f_n)| = \max_{f \in \mathscr{F}} E(f) \tag{13.10}$$

Together, (13.9) and (13.10) simply mean that the error is equal at all the extremal frequencies. Equation (13.9) further indicates that maxima and minima alternate (hence "alternation" theorem).

13.2 Strategy of the Remez Exchange Method

The alternation theorem given in the previous section tells us how to recognize an optimal set of c_k for Eq. (13.1) when we have one, but it does not tell us how to go about obtaining such c_k. The Remez exchange algorithm provides an approach for finding the FIR filter corresponding to the optimal c_k as follows:

1. Make an initial guess of the $r + 1$ extremal frequencies.

2. Compute the error function corresponding to the candidate set of extremal frequencies (see Sec. 13.3).

3. Search to find the extrema (and therefore the extremal frequencies) of the error function (see Sec. 13.4).

4. Adopt the extremal frequencies found in step 3 as the new set of candidate extremal frequencies and return to step 2.

5. Repeat steps 2, 3, and 4 until the extremal frequencies have converged (see Sec. 13.4).

6. Use the final set of extremal frequencies to compute $P(f)$ and the corresponding impulse response coefficients for the filter (see Sec. 13.5).

The error function mentioned in step 2 is computed as

$$E(f) = W(f)[D(f) - A(f)] \tag{13.11}$$

where $D(f)$ is given by Eq. (13.5) and $W(f)$ is given by (13.7). Although Eq. (13.1) gives the form of $A(f)$, some other means must be used to evaluate $A(f)$ since the coefficients c_k are unknown. We can obtain $A(f)$ from the extremal frequencies F_k using

$$A(f) = \begin{cases} \gamma_k & \text{for } f = F_0, F_1, \ldots, F_{r-1} \\[2ex] \dfrac{\sum_{k=0}^{r-1} \dfrac{\beta_k}{x - x_k} \gamma_k}{\sum_{k=0}^{r-1} \dfrac{\beta_k}{x - x_k}} & \text{otherwise} \end{cases} \tag{13.12}$$

The parameters needed for evaluation of (13.12) are given by

$$\beta_k = \prod_{\substack{i=0 \\ i \neq k}}^{r-1} \frac{1}{x_k - x_i}$$

$$\gamma_k = D(F_k) - (-1)^k \frac{\delta}{W(F_k)}$$

$$\delta = \frac{\sum_{k=0}^{r} \alpha_k D(F_k)}{\sum_{k=0}^{r} \dfrac{(-1)^k \alpha_k}{W(F_k)}}$$

$$\alpha_k = \prod_{\substack{i=0 \\ i \neq k}}^{r} \frac{1}{x_k - x_i}$$

$$x = \cos(2\pi f)$$

$$x_k = \cos(2\pi F_k)$$

If estimates of the extremal frequencies rather than their "true" values are used in the evaluation of $A(f)$, the resulting error function $E(f)$ will exhibit extrema at frequencies that are different from the original estimates. If the frequencies of these newly observed extrema are then used in a subsequent evaluation of $A(f)$, th new $E(f)$ will exhibit extrema at frequencies that are closer to the true extremal frequencies. If this process is performed repeatedly, the observed extremal frequencies will eventually converge to the true extremal frequencies, which can then be used to obtain $A(f)$ and the filter's impulse response.

Although $A(f)$ is defined over continuous frequency, computer evaluation of $A(f)$ must necessarily be limited to a finite number of discrete frequencies—therefore, $A(f)$ is evaluated over a closely spaced set or *dense grid* of frequencies. The convergence of the observed extremal frequencies will be limited by the granularity of this dense grid, but it has been empirically determined that an average grid density of 16 to 20 frequencies per extremum will be adequate for most designs. Since the maximization of $E(f)$ is only conducted over $f \in \mathcal{F}$, it is not necessary to evaluate $A(f)$ at all within the transition band (except for possibly at the very end, just to see what sort of transition-band response the final filter design actually provides). The frequency interval between consecutive points should be approximately the same in both the pass band and stop band. Furthermore, the grid should be constructed in such a way that frequency points are provided at $f = 0$, $f = F_p$, $f = F_s$, and $f = 0.5$. An integrated procedure for defining the dense grid and making the initial (equispaced) guesses for the candidate extremal frequencies is provided in Algorithm 13.1.

Algorithm 13.1   Constructing the dense-frequency grid

Step 1. Compute the number of candidate extremal frequencies to be placed in the pass band as

$$m_p = \left\lfloor \frac{rF_p}{0.5 + F_p - F_s} - 0.5 \right\rfloor$$

Step 2. Determine the candidate extremal frequencies within the pass band as

$$F_k = \frac{kF_p}{m_p} \quad k = 1, 2, \ldots, m_p$$

Step 3. Compute the number of candidate extremal frequencies to be placed in the stop band as

$$m_s = r + 1 - m_p$$

Step 4. Determine the candidate extremal frequencies within the stop band as

$$F_k = F_s + \frac{k(0.5 - F_s)}{m_s - 1} \quad k = 0, 1, \ldots, m_s - 1$$

Step 5. Determine the pass-band grid frequencies as

$$f_j = jI_p \qquad j = 0, 1, 2, \ldots, m_p L$$

where $I_p = \dfrac{F_p}{m_p L}$

L = average grid density (in points per extremum)

Step 6. Determine the stop-band grid frequencies as

$$f_j = F_s + nI_s \qquad n = 0, 1, \ldots, (m_s - 1)L$$

$$j = m_p L + n + 1$$

where $I_s = \dfrac{(0.5 - F_s)}{(m_s - 1)L}$

For computer calculations, the dense grid of frequencies can be implemented by the function **gridFreq( )** shown in Listing 13.1. A grid of actual frequency values is never really created—instead, most of the frequency bookkeeping is done using integers to represent the frequencies' locations within the grid. A call to **gridFreq( )** is used to convert an integer location index into the corresponding floating-point frequency value when needed for a calculation. Several parameters used by **gridFreq( )** are computed once and subsequently held constant. Since **gridFreq( )** will be called numerous times, these parameters are packed into a single array **gridParam[ ]** to minimize the calling overhead.

Generating the desired response and weighting functions

Based upon the requirements of the intended application, the desired response function $D(f)$ is defined in accordance with Eq. (13.5) for each frequency $f = f_j$ in the dense grid. For frequency-selective filters, $D(f)$ will usually take on only one of two values—unity in the pass band and zero in the stop band. The ideal lowpass response is generated by the **desLpfResp( )** function provided in Listing 13.2.

The pass-band ripple limit δ_1 and stop-band ripple limit δ_2, as shown in Fig. 13.1, are determined by the designer in a manner consistent with the requirements of the intended application. The weight function $W(f)$ is then computed in accordance with Eq. (13.7) for each frequency in the dense grid with $K = \delta_1/\delta_2$. The function **weightLp( )** shown in Listing 13.3 determines whether the frequency value provided as input lies in the stop band or pass band and then returns the appropriate value for $W(f)$.

13.3 Evaluating the Error

Algorithm 13.2 provides a step-by-step procedure for evaluating the error function defined by Eq. (13.11).

Algorithm 13.2 Evaluating the estimation error for the Remez exchange

Step 1. For $k = 0, 1, \ldots, r - 1$, use the candidate extremal frequencies F_k to compute β_k as

$$\beta_k = \prod_{\substack{i = 0 \\ i \neq k}}^{r-1} \frac{1}{\cos 2\pi F_k - \cos 2\pi F_i}$$

Step 2. For $k = 0, 1, \ldots, r - 1$, use the β_k from step 1 to compute α_k as

$$\alpha_k = \frac{\beta_k}{\cos 2\pi F_k - \cos 2\pi F_r}$$

Step 3. Use the α_k from step 2 and the extremal frequencies F_k to compute δ as

$$\delta = \frac{\sum_{k=0}^{r} \alpha_k D(F_k)}{\sum_{k=0}^{r} \frac{(-1)^k \alpha_k}{W(F_k)}}$$

where $D(f)$ and $W(f)$ are the desired response and weight functions discussed in Sec. 13.2.

Step 4. For $k = 0, 1, \ldots, r - 1$, use δ from step 3 to compute γ_k as

$$\gamma_k = D(F_k) - (-1)^k \frac{\delta}{W(F_k)}$$

Step 5. Use β_k from step 1, the γ_k from step 4, and the candidate extremal frequencies F_k to compute $P(f)$ for each frequency $f = f_j$ in the dense grid as

$$A(f_j) = \begin{cases} \gamma_k & \text{for } f = F_0, F_1, \ldots, F_{r-1} \\[2em] \dfrac{\sum_{k=0}^{r-1} \dfrac{\beta_k}{x_j - x_k} \gamma_k}{\sum_{k=0}^{r-1} \dfrac{\beta_k}{x_j - x_k}} & \text{otherwise} \end{cases}$$

where $x_j = \cos(2\pi f_j)$
$x_k = \cos(2\pi F_k)$

Step 6. For each frequency f_j in the dense grid, use $A(f_j)$ from step 5 to compute $E(f_j)$ as

$$E(f_j) = W(f_j)[D(f_j) - A(f_j)]$$

For computer evaluation, the error function is calculated by **remezError( )**, which makes use of **computeRemezA( )**. These two functions are provided in Listings 13.4 and 13.5, respectively. The function **computeRemezA( )** could have been made an integral part of **remezError( )** and designed to automatically generate $A( )$ and $E( )$ for all frequencies within the dense grid. However, a function in this form would not be useable for generating the uniformly spaced samples of the final $A( )$ that are needed to conveniently obtain the impulse response of the filter.

13.4   Selecting Candidate Extremal Frequencies

Once Eq. (13.11) has been evaluated, the values of $E(f_j)$ must be checked in order to determine what the values of F_k should be for the next iteration of the optimization algorithm. Based upon the particular frequencies being checked, the testing can be divided into the five different variations that are described in the paragraphs below. A C function, **remezSearch( )**, which performs this testing is provided in Listing 13.6.

Testing $E(f)$ for $f = 0$

If $E(0) > 0$ and $E(0) > E(f_1)$, then a ripple peak (local maximum) exists at $f = 0$. (Note that f_1 denotes the first frequency within the "dense grid" after $f = 0$, and due to the way we have defined the frequency spacing with the grid, we know that $f_1 = I_p$.) Even if a peak or valley exists at $f = 0$, it may be a *superfluous* extremum not needed for the next iteration. If a ripple peak does exist at $f = 0$, and $|E(0)| \geq |\rho|$, then the maximum is not superfluous and $f = f_0 = 0$ should be used as the first-candidate extremal frequency—in other words, set $F_0 = f_0 = 0$. Similarly, if $E(0) < 0$ and $E(0) < E(f_1)$, a ripple trough (ripple valley, local minimum) exists at $f = 0$. If $|E(0)| \geq |\rho|$, this minimum is not superfluous and we should set $F_0 = f_0 = 0$.

Testing $E(f)$ within the pass band and the stop band

The following discussion applies to testing of $E(f)$ for all values of f_j for which $f_0 < f_j < f_p$ or for which $f_s < f_j < 0.5$. A ripple peak exists at f_j if

$$E(f_j) > E(f_{j-1}) \quad \text{and} \quad E(f_j) > E(f_{j+1}) \quad \text{and} \quad E(f_j) > 0 \quad (13.13)$$

Equation (13.13) can be rewritten as (13.14) for frequencies in the pass band and as (13.15) for frequencies within the stop band:

$$E(f_j) > E(f_j - I_p) \quad \text{and} \quad E(f_j) > E(f_j + I_p) \quad \text{and} \quad E(f_j) > 0 \quad (13.14)$$

$$E(f_j) > E(f_j - I_s) \quad \text{and} \quad E(f_j) > E(f_j + I_s) \quad \text{and} \quad E(f_j) > 0 \quad (13.15)$$

A ripple trough exists at f_j if

$$E(f_j) < E(f_{j-1}) \quad \text{and} \quad E(f_j) < E(f_{j+1}) \quad \text{and} \quad E(f_j) < 0 \quad (13.16)$$

Equation (13.16) can be rewritten as (13.17) for frequencies in the pass band and as (13.18) for frequencies within the stop band:

$$E(f_j) < E(f_j - I_p) \quad \text{and} \quad E(f_j) < E(f_j + I_p) \quad \text{and} \quad E(f_j) < 0 \quad (13.17)$$

$$E(f_j) < E(f_j - I_s) \quad \text{and} \quad E(f_j) < E(f_j + I_s) \quad \text{and} \quad E(f_j) < 0 \quad (13.18)$$

If either (13.13) or (13.16) is satisfied, $f = f_j$ should be selected as a candidate extremal frequency—that is, set $F_k = f_j$ where k is the index of the next extremal frequency due to be specified.

Testing of $E(f)$ at the pass-band and stop-band edges

There is some disagreement within the literature regarding the testing of the pass-band and stop-band edge frequencies f_p and f_s. Some authors (such as Antoniou 1982) indicate the following testing strategy for f_p and f_s:

> If $E(f_p) > 0$ and $E(f_p) > E(f_p - I_p)$, then a ripple peak (local maximum) is deemed to exist at $f = f_p$ regardless of how $E(f)$ behaves in the transition band which lies immediately to the right of $f = f_p$. If a ripple peak does exist at $f = f_p$, and if $|E(f_p)| \geq |\rho|$, then the maximum is not superfluous and $f = f_p$ should be selected as a candidate extremal frequency—i.e., set $F_k = f_p$ where k is the index of the next extremal frequency due to be specified. Similarly, if $E(f_p) < 0$ and $E(f_p) < E(f_p - I_p)$, a ripple trough exists at $f = f_p$. If $|E(f_p)| \geq |\rho|$, this minimum is not superfluous and we should set $F_k = f_p$ where k is the index of the next extremal frequency due to be specified. If $E(f_s) > 0$ and $E(f_s) > E(f_s + I_s)$, then a ripple peak is deemed to exist at $f = f_s$ regardless of how $E(f)$ behaves in the transition band which lies immediately to the left of $f = f_s$. If a ripple peak does exist at $f = f_s$, and if $|E(f_s)| \geq |\rho|$, then the maximum is not superfluous and $f = f_s$ should be selected as a candidate extremal frequency—i.e., set $F_k = f_s$ where k is the index of the next extremal frequency due to be specified. Similarly, if $E(f_s) < 0$ and $E(f_s) < E(f_s + I_s)$, a ripple trough exists at $f = f_s$. If $|E(f_p)| \geq |\rho|$, this minimum is not superfluous and we should set $F_k = fs_p$ where k is the index of the next extremal frequency due to be specified.

Other authors (such as Parks and Burrus 1987) indicate that f_p and f_s are *always* extremal frequencies. In my experience the testing indicated by Antoniou is always satisfied, so f_p and f_s are always selected as extremal frequencies. I have opted to eliminate this testing both to reduce execution time and to avoid the danger of having small numerical inaccuracies cause one of these points to erroneously fail the test and thereby be rejected.

Testing of $E(f)$ for $f = 0.5$

If $E(0.5) > 0$ and $E(0.5) > E(0.5 - I_s)$, then a ripple peak exists at $f = 0.5$. If a ripple peak does exist at $f = 0.5$, and if $|E(0)| \geq |\rho|$, then the maximum is not superfluous and $f = f_0 = 0.5$ should be used as the final candidate extremal frequency. Similarly, if $E(0.5) < 0$ and $E(0.5) < E(0.5 - I_s)$, a ripple trough (ripple valley, local minimum) exists at $f = 0.5$. If $|E(0)| \geq |\rho|$, this minimum is not superfluous.

Rejecting superfluous candidate frequencies

The Remez algorithm requires that only $r + 1$ extremal frequencies be used in each iteration. However, when the search procedures just described are used, it is possible to wind up with more than $r + 1$ candidate frequencies. This situation can be very easily remedied by retaining only the $r + 1$ frequencies F_k for which $|E(F_k)|$ is the largest. The retained frequencies are renumbered from 0 to r before proceeding. An alternative approach is to reject the frequency corresponding to the smaller of $|E(F_0)|$ and $|E(F_r)|$, regardless of how these two values compare to the absolute errors at the other extrema. Since there is only one solution for a given set of filter specifications, both approaches should lead to the same result. However, one approach may lead to a faster solution or be less prone to numeric difficulties. This would be a good area for a small research effort.

Deciding when to stop

There are two schools of thought on deciding when to stop the exchange algorithm. The original criterion (Parks and McClellan 1972) examines the extremal frequencies and stops the algorithm when they do not change from one iteration to the next. This criterion is implemented in the C function **remezStop( )** provided in Listing 13.7. This approach has worked well for me, but it does have a potential flaw. Suppose that one of the true extremal frequencies for a particular filter lies at $f = F_T$, and due to the way the dense grid has been defined, F_T lies midway between two grid frequencies such that

$$F_T = \frac{f_n + f_{n+1}}{2}$$

It is conceivable that on successive iterations, the observed extremal frequency could alternate between f_j and f_{n+1} and therefore never allow the stopping criteria to be satisfied.

A different criterion, advocated by Antoniou (1982), uses values of the error function rather then the locations of the extremal frequencies. In theory, when the Remez algorithm is working correctly, each successive iteration will produce continually improving estimates of the correct extremal frequencies, and the values of $|E(F_k)|$ will become exactly equal for all values of k. However, due to the finite resolution of the frequency grid as well as finite precision arithmetic, the estimates may in fact never converge to exact equality. One remedy is to stop when the largest $|E(F_k)|$ and the smallest $|E(F_k)|$ differ by some reasonably small amount. The difference as a fraction of the largest $|E(F_k)|$ is given by

$$Q = \frac{\max|E(F_k)| - \min|E(F_k)|}{\max|E(F_k)|}$$

Typically, the iterations are stopped when $Q \le 0.01$. This second stopping criterion is implemented in the C function **remezStop2( )** provided in Listing 13.8.

13.5   Obtaining the Impulse Response

Back in Sec. 13.2, the final step in the Remez exchange design strategy consisted of using the final set of extremal frequencies to obtain the filter's impulse response. This can be accomplished by using Eq. (13.10) to obtain $P(f)$ from the set of extremal frequencies and then performing an inverse DFT on $P(f)$ to obtain the corresponding impulse response. An alternative approach involves deriving a dedicated inversion formula similar to the dedicated formulas presented in Sec. 12.3. For the case of the type 1 filter that has been considered thus far, the required inversion formula is

$$h[n] = h[-n] = \frac{1}{N}\left[A(0) + \sum_{k=1}^{r-1} 2A\left(\frac{2\pi k}{N}\right)\cos\left(\frac{2\pi kn}{N}\right)\right]$$

This formula is implemented via the **fsDesign( )** function (from Chap. 12), which is called by the C function **remezFinish( )** provided in Listing 13.9. Although the filter's final frequency response could be obtained using calls to **computRemezA( )**, I have found it more convenient to use **cgdFirResponse( )** from Chap. 10, since this function produces output in a form that is directly compatible with my plotting software.

13.6   Using the Remez Exchange Method

All of the constituent functions of the Remez method that have been presented in previous sections are called in the proper sequence by the function **remez( )**, which is presented in Listing 13.10. This function accepts the inputs listed in Table 13.1 and produces two outputs—**extFreq[ ]**, which is a vector containing the final estimates, and **h[ ]**, which is a vector containing the FIR filter coefficients.

Deciding on the filter length

To use the Remez exchange method, the designer must specify N, f_s, f_p, and the ratio δ_1/δ_2. The algorithm will provide the filter having the smallest values of $|\delta_1|$ and $|\delta_2|$ that can be achieved under these constraints. However, in many applications, the values specified are f_p, f_s, δ_1, and δ_2 with the

TABLE 13.1 Input Parameters for remez( ) Function

Mathematical symbol	C variable	Definition
N	**nn**	Filter length
r	**r**	Number of approximating functions
L	**gridDensity**	Average density of frequency grid (in grid points per extremal frequency) (must be an integer)
K	**kk**	Ripple ratio δ_1/δ_2
f_p	**freqP**	Pass-band edge frequency
f_s	**freqS**	Stop-band edge frequency

designer left free to set N as required. Faced with such a situation, the designer can use f_p, f_s, and $K = \delta_1/\delta_2$ as dictated by the application and design filters for increasing values of N until the δ_1 and δ_2 specifications are satisfied. An approximation of the required number of taps can be obtained by one of the formulas given below. For filters having pass bands of "moderate" width, the approximate number of taps required is given by

$$\tilde{N} = 1 + \frac{-20 \log \sqrt{\delta_1 \delta_1} - 13}{14.6(f_s - f_p)} \tag{13.19}$$

For filters with very narrow pass bands, (13.19) can be modified to be

$$\tilde{N} = \frac{0.22 - (20 \log \delta_2)/27}{(f_s - f_p)} \tag{13.20}$$

For filters with very wide pass bands, the required number of taps is approximated by

$$\tilde{N} = \frac{0.22 - (20 \log \delta_1)/27}{(f_s - f_p)} \tag{13.21}$$

Example 13.1 Suppose we wish to design a lowpass filter with a maximum pass-band ripple of $\delta_1 = 0.025$ and a minimum stop-band attenuation of 60 dB or $\delta_2 = 0.001$. The normalized cutoff frequencies for the pass band and stop band are, respectively, $f_p = 0.215$ and $f_s = 0.315$. Using (13.19) to approximate the required filter length N, we obtain

$$\tilde{N} = 1 + \frac{-20 \log\sqrt{(0.001)(0.025)} - 13}{14.6(0.315 - 0.215)}$$

$$= 23.6$$

The next larger odd length would be $N = 25$. If we run **remez( )** with the following inputs:

$$\textbf{nn} = 25 \qquad \textbf{r} = 13 \qquad \textbf{gridDensity} = 16$$

$$\textbf{kk} = 25.0 \qquad \textbf{freqP} = 0.215 \qquad \textbf{freqS} = 0.315$$

TABLE 13.2 Extremal Frequencies for Example 13.1

k	f_k
0	0.000000
1	0.042232
2	0.084464
3	0.126696
4	0.165089
5	0.199643
6	0.215000
7	0.315000
8	0.322708
9	0.343906
10	0.372813
11	0.407500
12	0.447969
13	0.500000

TABLE 13.3 Coefficients for 25-tap FIR Filter of Example 13.1

$h[0] = h[24] = -0.004069$

$h[1] = h[23] = -0.010367$

$h[2] = h[22] = -0.001802$

$h[3] = h[21] = 0.015235$

$h[4] = h[20] = 0.003214$

$h[5] = h[19] = -0.027572$

$h[6] = h[18] = -0.005119$

$h[7] = h[17] = 0.049465$

$h[8] = h[16] = 0.007009$

$h[9] = h[15] = -0.096992$

$h[10] = h[14] = -0.008320$

$h[11] = h[13] = 0.315158$

$h[12] = 0.508810$

we obtain the extremal frequencies listed in Table 13.2 and the filter coefficients listed in Table 13.3. The frequency response of the filter is shown in Figs. 13.2 and 13.3. The actual pass-band and stop-band ripple values of 0.0195 and 0.000780 are significantly better than the specified values of 0.025 and 0.001.

Example 13.2 The ripple performance of the 25-tap filter designed in Example 13.1 exhibits a certain amount of overachievement, and the estimate of the minimum number

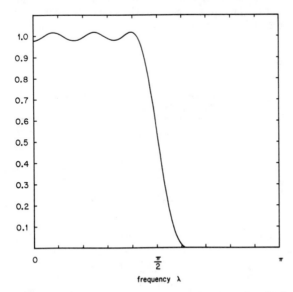

Figure 13.2 Magnitude response (as a fraction of peak) for the filter of Example 13.1.

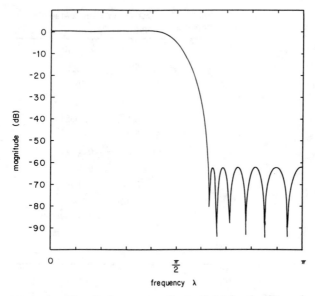

Figure 13.3 Magnitude response (in decibels) for the filter of Example 13.1.

of taps was closer to 23 than 25. Therefore, it would be natural for us to ask if we could in fact achieve the desired performance with a 23-tap filter. If we rerun **remez( )** with **nn** = 23, we obtain the extremal frequencies and filter coefficients listed in Tables 13.4 and 13.5. The frequency response of this filter is shown in Figs. 13.4 and 13.5. The pass-band ripple is approximately 0.034, and the stop-band ripple is approximately 0.00138—therefore, we conclude that a 23-tap filter does not satisfy the specified requirements.

TABLE 13.4 Extremal Frequencies for Example 13.2

k	f_k
0	0.000000
1	0.051510
2	0.103021
3	0.152292
4	0.194844
5	0.215000
6	0.315000
7	0.324635
8	0.349688
9	0.382448
10	0.419062
11	0.459531
12	0.500000

TABLE 13.5 Coefficients for 23-tap FIR Filter of Example 13.2

$h[0] = h[22] = -0.000992$

$h[1] = h[21] = \ \ \ 0.007452$

$h[2] = h[20] = \ \ \ 0.018648$

$h[3] = h[19] = \ \ \ 0.002873$

$h[4] = h[18] = -0.026493$

$h[5] = h[17] = -0.003625$

$h[6] = h[16] = \ \ \ 0.048469$

$h[7] = h[15] = \ \ \ 0.005314$

$h[8] = h[14] = -0.096281$

$h[9] = h[13] = -0.006601$

$h[10] = h[12] = -0.314911$

$h[11] = 0.507077$

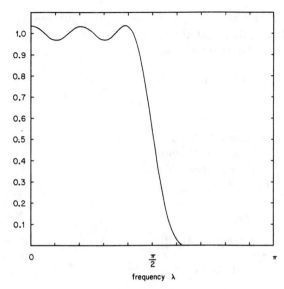

Figure 13.4 Magnitude response (as a fraction of peak) for the filter of Example 13.2.

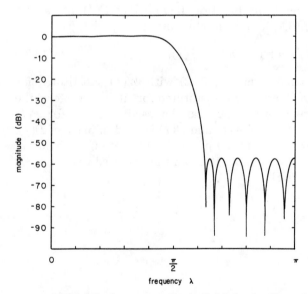

Figure 13.5 Magnitude response (in decibels) for the filter of Example 13.2.

13.7 Extension of the Basic Method

So far we have considered use of the Remez exchange method for odd-length, linear phase FIR filters having even-symmetric impulse responses (that is, type 1 filters). The Remez method was originally adapted specifically for the design of type 1 filters (Parks and McClellan 1972). However, in a subsequent paper, Parks and McClellan (1973) noted that the amplitude response of any constant group-delay FIR filter can be expressed as

$$A(f) = Q(f)\,P(f)$$

where $P(f) = \sum_{k=0}^{r-1} c_k \cos(2\pi kf)$

$$Q(f) = \begin{cases} 1 & h[n] \text{ symmetric, } N \text{ odd} \\ \cos \pi f & h[n] \text{ symmetric, } N \text{ even} \\ \sin 2\pi f & h[n] \text{ antisymmetric, } N \text{ odd} \\ \sin \pi f & h[n] \text{ antisymmetric, } N \text{ even} \end{cases}$$

Recall that the error $E(f)$ was defined as

$$E(f) = W(f)[D(f) - A(f)] \qquad (13.22)$$

If we substitute $Q(f)P(f)$ and factor out $Q(f)$, we obtain

$$E(f) = W(f)\,Q(f)\left[\frac{D(f)}{Q(f)} - P(f)\right]$$

We can then define a new weighting function $\hat{W}(f) = W(f)Q(f)$ and a new desired response $\hat{D}(f) = D(f)/Q(f)$, and thereby obtain

$$E(f) = \hat{W}(f)[\hat{D}(f) - P(f)] \qquad (13.23)$$

Equation (13.23) is of the same form as (13.22) with $\hat{W}(f)$ substituted for $W(f)$, $\hat{D}(f)$ substituted for $D(f)$, and $P(f)$ substituted for $A(f)$. Therefore, the procedures developed in previous sections can be used to solve for $P(f)$ provided that $\hat{W}(f)$ is used in place of $W(f)$ and $\hat{D}(f)$ is used in place of $D(f)$. Once this $P(f)$ is obtained, we can multiply by the appropriate $Q(f)$ to obtain $A(f)$. The appropriate formula from Table 12.2 can then be used to obtain the impulse response coefficients $h[n]$.

Listing 13.1   gridFreq( )

```
/***********************************/
/*                                 */
/*    Lisitng 13.1                 */
/*                                 */
/*    gridFreq()                   */
/*                                 */
/***********************************/

real gridFreq(   real gridParam[],
                 int gI)
{
real work;
static real incP, incS, freqP, freqS;
static int r, gridDensity, mP, mS, gP;

if(gridParam[0] == 1.0) {
    gridParam[0] = 0.0;
    freqP = gridParam[1];
    freqS = gridParam[2];
    r = gridParam[3];
    gridDensity = gridParam[4];
    work = (0.5 + freqP - freqS)/r;
    mP = floor(0.5 + freqP/work);
    gridParam[5] = mP;
    gP = mP * gridDensity;
    gridParam[7] = gP;
    mS = r +1 - mP;
    gridParam[6] = mS;
    incP = freqP / gP;
    incS = (0.5-freqS) / ((mS-1) * gridDensity);
    }
else {
    work = (gI<=gP) ? (gI*incP) : (freqS+(gI-(gP+1))*incS);
    }
return(work);
}
```

Listing 13.2   desLpfResp( )

```
/**********************************/
/*                                */
/*    Listing 13.2                */
/*                                */
/*    desLpfResp()                */
/*                                */
/**********************************/

real desLpfResp( real freqP, real freq)
{
real result;
result = 0.0;
if(freq <= freqP) result = 1.0;
return(result);
}
```

Listing 13.3   weightLp( )

```
/**********************************/
/*                                */
/*    Listing 13.3                */
/*                                */
/*    weightLp()                  */
/*                                */
/**********************************/

real weightLp( real kk, real freqP, real freq)
{
real result;

result = 1.0;
if(freq <= freqP) result = 1.0/kk;
return(result);
}
```

Listing 13.4   remezError( )

```
/**********************************/
/*                                */
/*    Listing 13.4                */
/*                                */
/*    remezError()                */
/*                                */
/**********************************/

void remezError( real gridParam[],
                 int gridMax,
                 int r,
                 real kk,
                 real freqP,
                 int iFF[],
                 real ee[])
{
int j;
real freq,aa;

aa = computeRemezA(  gridParam, gridMax, r, kk,
                     freqP, iFF, 1, 0.0);

for( j=0; j<=gridMax; j++) {
    freq = gridFreq(gridParam,j);
    aa = computeRemezA(  gridParam,
                         gridMax, r, kk, freqP,
                         iFF, 0,freq);
    ee[j] = weightLp(kk,freqP,freq) *
                (desLpfResp(freqP,freq) - aa);
    }
return;
}
```

Listing 13.5   computeRemezA( )

```
/**********************************/
/*                                */
/*    Listing 13.5                */
/*                                */
/*    computeRemezA()             */
/*                                */
/**********************************/

real computeRemezA(  real gridParam[],
                     int gridMax,
```

```
                    int r,
                    real kk,
                    real freqP,
                    int iFF[],
                    int initFlag,
                    real contFreq)
{
static int i, j, k, sign;
static real freq, denom, numer, alpha, delta;
static real absDelta, xCont, term;
static real x[50], beta[50], gamma[50];
real aa;

if(initFlag) {
    for(j=0; j<=r; j++) {
        freq = gridFreq(gridParam,iFF[j]);
        x[j] = cos(TWO_PI * freq);
        }

    /*  compute delta  */
    denom = 0.0;
    numer = 0.0;
    sign = -1;
    for( k=0; k<=r; k++) {
        sign = -sign;
        alpha = 1.0;
            for( i=0; i<=(r-1); i++) {
            if(i==k) continue;
            alpha = alpha / (x[k] - x[i]);
            }

    beta[k] = alpha;
    if( k != r ) alpha = alpha/(x[k] - x[r]);
    freq =  gridFreq(gridParam,iFF[k]);
    numer = numer + alpha * desLpfResp(freqP,freq);
    denom = denom + sign*(alpha/
                        weightLp(kk, freqP, freq));
    }
delta = numer/denom;
absDelta = fabs(delta);

sign = -1;
for( k=0; k<=r-1; k++) {
    sign = -sign;
    freq = gridFreq(gridParam,iFF[k]);
    gamma[k] = desLpfResp(freqP, freq) - sign * delta /
                    weightLp(kk,freqP,freq);
    }
```

```
        }
    else {
        xCont = cos(TWO_PI * contFreq);
        numer = 0.0;
        denom = 0.0;
        for( k=0; k<r; k++) {
            term = xCont - x[k];
            if(fabs(term)<1.0e-7) {
                aa = gamma[k];
                goto done;
                }
            else {
                term = beta[k]/(xCont - x[k]);
                denom += term;
                numer += gamma[k]*term;
                }
            }
        aa = numer/denom;
        }
done:
return(aa);
}
```

Listing 13.6   remezSearch( )

```
/**********************************/
/*                                */
/*    Listing 13.6                */
/*                                */
/*    remezSearch()               */
/*                                */
/**********************************/

void remezSearch(real ee[],
                 real absDelta,
                 int gP,
                 int iFF[],
                 int gridMax,
                 int r,
                 real gridParam[])
{
```

```
int i,j,k,extras,indexOfSmallest;
real smallestVal;

k=0;

/* test for extremum at f=0  */
if( ( (ee[0]>0.0) && (ee[0]>ee[1]) && (fabs(ee[0])>=absDelta) ) ||
    ( (ee[0]<0.0) && (ee[0]<ee[1]) && (fabs(ee[0])>=absDelta) ) ) {
    iFF[k]=0;
    k++;
    }

/*  search for extrema in passband  */
for(j=1; j<gP; j++) {
    if( ( (ee[j]>=ee[j-1]) && (ee[j]>ee[j+1]) && (ee[j]>0.0) ) ||
        ( (ee[j]<=ee[j-1]) && (ee[j]<ee[j+1]) && (ee[j]<0.0) )) {
        iFF[k] = j;
        k++;
        }
    }

/* pick up an extremal frequency at passband edge  */
    iFF[k]=gP;
    k++;

/* pick up an extremal frequency at stopband edge  */
j=gP+1;
    iFF[k]=j;
    k++;

/*  search for extrema in stopband  */

for(j=gP+2; j<gridMax; j++) {
    if( ( (ee[j]>=ee[j-1]) && (ee[j]>ee[j+1]) && (ee[j]>0.0) ) ||
        ( (ee[j]<=ee[j-1]) && (ee[j]<ee[j+1]) && (ee[j]<0.0) )) {
        iFF[k] = j;
        k++;
        }
    }
/* test for extremum at f=0.5  */
j = gridMax;
if( ( (ee[j]>0.0) && (ee[j]>ee[j-1]) && (fabs(ee[j])>=absDelta) ) ||
    ( (ee[j]<0.0) && (ee[j]<ee[j-1]) && (fabs(ee[j])>=absDelta) ) ) {
    iFF[k]=gridMax;
    k++;
    }
/*-----------------------------------------------------*/
/*  find and remove superfluous extremal frequencies  */
```

```
if( k>r+1) {
    extras = k - (r+1);
    for(i=1; i<=extras; i++) {
        smallestVal = fabs(ee[iFF[0]]);
        indexOfSmallest = 0;
        for(j=1; j< k; j++) {
            if(fabs(ee[iFF[j]]) >= smallestVal) continue;
            smallestVal = fabs(ee[iFF[j]]);
            indexOfSmallest = j;
            }
        k--;
        for(j=indexOfSmallest; j<k; j++) iFF[j] = iFF[j+1];
        }
    }
return;
}
```

Listing 13.7   remezStop( )

```
/*********************************/
/*                               */
/*    Listing 13.7               */
/*                               */
/*    remezStop()                */
/*                               */
/*********************************/

int remezStop(    int iFF[],
                  int r)
{
static int oldIFF[50];
int j,result;

result = 1;
for(j=0; j<=r; j++) {
    if(iFF[j] != oldIFF[j]) result = 0;
    oldIFF[j] = iFF[j];
    }
return(result);
}
```

Listing 13.8   remezStop2( )

```
/**********************************/
/*                                */
/*    Listing 13.8                */
/*                                */
/*    remezStop2()                */
/*                                */
/**********************************/

int remezStop2(  real ee[],
                 int iFF[],
                 int r)
{
real biggestVal, smallestVal,qq;
int j,result;

result = 0;
biggestVal = fabs(ee[iFF[0]]);
smallestVal = fabs(ee[iFF[0]]);
for(j=1; j<=r; j++) {
    if(fabs(ee[iFF[j]]) < smallestVal) smallestVal = fabs(ee[iFF[j]]);
    if(fabs(ee[iFF[j]]) > biggestVal) biggestVal = fabs(ee[iFF[j]]);
    }
qq = (biggestVal - smallestVal)/biggestVal;
if(qq<0.01) result=1;
return(result);
}
```

Listing 13.9   remezFinish( )

```
/**********************************/
/*                                */
/*    Listing 13.9                */
/*                                */
/*    remezFinish()               */
/*                                */
/**********************************/

void remezFinish(real extFreq[],
                 int nn,
                 int r,
                 real freqP,
                 real kk,
                 real aa[],
                 real h[])
{
```

```
int k,n, gridMax, iFF[1];
real freq,sum;
static real gridParam[1];

for(k=0; k<r; k++) {
    freq = (real) k/ (real) nn;
    aa[k] = computeRemezA(    gridParam, gridMax, r, kk,
                              freqP, iFF, 0,freq);
    }
fsDesign( nn, 1, aa, h);
return;
}
```

Listing 13.10   remez( )

```
/*********************************/
/*                               */
/*    Listing 13.10              */
/*                               */
/*    remez()                    */
/*                               */
/*********************************/

void remez(   int nn,
              int r,
              int gridDensity,
              real kk,
              real freqP,
              real freqS,
              real extFreq[],
              real h[])
{
int m, gridMax, j, mP, gP, mS;
real absDelta,freq;
static real gridParam[10];
static int iFF[50];
static real ee[1024];

/*------------------------------*/
/*  set up frequency grid       */
gridParam[0] = 1.0;
gridParam[1] = freqP;
gridParam[2] = freqS;
gridParam[3] = r;
gridParam[4] = gridDensity;
freq = gridFreq(gridParam,0);
```

```
mP = gridParam[5];
mS = gridParam[6];
gP = gridParam[7];
freqP = freqP + (freqP/(2.0*gP));
gridMax = 1 + gridDensity*(mP+mS-1);
/*----------------------------------------------*/
/*  make initial guess of extremal frequencies  */

for(j=0; j<mP; j++) iFF[j] = (j+1)* gridDensity;

for(j=0; j<mS; j++) iFF[j+mP] = gP + 1 + j * gridDensity;

/*-----------------------------------------------------*/
/*  find optimal locations for extremal frequencies    */

for(m=1;m<=20;m++) {

    remezError(  gridParam, gridMax, r, kk, freqP, iFF, ee);

    remezSearch( ee, absDelta, gP, iFF, gridMax, r, gridParam);

    remezStop2(ee,iFF,r);
    if(remezStop(iFF,r)) break;
    }

for(j=0; j<=r; j++) {
    extFreq[j] = gridFreq(gridParam,iFF[j]);
    }
remezFinish( extFreq, nn, r, freqP,kk, ee, h);
return;
}
```

IIR Filters

The general form for an *infinite impulse response* (IIR) filter's output $y[k]$ at time k is given by

$$y[n] = \sum_{n=1}^{N} a_n y[k-n] + \sum_{m=0}^{M} b_m x[k-m] \tag{14.1}$$

This equation indicates that the filter's output is a linear combination of the present input, the M previous inputs, and the N previous outputs. The corresponding system function is given by

$$H(z) = \frac{\sum_{m=0}^{M} b_m z^{-m}}{1 - \sum_{n=1}^{N} a_n z^{-n}} \tag{14.2}$$

where at least one of the a_n is nonzero and at least one of the roots of the denominator is not exactly cancelled by one of the roots of the numerator. For a stable filter, all the poles of $H(z)$ must lie inside the unit circle, but the zeros can lie anywhere in the z plane. It is usual for M, the number of zeros, to be less than or equal to N, the number of poles. Whenever the number of zeros exceeds the number of poles, the filter can be separated into an FIR filter with $M - N$ taps in cascade with an IIR filter with N poles and N zeros. Therefore, IIR design techniques are conventionally restricted to cases for which $M \leq N$.

Except for the special case in which all poles lie on the unit circle (in the z plane), it is not possible to design an IIR filter having exactly linear phase. Therefore, unlike FIR design procedures that are concerned almost exclusively with the magnitude response, IIR design procedures are concerned with both the magnitude response and phase response.

14.1   Frequency Response of IIR Filters

The frequency response of an IIR filter can be computed from the coefficients a_n and b_m as

$$H[k] = \frac{\sum_{m=0}^{L-1} \beta_m \exp(j2\pi mk/L)}{\sum_{n=0}^{L-1} \alpha_n \exp(j2\pi k/L)} \qquad (14.3)$$

where $\alpha_n = \begin{cases} 1 & n=0 \\ -a_n & 0 < n \le N \\ 0 & N < n \end{cases}$

$\beta_m = \begin{cases} b_m & 0 \le m \le M \\ 0 & M < m \end{cases}$

A C function that uses (14.3) to compute the response for an IIR filter is provided in Listing 14.1.

14.2   IIR Realizations

A direct realization of Eq. (14.1) is shown in Fig. 14.1 using the signal flow graph notation introduced in Sec. 4.4. The structure shown is known as the *direct form I realization* or *direct form I structure* for the IIR system represented by (14.1). Examination of the figure reveals that the system can be viewed as two systems in cascade—the first system using $x[k-M]$ through $x[k]$ to generate an intermediate signal that we will call $w[k]$ and the second

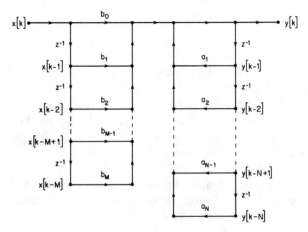

Figure 14.1 Signal flow graph of direct form I realization for an IIR system.

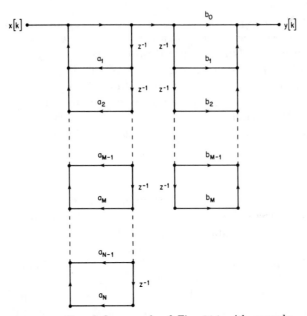

Figure 14.2 Signal flow graph of Fig. 14.1 with cascade order reversed.

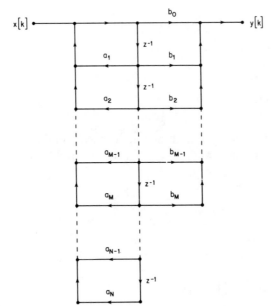

Figure 14.3 Signal flow graph of direct form II realization for an IIR system.

system using $w[k]$ and $y[k - N]$ through $y[k - 1]$ to generate $y[k]$. Since these two systems are LTI systems, the order of the cascade can be reversed to yield the equivalent system shown in Fig. 14.2. Examination of this figure reveals that the unit delays in parallel running down the center of the diagram can be paired such that within a pair the two delays each take the same input signal. This fact can be exploited to merge the two delay chains into a single chain as shown in Fig. 14.3. The structure shown in this figure is known as the *direct form II realization* of the IIR system represented by (14.1).

14.3   Impulse Invariance

The basic idea behind the impulse-invariance approach is a very simple one—the unit sample response of the digital filter is set equal to a sequence of uniformly spaced samples from the impulse response of an analog filter:

$$h[n] = h_a(nT) \qquad (14.4)$$

(An analog filter used in this context is usually refered to as a "prototype" filter.) This approach is conceptually simple, but from a practical viewpoint, evaluation of (14.4) is not a straightforward matter. By definition, for an *infinite* impulse response filter, the sequence $h[n]$ will be nonzero over an infinite domain of n. Furthermore, based on the s-plane-to-z-plane mapping discussed in Sec. 9.2, we can conclude that the imposition of (14.4) will not result in a simple relationship between the frequency response corresponding to $h[n]$ and the frequency response corresponding to $h_a(t)$. In fact, this relationship can be shown to be

$$H(e^{j\lambda}) = \frac{1}{T} \sum_{k=-\infty}^{\infty} H_a\left(j\frac{\lambda + 2\pi k}{T}\right) \qquad (14.5)$$

where $h[n] \overset{\text{DTFT}}{\longleftrightarrow} H(e^{j\lambda})$

$\qquad h_a(t) \overset{\text{FT}}{\longleftrightarrow} H_a(j\omega)$

Put simply, Eq. (14.5) indicates that $H(e^{j\lambda})$ will be an aliased version of $H_a(j\omega)$. The only way the aliasing can be avoided is if $H_a(j\omega)$ is band limited such that

$$H_a(j\omega) = 0 \qquad \text{for } |\omega| \geq \frac{\pi}{T} \qquad (14.6)$$

If (14.6) is satisfied, then

$$H(e^{j\lambda}) = \frac{1}{T} H_a\left(j\frac{\lambda}{T}\right) \qquad |\lambda| \leq \pi \qquad (14.7)$$

For a practical analog filter, Eq. (14.6) will never be satisfied exactly, but the impulse-invariance method can be used to advantage with responses that are nonzero but negligible beyond some frequency.

The transfer function of the analog prototype filter can be expressed in the form of a partial-fraction expansion as

$$H_a(s) = \sum_{k=1}^{N} \frac{A_k}{s - s_k} \tag{14.8}$$

where the s_k are the poles of $H_a(s)$ and the A_k are given by

$$A_k = [(s - s_k)H_a(s)]|_{s = s_k}$$

Based on transform pair 8 from Table 2.2, the impulse response can then be written as

$$h_a(t) = \sum_{k=1}^{N} A_k e^{s_k t} u(t) \tag{14.9}$$

The unit-sample response of the digital filter is then formed by sampling the prototype filter's impulse response to obtain

$$h[n] = \sum_{k=1}^{N} A_k (e^{s_k T})^n u(t) \tag{14.10}$$

The corresponding system function for the digital filter $H(z)$ is obtained as the z transform of (14.10):

$$H(z) = \sum_{k=1}^{N} \frac{A_k}{1 - e^{s_k T} z^{-1}} \tag{14.11}$$

Based on the foregoing, we can state the following algorithm for impulse-invariant design of an IIR filter.

Algorithm 14.1   Impulse-invariant design of IIR filters

Step 1. Obtain the transfer function $H_a(s)$ for the desired analog prototype filter. (The material provided in Chaps. 3 through 6 will prove useful here.)

Step 2. For $k = 1, 2, \ldots, N$, determine the poles s_k of $H_a(s)$ and compute the coefficients A_k using

$$A_k = [(s - s_k)H_a(s)]|_{s = s_k} \tag{14.12}$$

Step 3. Using the coefficients A_k obtained in step 2, generate the digital filter system function $H(z)$ as

$$H(z) = \sum_{k=1}^{N} \frac{A_k}{1 - \exp(s_k T)z^{-1}} \tag{14.13}$$

where T is the sampling interval of the digital filter.

Step 4. The result obtained in step 3 will be a sum of fractions. Obtain a common denominator, and express $H(z)$ as a ratio of polynomials in z^{-1} in the form

$$H(z) = \frac{\sum_{k=0}^{M} b_k z^{-k}}{1 - \sum_{k=1}^{N} a_k z^{-k}} \qquad (14.14)$$

Step 5. Use the a_k and b_k obtained in step 4 to realize the filter in any of the structures given in Sec. 14.1.

Example 14.1 Use the technique of impulse invariance to derive a lowpass IIR digital filter from a second-order Butterworth analog filter with a 3-dB cutoff frequency of 3 KHz. The sampling rate for the digital filter is 30,000 samples per second.

solution From Sec. 3.1 we obtain the normalized-transfer function for a second-order Butterworth filter as

$$H(s) = \frac{1}{(s - s_1)(s - s_2)}$$

where $s_1 = \cos \dfrac{3\pi}{4} + j \sin \dfrac{3\pi}{4}$

$$= \frac{-\sqrt{2}}{2} + j \frac{\sqrt{2}}{2}$$

$$s_2 = \cos \frac{5\pi}{4} + j \sin \frac{5\pi}{4}$$

$$= \cos \frac{3\pi}{4} - j \sin \frac{3\pi}{4}$$

$$= \frac{-\sqrt{2}}{2} - j \frac{\sqrt{2}}{2}$$

The specified cutoff frequency of $f = 3000$ yields $\omega_c = 6000\pi$, and the denormalized response (see Sec. 2.9) is given by

$$H_a(s) = \frac{\omega_c^2}{(s - \omega_c s_1)(s - \omega_c s_2)}$$

$$= \frac{\omega_c^2}{[s + \omega_c(\sqrt{2}/2) - j\omega_c(\sqrt{2}/2)][s + \omega_c(\sqrt{2}/2) + j\omega_c(\sqrt{2}/2)]}$$

The partial-fraction expansion of $H_a(s)$ is given by

$$H_a(s) = \frac{A_1}{s + \omega_c(\sqrt{2}/2) - j\omega_c(\sqrt{2}/2)} + \frac{A_2}{s + \omega_c(\sqrt{2}/2) + j\omega_c(\sqrt{2}/2)}$$

where $A_1 = \dfrac{-j\sqrt{2}}{2\omega_c}$

$$A_2 = \frac{j\sqrt{2}}{2\omega_c}$$

Using these values for A_1 and A_2 plus the fact that

$$\omega_c T = \frac{6000\pi}{30,000} = \frac{\pi}{5}$$

we obtain from Eq. (14.13) the discrete system function $H(z)$ as

$$H(z) = \frac{-j\sqrt{2}/(2\omega_c)}{1 - \exp\!\left(\dfrac{-\pi\sqrt{2}}{10} + j\dfrac{\pi\sqrt{2}}{10}\right)z^{-1}} + \frac{j\sqrt{2}/(2\omega_c)}{1 - \exp\!\left(\dfrac{-\pi\sqrt{2}}{10} - j\dfrac{\pi\sqrt{2}}{10}\right)z^{-1}}$$

$$= \frac{2.06797 \times 10^{-5}z^{-1}}{1 - 1.158045z^{-1} + 0.4112407z^{-2}}$$

Programming considerations

Step 1. Butterworth, Chebyshev, and Bessel filters are "all-pole" filters—their transfer functions have no finite zeros. Closed-form expressions are available for the poles of Butterworth [Eq. (3.2)] and Chebyshev [Eq. (4.4)] filters. The poles of Bessel filters can be readily obtained by finding the roots of the denominator polynomial as discussed in Chap. 6. The transfer function for an elliptical filter has both poles and zeros. The poles are readily available by using the quadratic formula to find the denominator roots for each factor in Eq. (5.22). The zeros $\pm j\alpha\sqrt{a_i}$ are obtained by inspection of Eq. (5.22). The software for performing the impulse-invariance transformation is therefore designed to accept $H_a(s)$ specified as an array of poles and an array of zeros.

Step 2. Evaluation of A_k for step 2 of the algorithm is straightforward. The coefficients A_k can be written as $A_k = N_{Ak}/D_{Ak}$ where the numerator N_{Ak} is obtained as

$$N_{Ak} = \begin{cases} H_0 \displaystyle\prod_{m=1}^{M} (p_k - q_m) & M \neq 0 \\[2mm] H_0 & M = 0 \end{cases}$$

and q_m is the mth zero of $H_a(s)$, p_k is the kth pole of $H_a(s)$, and M is the total number of zeros. Equation (14.12) can be evaluated using simple arithmetic—there is no symbolic manipulation needed. The denominator D_{Ak} is obtained as

$$D_{Ak} = \prod_{\substack{n=1 \\ n \neq k}}^{N} (p_k - p_n)$$

Step 3. Evaluation of $H(z)$ is more than plain, straightforward arithmetic. At this point, for each value of k, the coefficient A_k is known and the coefficient $\exp(s_k T)$ can be evaluated. However, z remains a variable and hence will demand some special consideration. To simplify the notation in the subsequent development, let us rewrite $H(z)$ as

$$H(z) = \sum_{k=1}^{N} \frac{A_k}{1 + \beta_k z^{-1}} \tag{14.15}$$

where $\beta_k = -\exp(s_k T)$

Step 4. For the summation in (14.15), the common denominator will be the product of each summand's denominator:

$$D(z) = \prod_{k=1}^{N} (1 + \beta_k z^{-1}) \tag{14.16}$$

To see how (14.16) can be easily evaluated by computer, let's examine the sequence of partial products $\{D_k(z)\}$ encountered in the evaluation:

$$D_1(z) = (1 + \beta_1 z^{-1})$$

$$D_2(z) = (1 + \beta_2 z^{-1}) D_1(z) = D_1(z) + \beta_2 z^{-1} D_1(z)$$

$$D_3(z) = (1 + \beta_3 z^{-1}) D_2(z) = D_2(z) + \beta_3 z^{-1} D_2(z)$$

$$D_4(z) = (1 + \beta_4 z^{-1}) D_3(z) = D_3(z) + \beta_4 z^{-1} D_3(z)$$

$$\vdots$$

$$D(z) = D_N(z) = (1 + \beta_N z^{-1}) D_{N-1}(z) = D_{N-1}(z) + \beta_N z^{-1} D_{N-1}(z)$$

Examination of this sequence reveals that the partial product $D_k(z)$ at iteration k can be expressed in terms of the partial product $D_{k-1}(z)$ as

$$D_k(z) = D_{k-1}(z) + \beta_k z^{-1} D_{k-1}(z)$$

The partial product $D_{k-1}(z)$ will be a $(k-1)$-degree polynomial in z^{-1}:

$$D_{k-1}(z) = \delta_0 (z^{-1})^0 + \delta_1 (z^{-1})^1 + \delta_2 (z^{-1})^2 + \cdots + \delta_{k-1} (z^{-1})^{k-1}$$

The product $\beta_k z^{-1} D_{k-1}(z)$ is then given by

$$\beta_k z^{-1} D_{k-1}(z) = \delta_0 \beta_k (z^{-1})^1 + \delta_1 \beta_k (z^{-1})^2 + \delta_2 \beta_k (z^{-1})^3 + \cdots + \delta_{k-1} \beta_k (z^{-1})^k$$

and $D_k(z)$ is given by

$$D_k(z) = \delta_0 (z^{-1})^0 + (\delta_1 + \delta_0 \beta_k)(z^{-1})^1 + (\delta_2 + \delta_1 \beta_k)(z^{-1})^2 + \cdots$$
$$+ (\delta_{k-1} + \delta_{k-2} \beta_k)(z^{-1})^{k-1} + \delta_{k-1} \beta_k (z^{-1})^k$$

Therefore, we can conclude that if δ_n is the coefficient for the $(z^{-1})^n$ term in $D_{k-1}(z)$, then the coefficient for the $(z^{-1})^n$ term in $D_k(z)$ is $(\delta_n + \delta_{n-1} \beta_k)$ with the proviso that $\delta_k \triangleq 0$ in $D_{k-1}(z)$. The polynomial $D_{k-1}(z)$ can be represented in the computer as an array of k coefficients, with the array index corresponding to the subscript on δ and the superscript (exponent) on (z^{-1}): **delta[0]** $= \delta_0$, **delta[1]** $= \delta_1$, and so on. The coefficients for the partial product $D_k(z)$ can be obtained from the coefficients for $D_{k-1}(z)$ as indicated by the following fragment of pseudocode:

```
for( j = k; j >= 1; j−−)
    {delta[j] = delta[j] + beta * delta[j−1];}
```

The loop is executed in reverse order so that the coefficients can be updated "in place" without prematurely overwriting the old values. Notice that I referred to the fragment shown above as "pseudocode." In actuality, both **delta[ ]** and **beta** are complex valued; and the arithmetic operations shown in the fragment are incorrect. The following code fragment performs the complex arithmetic correctly, but all the complex functions tend to obscure the algorithm that is more clearly conveyed by the pseudocode above:

```
for( j = k; j >= 1; j−−)
    {delta[j] = cAdd(delta[j], cMult(beta, delta[j−1]));}
```

If this fragment is placed within an outer loop with k ranging from 1 to **numPoles**, the final values in **delta[n]** will be the coefficients a_n for Eq. (14.14).

For the summation in Eq. (14.13), the numerator can be computed as

$$N(z) = \sum_{k=1}^{N} \left[A_k \prod_{\substack{n=1 \\ n \neq k}}^{N} (1 - \beta_n z^{-1}) \right] \qquad (14.17)$$

For each value of k, the product in (14.17) can be evaluated in a manner similar to the way in which the denominator is evaluated. The major difference is that the factor $(1 - \beta_k z^{-1})$ is not included in the product. It is then a simple matter to add the coefficients of each of the N products to obtain the coefficients for the numerator polynomial $N(z)$. A complete function for computing the coefficients a_n and b_n is provided in Listing 14.2.

14.4 Step Invariance

One major drawback to filters designed via the impulse-invariance method is their sensitivity to the specific characteristics of the input signal. The digital filter's unit-sample response is a sampled version of the prototype filter's impulse response. However, the prototype filter's response to an arbitrary input cannot in general be sampled to obtain the digital filter's response to a sampled version of the same arbitrary input. In many applications a filter's step response is of more concern than is the filter's impulse response. In such cases, the impulse-invariance technique can be modified to design a digital filter based on the principle of step invariance.

Algorithm 14.2   Step-invariant design of IIR filters

Step 1.   Obtain the transfer function $H_a(s)$ for the desired analog prototype filter.

Step 2.   Multiply $H_a(s)$ by $1/s$ to obtain $G_a(s)$, the filter's response to the unit step function.

Step 3.   For $k = 1, 2, \ldots, N$, determine the poles s_k of $G_a(s)$ and compute the coefficients A_k using

$$A_k = [(s - s_k)G_a(s)]\big|_{s = s_k}$$

Step 4.   Using the coefficients A_k obtained in step 3, generate the system function $G(z)$ as

$$G(z) = \sum_{k=1}^{N} \frac{A_k}{1 - \exp(s_k T)z^{-1}}$$

Step 5.   Multiply $G(z)$ by $(1 - z^{-1})$ to remove the z transform of a unit step and thereby obtain $H(z)$ as

$$H(z) = (1 - z^{-1}) \sum_{k=1}^{N} \frac{A_k}{1 - \exp(s_k T)z^{-1}}$$

Step 6.   Obtain a common denominator for the terms in the summation of step 5, and express $H(z)$ as a ratio of polynomials in z^{-1} in the form

$$G(z) = \frac{\sum_{k=0}^{M} b_k z^{-k}}{1 - \sum_{k=1}^{N} a_k z^{-k}}$$

Step 7.   Use the a_k and b_k obtained in step 6 to realize the filter in any of the structures given in Sec. 14.1.

Programming considerations

The step-invariance method is similar to the impulse-invariance method, with two important differences. In step 2 of Algorithm 14.2, the transfer function $H_a(s)$ is multiplied by $1/s$. Assuming that $H_a(s)$ is represented in terms of its poles and zeros, multiplication by $1/s$ is accomplished by simply adding a pole at $s = 0$. (Strictly speaking, if the analog filter has a zero at $s = 0$, multiplication by $1/s$ creates a pole at $s = 0$, which cancels the zero. However, since none of the analog prototype filters within the scope of this book have zeros at $s = 0$, we shall construct the software without provisions for handling a zero at $s = 0$.)

In step 5 of Algorithm 14.2, the system function $G(z)$ is multiplied by $(1 - z^{-1})$ to remove the z transform of a unit step and thereby obtain the system function $H(z)$. Conceptually, this multiplication is appropriately located in step 5. However, for ease of implementation it makes sense to defer the multiplication until after the coefficients a_n and b_n are generated in step 6. A function modified to perform the step-invariance technique is provided in Listing 14.3.

Listing 14.1   iirResponse( )

```
/***********************************/
/*                                 */
/*    Listing 14.1                 */
/*                                 */
/*    iirResponse()                */
/*                                 */
/***********************************/


void iirResponse(struct complex a[],
                 int bigN,
                 struct complex b[],
                 int bigM,
                 int numberOfPoints,
                 logical dbScale,
                 real magnitude[],
                 real phase[])
{
static struct complex response[MAXPOINTS];
int k, n, m;
real sumRe, sumIm, phi;

/*-----------------------------------------------------*/
/*  compute DFT of H(z) numerator                      */

for( m=0; m<numberOfPoints; m++) {
    sumRe = 0.0;
    sumIm = 0.0;
    printf("\r%d  000",m);
    for(n=0; n<=bigM; n++) {
        printf("\b\b\b%3d",n);
        phi = 2.0 * PI * m * n / (2.0*numberOfPoints);
        printf("b[%d] = (%e, %e)\n",n,b[n].Re,b[n].Im);
        sumRe += b[n].Re * cos(phi) + b[n].Im * sin(phi);
        sumIm += b[n].Im * cos(phi) - b[n].Re * sin(phi);
        }
    response[m] = cmplx(sumRe, sumIm);
    printf("response = (%e, %e)\n",response[m].Re, response[m].Im);
    }


/*-----------------------------------------------------*/
/*  compute DFT of H(z) denominator                    */

for( m=0; m<numberOfPoints; m++) {
    sumRe = 1.0;
    sumIm = 0.0;
```

```
      for(n=1; n<=bigN; n++) {
          phi = 2.0 * PI * m * n / (2.0*numberOfPoints);
          sumRe += -a[n].Re * cos(phi) - a[n].Im * sin(phi);
          sumIm += -a[n].Im * cos(phi) + a[n].Re * sin(phi);
          }
      response[m] = cDiv(response[m],cmplx(sumRe, sumIm));
      }
/*-------------------------------------------------*/
/*  compute magnitude and phase of response        */

for( m=0; m<numberOfPoints; m++) {
    phase[m] = arg(response[m]);
    if(dbScale)
        {magnitude[m] = 20.0 * log10(cAbs(response[m]));}
    else
        {magnitude[m] = cAbs(response[m]);}
    printf("mag = %e\n",magnitude[m]);
    }
return;
}
```

Listing 14.2   impulseInvar( )

```
/**********************************/
/*                                */
/*    Listing 14.2                */
/*                                */
/*    impulseInvar()              */
/*                                */
/**********************************/


void impulseInvar(    struct complex pole[],
                      int numPoles,
                      struct complex zero[],
                      int numZeros,
                      real hZero,
                      real bigT,
                      struct complex a[],
                      struct complex b[])
{
int k, n, j, maxCoef;
struct complex delta[MAXPOLES];
struct complex bigA[MAXPOLES];
struct complex beta, denom, numer, work2;
```

```
for(j=0; j<MAXPOLES; j++) {
    delta[j] = cmplx(0.0,0.0);
    a[j] = cmplx(0.0,0.0);
    b[j] = cmplx(0.0,0.0);
    }
/*----------------------------------------------------*/
/*  compute partial fraction expansion coefficients  */
for( k=1; k<=numPoles; k++) {
    numer = cmplx(hZero,0.0);
    for(n=1; n<=numZeros; n++)
        { numer = cMult(numer, cSub(pole[n], zero[n]));}
    denom = cmplx(1.0,0.0);
    for( n=1; n<=numPoles; n++) {
        if(n==k) continue;
        denom = cMult(denom, cSub(pole[k],pole[n]));
        }
    bigA[k] = cDiv(numer,denom);
    }
/*----------------------------------------*/
/*  compute numerator coefficients      */
for( k=1; k<=numPoles; k++) {
    delta[0] = cmplx(1.0, 0.0);
    for(n=1; n<MAXPOLES; n++)
        {delta[n] = cmplx(0.0,0.0);}
    maxCoef = 0;
    for( n=1; n<=numPoles; n++) {
        if(n==k) continue;
        maxCoef++;
        beta = sMult(-1.0, cExp(sMult(bigT,pole[n])));
        for(j=maxCoef; j>=1; j--)
            { delta[j] = cAdd( delta[j], cMult( beta, delta[j-1]));}
        }
    for( j=0; j<numPoles; j++)
        { b[j] = cAdd(b[j], cMult( bigA[k], delta[j])); }
    }

/*----------------------------------------*/
/*  compute denominator deltaficients    */
a[0] = cmplx(1.0,0.0);
for( n=1; n<=numPoles; n++) {
    beta = sMult(-1.0, cExp(sMult(bigT,pole[n])));
    for( j=n; j>=1; j--)
        { a[j] = cAdd( a[j], cMult( beta, a[j-1]));}
    }
for( j=1; j<=numPoles; j++)
    { a[j] = sMult(-1.0,a[j]);}
return;
}
```

Listing 14.3   stepInvar( )

```
/**********************************/
/*                                */
/*    Listing 14.3                */
/*                                */
/*    stepInvar()                 */
/*                                */
/**********************************/

void stepInvar(  struct complex pole[],
                 int numPoles,
                 struct complex zero[],
                 int numZeros,
                 real hZero,
                 real bigT,
                 struct complex a[],
                 struct complex b[])
{
int k, n, j, maxCoef;
struct complex delta[MAXPOLES];
struct complex bigA[MAXPOLES];
struct complex beta, denom, numer, work2;

for(j=0; j<MAXPOLES; j++) {
    delta[j] = cmplx(0.0,0.0);
    a[j] = cmplx(0.0,0.0);
    b[j] = cmplx(0.0,0.0);
    }
pole[0] = cmplx(0.0,0.0);
/*-----------------------------------------------------*/
/* compute partial fraction expansion coefficients */
for( k=0; k<=numPoles; k++) {
    numer = cmplx(hZero,0.0);
    for(n=1; n<=numZeros; n++)
        { numer = cMult(numer, cSub(pole[n], zero[n]));}
    denom = cmplx(1.0,0.0);
    for( n=0; n<=numPoles; n++) {
        if(n==k) continue;
        denom = cMult(denom, cSub(pole[k],pole[n]));
        }
    bigA[k] = cDiv(numer,denom);
    }
/*-----------------------------------------*/
/* compute numerator coefficients      */
for( k=1; k<=numPoles; k++) {
    delta[0] = cmplx(1.0, 0.0);
    for(n=1; n<MAXPOLES; n++)
```

```
            {delta[n] = cmplx(0.0,0.0);}
    maxCoef = 0;
    for( n=0; n<=numPoles; n++) {
        if(n==k) continue;
        maxCoef++;
        beta = sMult(-1.0, cExp(sMult(bigT,pole[n])));
        for(j=maxCoef; j>=1; j--)
            { delta[j] = cAdd( delta[j], cMult( beta, delta[j-1]));}
        }
    for( j=0; j<numPoles; j++)
        { b[j] = cAdd(b[j], cMult( bigA[k], delta[j])); }

/* multiply by 1-z**(-1)   */
    beta = cmplx(-1.0,0.0);
    for(j=numPoles+1; j>=1; j--) {
        b[j] = cAdd(b[j], cMult(beta, b[j-1]));}


    }

/*-------------------------------------*/
/*  compute denominator coefficients   */
a[0] = cmplx(1.0,0.0);
for( n=1; n<=numPoles; n++) {
    beta = sMult(-1.0, cExp(sMult(bigT,pole[n])));
    for( j=n; j>=1; j--)
        { a[j] = cAdd( a[j], cMult( beta, a[j-1]));}
    }
for( j=1; j<=numPoles; j++)
    { a[j] = sMult(-1.0,a[j]);}
return;
}
```

15

IIR Filters via the Bilinear Transformation

A popular technique for the design of IIR digital filters is the *bilinear transformation method*, which offers several advantages over the other techniques presented in the previous chapter.

15.1 Bilinear Transformation

The bilinear transformation converts the transfer function for an analog filter into the system function for a digital filter by making the substitution

$$s \to \frac{2}{T} \frac{1 - z^{-1}}{1 + z^{-1}}$$

If the analog prototype filter is stable, the bilinear transformation will result in a stable digital filter.

Algorithm 15.1 Bilinear transformation

Step 1. Obtain the transfer function $H_a(s)$ for the desired analog prototype filter.

Step 2. In the transfer function obtained in step 1, make the substitution

$$s = \frac{2}{T} \frac{1 - z^{-1}}{1 + z^{-1}}$$

where T is the sampling interval of the digital filter. Call the resulting digital system function $H(z)$.

Step 3. The analog prototype filter's transfer function $H_a(s)$ will, in general, be a ratio of polynomials in s. Therefore, the system function $H(z)$ obtained in step 2 will, in general, contain various powers of the ratio $(1-z^{-1})/$ $(1+z^{-1})$ in both the numerator and the denominator. Multiply both the numerator and denominator by the highest power of $1+z^{-1}$, and collect terms to obtain $H(z)$ as a ratio of polynomials in z^{-1} of the form

$$H(z) = \frac{\sum_{k=0}^{M} b_k z^{-k}}{1 - \sum_{k=1}^{N} a_k z^{-k}} \tag{15.1}$$

Step 4. Use the a_k and b_k obtained in step 3 to realize the filter in any of the structures given in Sec. 14.1.

Example 15.1 Use the bilinear transform to obtain an IIR filter from a second-order Butterworth analog filter with a 3-dB cutoff frequency of 3 KHz. The sampling rate for the digital filter is 30,000 samples per second.

solution The analog prototype filter's transfer function is given by

$$H_a(s) = \frac{\omega_c^2}{s^2 + \sqrt{2}\omega_c s + \omega_c^2}$$

where $\omega_c = 6000\pi$. Making the substitution $s = 2(1-z^{-1})/(T(1+z^{-1}))$ yields

$$H(z) = \frac{\omega_c^2}{\left(\frac{2}{T}\right)^2\left(\frac{1-z^{-1}}{1+z^{-1}}\right)^2 + \sqrt{2}\omega_c\left(\frac{2}{T}\right)\left(\frac{1-z^{-1}}{1+z^{-1}}\right) + \omega_c^2}$$

where $T = 1/30{,}000$. After the appropriate algebraic simplifications and making use of the fact that

$$\omega_c T = \frac{6000\pi}{30{,}000} = \frac{\pi}{5}$$

we obtain the desired form of $H(z)$ as

$$H(z) = \frac{0.063964 + 0.127929z^{-1} + 0.063964z^{-2}}{1 - 1.168261z^{-1} + 0.424118z^{-2}} \tag{15.2}$$

Comparison of (15.1) and (15.2) reveals that

$$a_1 = -1.168261 \qquad a_2 = 0.424118$$

$$b_0 = 0.063964 \qquad b_1 = 0.127929 \qquad b_2 = 0.063964$$

15.2   Factored Form of the Bilinear Transformation

Often an analog prototype filter will be specified in terms of its poles and zeros—that is, the numerator and denominator of the filter's transfer function will be in factored form. The bilinear transformation can be applied directly to this factored form. An additional benefit of this approach is that the process of finding the *digital* filter's poles and zeros is greatly simplified. Each factor in the numerator of the analog filter's transfer function will be of the form $(s - q_n)$, and each factor of the denominator will be of the form

$(s - p_n)$, where q_n and p_n are, respectively, the nth zero and nth pole of the filter. When the bilinear transform is applied, the corresponding factors become

$$\left(\frac{2}{T}\frac{1 - z^{-1}}{1 + z^{-1}} - q_n\right) \quad \text{and} \quad \left(\frac{2}{T}\frac{1 - z^{-1}}{1 + z^{-1}} - p_n\right)$$

The zeros of the digital filter are obtained by finding the values of z for which

$$\frac{2}{T}\frac{1 - z^{-1}}{1 + z^{-1}} - q_n = 0$$

The desired values of z are given by

$$z_z = \frac{2 + q_n T}{2 - q_n T} \tag{15.3}$$

In a similar fashion, the poles of the digital filter are obtained from the poles of the analog filter using

$$z_p = \frac{2 + p_n T}{2 - p_n T} \tag{15.4}$$

The use of (15.3) and (15.4) is straightforward for the analog filter's *finite* poles or zeros. Usually, only the finite poles and zeros of a filter are considered, but in the present context, *all* poles and zeros of the analog filter must be considered. The analog filter's infinite zeros will map into zeros of $z = -1$ for the digital filter.

Algorithm 15.2   Bilinear transformation for transfer functions in factored form

Step 1. For the desired analog prototype filter, obtain the transfer function $H_a(s)$ in the factored form given by

$$H_a(s) = H_0 \frac{\prod_{m=1}^{M}(s - q_m)}{\prod_{n=1}^{N}(s - p_n)}$$

Step 2. Obtain the poles z_{pn} of the analog filter from the poles p_n of the analog filter using

$$z_{pn} = \frac{2 + p_n T}{2 - p_n T} \quad n = 1, 2, \ldots, N$$

Step 3. Obtain the zeros z_{zm} of the digital filter from the zeros q_m of the analog filter using

$$z_{zm} = \frac{2 + q_m T}{2 - q_m T} \quad m = 1, 2, \ldots, M$$

Step 4. Using the values of z_{pn} obtained in step 2 and the values of z_{zm} obtained in step 3, form $H(z)$ as

$$H(z) = H_0 \frac{T^N}{\prod_{n=1}^{N}(2 - p_n T)} \cdot \frac{(z+1)^{N-M}\prod_{m=1}^{M}(z - z_{zm})}{\prod_{n=1}^{N}(z - z_{pn})} \qquad (15.5)$$

The factor $(z+1)^{N-M}$ supplies the zeros at $z = -1$, which correspond to the zeros at $s = \infty$ for analog filter's having $M < N$. The first rational factor in Eq. (15.5) is a constant gain factor that is needed to obtain results which exactly match the results obtained via Algorithm 15.1. However, in practice, this factor is often omitted to yield

$$H(z) = H_0 \frac{(z+1)^{N-M}\prod_{m=1}^{M}(z - z_{zm})}{\prod_{n=1}^{N}(z - z_{pn})}$$

Example 15.2 The Butterworth filter of Example 15.1 has a transfer function given in factored form as

$$H_a(s) = \frac{\omega_c^2}{[s + \omega_c(\sqrt{2}/2) - j\omega_c(\sqrt{2}/2)][s + \omega_c(\sqrt{2}/2) + j\omega_c(\sqrt{2}/2)]}$$

Apply the bilinear transform to this factored form to obtain the IIR filter's system function $H(z)$.

solution The analog filter has poles at

$$s = \omega_c \frac{-\sqrt{2}}{2} \pm j\omega_c \frac{\sqrt{2}}{2}$$

Using (15.4), we then obtain the poles of the digital filter as

$$z_{P_1} = \frac{2 + \left(\dfrac{-\sqrt{2}}{2} + j\dfrac{\sqrt{2}}{2}\right)\omega_c T}{2 - \left(\dfrac{-\sqrt{2}}{2} + j\dfrac{\sqrt{2}}{2}\right)\omega_c T}$$

$$= 0.584131 + 0.28794j$$

$$z_{P_2} = \frac{2 + \left(\dfrac{-\sqrt{2}}{2} - j\dfrac{\sqrt{2}}{2}\right)\omega_c T}{2 - \left(\dfrac{-\sqrt{2}}{2} - j\dfrac{\sqrt{2}}{2}\right)\omega_c T}$$

$$= 0.584131 - 0.287941j$$

The two zeros at $s = \infty$ map into two zeros at $z = -1$. Thus the system function is given by

$$H(z) = H_c \frac{(z+1)^2}{(z - 0.584131 + 0.287941j)(z - 0.584131 - 0.287941j)}$$

where $H_c = \dfrac{H_0 T^2}{(2 - p_1 T)(2 - p_2 T)}$

$$= \frac{(6000\pi)^2}{(30{,}000)^2\left(2 + \dfrac{\pi\sqrt{2}}{10} - j\dfrac{\pi\sqrt{2}}{10}\right)\left(2 + \dfrac{\pi\sqrt{2}}{10} + j\dfrac{\pi\sqrt{2}}{10}\right)}$$

$$= 0.063964$$

If the numerator and denominator factors are multiplied out and all terms are divided by z^2, we obtain

$$H(z) = \frac{0.063964(1 + 2z^{-1} + z^{-2})}{1 - 1.168261z^{-1} + 0.424118z^{-2}} \tag{15.6}$$

which matches the result of Example 15.1.

15.3 Properties of the Bilinear Transformation

Assume that the analog prototype filter has a pole at $s_P = \sigma + j\omega$. The corresponding IIR filter designed via the bilinear transformation will have a pole at

$$z_P = \frac{2 + sT}{2 - sT}$$

$$= \frac{2 + (\sigma + j\omega)T}{2 - (\sigma + j\omega)T}$$

$$= \frac{2 + \sigma T + j\omega T}{2 - \sigma T - j\omega T}$$

The magnitude and angle of this pole are given by

$$|z_P| = \sqrt{\frac{(2 + \sigma T)^2 + (\omega T)^2}{(2 - \sigma T)^2 + (\omega T)^2}} \tag{15.7}$$

$$\arg(z_P) = \tan^{-1}\!\left(\frac{\omega T}{2 + \sigma T}\right) - \tan^{-1}\!\left(\frac{-\omega T}{2 - \sigma T}\right)$$

The poles of a stable analog filter must lie in the left half of the s plane—that is, $\sigma < 0$. When $\sigma < 0$, the numerator of (15.7) will be smaller than the denominator, and thus $|z_P| < 1$. This means that analog poles in the left half of the s plane map into digital poles inside the unit circle of the z plane—stable analog poles map into stable digital poles. Poles that lie on the $j\omega$ axis of the s plane have $\sigma = 0$ and consequently map into z-plane poles which have unity magnitude and hence lie on the unit circle. Analog poles at $s = 0$ map into digital poles at $z = 1$, and analog poles at $s = \pm j\infty$ map into digital poles at $z = -1$.

Frequency warping

The mapping of the s plane's $j\omega$ axis into the z plane's unit circle is a highly nonlinear mapping. The analog frequency ω_0 can range from $-\infty$ to $+\infty$, but the digital frequency ω_d is limited to the range $\pm\pi$. The relationship between ω_a and ω_d is given by

$$\omega_d = 2\tan^{-1}\frac{\omega_a T}{2} \qquad (15.8)$$

If an analog prototype filter with a cutoff frequency of ω_a is used to design a filter via the bilinear transformation, the resulting digital filter will have a cutoff frequency of ω_d, where ω_d is related to ω_a via (15.8).

Example 15.3 A lowpass filter with a 3-dB frequency of 3 kHz is used as the prototype for an IIR filter with a sampling rate of 30,000 samples per second. What will be the 3-dB frequency of the digital filter designed via the bilinear transformation?

solution Equation (15.8) yields

$$\omega_d = 2\tan^{-1}\frac{(6000\pi)(1/30,000)}{2}$$

$$= 0.6088$$

Since $\omega_d = \pi$ corresponds to a frequency of $30,000/2 = 15,000$ Hz, the cutoff frequency of the filter is given by

$$\omega_c = \frac{0.6088}{\pi}(15,000) = 2906.8 \text{ Hz}$$

The frequency-warping effects become more severe as the frequency of interest increases relative to the digital filter's sampling rate.

Example 15.4 Consider the case of an analog filter with a 3-dB frequency of 3 kHz used as the prototype for an IIR filter designed via the bilinear transformation. Determine the impact on the 3-dB frequency if the sampling rate is changed from 10,000 samples per second to 30,000 samples per second in steps of 1000 samples per second.

solution The various sampling rates and the corresponding warped 3-dB frequencies are listed in Table 15.1.

Fortunately, it is a simple matter to counteract the effects of frequency warping by prewarping the critical frequencies of the analog prototype filter in such a way that the warping caused by the bilinear transformation restores the critical frequencies to their original intended values. Equation (15.8) can be inverted to yield the equation needed for this prewarping:

$$\omega_a = \frac{2}{T}\tan\frac{\omega_d}{2} \qquad (15.9)$$

Example 15.5 We wish to design an IIR filter with a 3-dB frequency of 3 kHz and a sampling rate of 30,000 samples per second. Determine the prewarped 3-dB frequency required for the analog prototype filter.

TABLE 15.1   Warped Cutoff Frequencies for Example 15.4

Sampling rate	Cutoff frequency, Hz	% error
10,000	2405.8	−19.81
11,000	2480.5	−17.32
12,000	2543.1	−15.23
13,000	2595.8	−13.47
14,000	2640.4	−11.99
15,000	2678.5	−10.72
16,000	2711.1	−9.63
17,000	2739.3	−8.69
18,000	2763.6	−7.88
19,000	2784.9	−7.17
20,000	2803.5	−6.55
21,000	2819.9	−6.00
22,000	2834.4	−5.52
23,000	2847.2	−5.09
24,000	2858.7	−4.71
25,000	2868.9	−4.37
26,000	2878.1	−4.06
27,000	2886.4	−3.79
28,000	2893.8	−3.54
29,000	2900.6	−3.31
30,000	2906.8	−3.11

solution   Since $\omega_d = \pi$ corresponds to a frequency of $30,000/2 = 15,000$ Hz, a frequency of 3 kHz corresponds to a ω_d of

$$\omega_d = \frac{3000\pi}{15,000} = \frac{\pi}{5}$$

The prototype analog frequency ω_a is obtained by using this value of ω_d in Eq. (15.9):

$$\omega_a = \frac{2}{(1/30,000)} \tan \frac{\pi}{10} = 19,495.18$$

The analog prototype filter must have a 3-dB frequency of $19,495.18/(2\pi) = 3102.75$ Hz in order for the IIR filter to have a 3-dB frequency of 3 kHz after warping.

15.4   Programming the Bilinear Transformation

Assume that the transfer function of the analog prototype filter is in the form given by

$$H_a(s) = H_0 \frac{\prod_{m=1}^{M} (s - q_m)}{\prod_{n=1}^{N} (s - p_n)}$$

where p_n and q_n denote, respectively, the filter's poles and zeros. To generate a digital filter via the bilinear transformation, we make the substitution

$$s = \frac{2}{T}\left(\frac{1 - z^{-1}}{1 + z^{-1}}\right)$$

and obtain

$$H(z) = H_0 \frac{\prod_{m=1}^{M}\left[\frac{2}{T}\left(\frac{1 - z^{-1}}{1 + z^{-1}}\right) - q_m\right]}{\prod_{n=1}^{N}\left[\frac{2}{T}\left(\frac{1 - z^{-1}}{1 + z^{-1}}\right) - p_n\right]}$$

which, after some algebraic manipulation, can be put into the form

$$H(z) = H_0 \frac{(1 + z^{-1})^{N-M}\prod_{m=1}^{N}\left[\left(\frac{2}{T} - q_m\right) - \left(\frac{2}{T} + q_m\right)z^{-1}\right]}{\prod_{n=1}^{N}\left[\left(\frac{2}{T} - p_n\right) - \left(\frac{2}{T} + p_n\right)z^{-1}\right]}$$

Thus, the denominator of $H(z)$ is given by

$$D(z) = \prod_{n=1}^{N}(\gamma_n + \delta_n z^{-1}) \qquad (15.10)$$

where $\gamma_n = \dfrac{2}{T} - p_n$

$\delta_n = \dfrac{-2}{T} - p_n$

To see how (15.10) can be easily evaluated by computer, let's examine the sequence of partial products $\{D_k(z)\}$ encountered in the evaluation:

$D_1(z) = (\gamma_1 + \delta_1 z^{-1})$

$D_2(z) = (\gamma_2 + \delta_2 z^{-1})D_1(z) = \gamma_2 D_1(z) + \delta_2 z^{-1} D_1(z)$

$D_3(z) = (\gamma_3 + \delta_3 z^{-1})D_2(z) = \gamma_3 D_2(z) + \delta_3 z^{-1} D_2(z)$

$D_4(z) = (\gamma_4 + \delta_4 z^{-1})D_3(z) = \gamma_4 D_3(z) + \delta_4 z^{-1} D_3(z)$

$\qquad \vdots$

$D(z) = D_N(z) = (\gamma_N + \delta_N z^{-1})D_{N-1}(z) = \gamma_N D_{N-1}(z) + \delta_N z^{-1} D_{N-1}(z)$

Examination of this sequence reveals that the partial product $D_k(z)$ at iteration k can be expanded in terms of the partial product $D_{k-1}(z)$ as

$$D_k(z) = \gamma_k D_{k-1}(z) + \delta_k z^{-1} D_{k-1}(z)$$

The partial product $D_{k-1}(z)$ will be a $(k-1)$-degree polynomial in z^{-1}:

$$D_{k-1}(z) = \mu_0(z^{-1})^0 + \mu_1(z^{-1})^1 + \mu_2(z^{-1})^2 + \cdots + \mu_{k-1}(z^{-1})^{k-1}$$

The products $\gamma_k D_{k-1}(z)$ and $\delta_k z^{-1} D_{k-1}(z)$ are then given by

$$\gamma_k D_{k-1}(z) = \gamma_k \mu_0 (z^{-1})^0 + \gamma_k \mu_1 (z^{-1})^1 + \gamma_k \mu_2 (z^{-1})^2 + \cdots + \gamma_k \mu_{k-1} (z^{-1})^{k-1}$$

$$\delta_k z^{-1} D_{k-1}(z) = \delta_k \mu_0 (z^{-1})^1 + \delta_k \mu_1 (z^{-1})^2 + \delta_k \mu_2 (z^{-1})^3 + \cdots + \delta_k \mu_{k-1} (z^{-1})^k$$

and $D_k(z)$ is given by

$$D_k(z) = \gamma_k \mu_0 (z^{-1})^0 + (\gamma_k \mu_1 - \delta_k \mu_0)(z^{-1})^1 + (\gamma_k \mu_2 - \delta_k \mu_1)(z^{-1})^2 + \cdots$$
$$+ (\gamma_k \mu_{k-1} - \delta_k \mu_{k-2})(z^{-1})^{k-1} - \delta_k \mu_{k-1}(z^{-1})^k$$

Therefore, we can conclude that if μ_n is the coefficient for the $(z^{-1})^n$ term in $D_{k-1}(z)$, then the coefficient for the $(z^{-1})^n$ term in $D(z)$ is $(\gamma_k \mu_n + \delta_k \mu_{n-1})$ with the proviso that $\mu \triangleq 0$ in $D_{k-1}(z)$. The polynomial $D_{k-1}(z)$ is represented in the computer as an array of k coefficients, with the array index corresponding to the subscript on μ and the superscript (exponent) on (z^{-1}). Thus, array element **mu[0]** contains μ_0, array element **mu[1]** contains μ_1, and so forth. The coefficients for the partial product $D_k(z)$ can be obtained from the coefficients for $D_{k-1}(z)$, as indicated by the following fragment of pseudocode:

```
for( j = k; j >= 1; j--)
    {mu[j] = gamma * mu[j] + beta * mu[j-1];}
```

The loop is executed in reverse order so that the coefficients can be updated "in place" without prematurely overwriting the old values. Notice that I referred to the fragment shown above as "pseudocode." In actuality, **mu[ ]**, **gamma**, and **delta** are each complex valued; and the arithmetic operations shown in the fragment are incorrect. The following code fragment performs the complex arithmetic correctly, but all the complex functions tend to obscure the algorithm which is more clearly conveyed by the pseudocode above:

```
for( j = k; j >= 1; j--)
    {mu[j] = cSub(cMult(gamma, mu[j], cMult(delta, mu[j-1]));}
```

If this fragment is placed within an outer loop with k ranging from 1 to **numPoles**, the final values in **mu[n]** will be the coefficients a_n for Eq. (15.1). A similar loop can be developed for the numerator product $N(z)$ given by

$$N(z) = \prod_{m=1}^{M} (\alpha_m - \beta_m z^{-1}) \tag{15.11}$$

where $\alpha_m = \dfrac{-2}{T} + q_m$

$\beta_m = \dfrac{-2}{T} - q_m$

A C program for computation of the bilinear transformation is provided in Listing 15.1.

Listing 15.1   bilinear( )

```
/*********************************/
/*                               */
/*    Listing 15.1               */
/*                               */
/*    bilinear()                 */
/*                               */
/*********************************/


void bilinear(   struct complex pole[],
                 int numPoles,
                 struct complex zero[],
                 int numZeros,
                 real hZero,
                 real bigT,
                 struct complex a[],
                 struct complex b[])
{
int j,k,m,n, maxCoef;
real hC;
struct complex mu[MAXPOLES];
struct complex alpha, beta, gamma, delta, eta;
struct complex work, cTwo;

for(j=0; j<MAXPOLES; j++) {
    mu[j] = cmplx(0.0,0.0);
    a[j] = cmplx(0.0,0.0);
    b[j] = cmplx(0.0,0.0);
    }
/*-----------------------------------*/
/* compute constant gain factor      */
hC = 1.0;
work = cmplx(1.0,0.0);
cTwo = cmplx(2.0,0.0);
for(n=1; n<=numPoles; n++) {
    work = cMult(work, cSub(cTwo, sMult(bigT,pole[n])));
    hC = hC * bigT;
    }
hC = hZero * hC / work.Re;
/*-----------------------------------*/
/* compute numerator coefficients    */
mu[0] = cmplx(1.0, 0.0);
maxCoef = 0;
for( m=1; m<=(numPoles-numZeros); m++) {
    maxCoef++;
```

```
        for( j=maxCoef; j>=1; j--)
            { mu[j] = cAdd( mu[j], mu[j-1]);}
        }
    for( m=1; m<=numZeros; m++) {
        maxCoef++;
        alpha = cAdd(cmplx( (-2.0/bigT), 0.0), zero[n]);
        beta = cSub(cmplx( (-2.0/bigT), 0.0), pole[n]);
        for(j=maxCoef; j>=1; j--)
            { mu[j] = cAdd( mu[j], cMult( beta, mu[j-1]));}
        }
    for( j=0; j<=numPoles; j++) b[j] = sMult(hC, mu[j]);

    /*-------------------------------------*/
    /* compute denominator coefficients   */
    mu[0] = cmplx(1.0,0.0);
    for(n=1; n<MAXPOLES; n++)
        {mu[n] = cmplx(0.0,0.0);}
    for( n=1; n<=numPoles; n++) {
        gamma = cSub(cmplx( (2.0/bigT), 0.0), pole[n]);
        delta = cSub(cmplx( (-2.0/bigT), 0.0), pole[n]);
        eta = cDiv( delta, gamma);
        for( j=n; j>=1; j--)
            { mu[j] = cAdd( mu[j], cMult(eta, mu[j-1]));}
        }
    for( j=1; j<=numPoles; j++)
        { a[j] = sMult(-1.0, mu[j] );}
    return;
    }
```

16

Practical Considerations

All of the digital filter designs presented up until now have been based on infinite-precision mathematics. That is, we have assumed that all of the signal samples, filter coefficients, and results of mathematical computations are represented exactly or with *infinite precision*. In most cases we have used the **double** data type in C to approximate such precision. In Think C for the Apple Macintosh, the **double** data type has a 64-bit mantissa that provides approximately 19 decimal digits of precision. In Turbo C for the PC, the **double** data type has a 52-bit mantissa that provides approximately 15 decimal digits of precision. For most practical situations, either 15 or 19 digits of precision is a reasonable approximation to infinite precision. Furthermore, the **double** type is a floating-point format and thus provides good dynamic range in addition to high precision.

Although floating-point formats are used in some digital filters, cost and speed considerations will often dictate the use of fixed-point formats having a relatively short word length. Such formats will force some precision to be lost in representations of the signal samples, filter coefficients, and computation results. A digital filter designed under the infinite-precision assumption will not perform up to design expectations if implemented with short-word-length, fixed-point arithmetic. In many cases, the degradations can be so severe as to make the filter unuseable. This chapter examines the various types of degradations caused by finite-precision implementations and explores what can be done to achieve acceptable filter performance in spite of the degradations.

16.1 Binary Representation of Numeric Values

Fixed-point formats

Binary fixed-point representation of numbers enjoys widespread use in digital signal processing applications where there is usually some control over the range of values that must be represented. Typically, all of the coefficients $h[n]$ for a digital filter will be scaled such that

$$|h[n]| \le 1.0 \qquad \text{for } n = 1, 2, \ldots, N \qquad (16.1)$$

Once scaled in this way, each coefficient can be expressed as

$$h = b_0 2^0 + b_1 2^{-1} + b_2 2^{-2} + \cdots \qquad (16.2)$$

where each of the b_n is a single bit; that is, $b_n \in \{0, 1\}$. If we limit our representation to a length of $L + 1$ bits, the coefficients can be represented as a fixed-point binary number of the form shown in Fig. 16.1. As shown in the figure, a small triangle is often used to represent the binary point so that it cannot be easily confused with a decimal point. The expansion of Eq. (16.2) can then be written as

$$h = \sum_{k=0}^{L} b_k 2^{-k} \qquad (16.3)$$

The bit shown to the left of the binary point in Fig. 16.1 is necessary to represent coefficients for which the equality in (16.1) holds, but its presence complicates the implementation of arithmetic operations. If we eliminate the need to exactly represent coefficients that equal unity, we can use the fixed-point fractional format shown in Fig. 16.2. Using this scheme, some values are easy to write:

$$\tfrac{1}{2} = {}_\triangle 1000$$

$$\tfrac{3}{8} = {}_\triangle 01100$$

$$\tfrac{5}{64} = {}_\triangle 000101$$

Some other values are not so easy. Consider the case of $\frac{1}{10}$, which expands as

$$\tfrac{1}{10} = 2^{-4} + 2^{-5} + 2^{-8} + 2^{-9} + 2^{-12} + 2^{-13} + \cdots$$

$$= \sum_{k=1}^{\infty} (2^{-4k} + 2^{-4k-1})$$

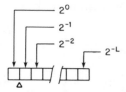

Figure 16.1 Fixed-point binary number format.

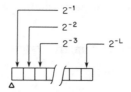

Figure 16.2 Alternative fixed-point binary number format.

The corresponding fixed-point binary representation is a repeating fraction given by

$$\frac{1}{10} = {}_\Delta 0001 1\overline{0011} \cdots$$

If we are limited to a 16-bit fixed-point binary representation, we can truncate the fraction after 16 bits to obtain

$$\frac{1}{10} \cong {}_\Delta 0001100110011001$$

The actual value of this 16-bit representation is

$$2^{-4} + 2^{-5} + 2^{-8} + 2^{-9} + 2^{-12} + 2^{-13} + 2^{-16} = \frac{6553}{65,536} \cong 0.099990845$$

Thus the value represented in 16 bits is too small by approximately 9.155×10^{-6}.

Instead of truncating, we could use a rounding approach. Rounding a binary value is easy—just add 1 to the first (leftmost) bit that is not being retained in the rounded format. In the current example we add 1 to bit 16. This generates a carry into b_{15} which propagates into b_{14} to yield

$$_\Delta 0001100110011010 = \frac{6554}{65,536} \cong 0.100006104$$

This value is too big by approximately 6.1×10^{-6}.

In many DSP applications where design simplicity, low cost, or high speed is important, the word length may be significantly shorter than 16 bits, and the error introduced by either truncating or rounding the coefficients can be quite severe, as we will see in Sec. 16.2.

Floating-point formats

A fixed-point fractional format has little use in a general-purpose computer where there is little or no a priori control over the range of values that may need to be represented. Clearly, any time a value equals or exceeds 1.0, it cannot be represented in the format of Fig. 16.2. Floating-point formats remove this limitation by effectively allowing the binary point to shift position as needed. For floating-point representations, a number is typically expanded in the form

$$h = 2^a \sum_{k=0}^{L} b_k 2^{-k}$$

In Think C for the Macintosh, a floating-point value has the form shown in Fig. 16.3. The fields denoted i and f contain a fixed-point value of the form shown in Fig. 16.1 where the binary point is assumed to lie between i and the most significant bit of f. This fixed-point value is referred to as the *mantissa*.

Figure 16.3 Floating-point binary number format used in Think C for the Macintosh.

If the bits in field f are designated from left to right as $f_1, f_2, \ldots, f_{63}$, the value of the mantissa is given by

$$m = i + \sum_{k=1}^{63} f_k 2^{-k}$$

The field denoted as e is a 15-bit integer value used to indicate the power of 2 by which the numerator must be multiplied in order to obtain the value being represented. This can be a positive or negative power of 2, but rather than using a sign in conjunction with the exponent, most floating-point formats use an offset. A 15-bit binary field can have values ranging from 0 to 32,767. Values from 0 to 16,382 are interpreted as negative powers of 2, and values from 16,384 to 32,766 are interpreted as positive powers of 2. The value 16,383 is interpreted as $2^0 = 1$, and the value 32,767 is reserved for representing infinity and specialized values called **NaN** (*not-a-number*). The sign bit denoted by s is the sign of the overall number. Thus the value represented by a floating-point number in the format of Fig. 16.3 can be obtained as

$$v = (-1)^s \, 2^{(e-16,383)} \left(i + \sum_{k=1}^{63} f_k 2^{-k} \right)$$

provided $e \neq 32,767$.

   Suppose we wish to represent $\frac{1}{10}$ in the floating-point format of Fig. 16.3. One way to accomplish this is to set the mantissa equal to a 64-bit fixed-point representation of $\frac{1}{10}$ and set $e = 16,383$ to indicate a multiplier of unity. Using the hexadecimal notation discussed previously, we can write the results of such an approach as

$$s = 0$$

$$e = 0x3fff$$

$$i = 0$$

$$f = 0x0ccccccccccccccc$$

With the various fields packed together, the resulting 80-bit floating-point representation of $\frac{1}{10}$ is $W = 0x3fff0cccccccccccccccc$. Slightly more precision can be squeezed into the representation if we shift f 4 places to the left and modify e to indicate multiplication by 2^{-4}. Such an approach yields

$$W = 0x3ffbcccccccccccccccc$$

Numbers greater than 1.0 present no problem for this format. The value 57 is represented as

$$s = 0$$

$$e = 0\text{x}4004 \qquad (\text{that is, } 2^5)$$

$$i = 1$$

$$f = 0\text{x}6400000000000000$$

$$W = 0\text{x}4004\text{e}400000000000000$$

In other words, this representation stores 57 by making use of the fact

$$57 = 2^5(2^0 + 2^{-1} + 2^{-2} + 2^{-5})$$

16.2   Quantized Coefficients

When the coefficients of a digital filter are quantized, the filter becomes a different filter. The resulting filter is still a discrete-time linear time-invariant system—it's just not the system we set out to design. Consider the 21-tap lowpass filter using a von Hann window that was designed in Example 11.6. The coefficients of this filter are reproduced in Table 16.1. The values given in the table, having 15 decimal digits in the fractional part, will be used as the baseline approximation to the coefficients' infinite-precision values. Let's force the coefficient values into a fixed-point fractional format having a 16-bit magnitude plus 1 sign bit. After truncating the bits in excess of 16, the coefficient values listed in Table 16.2 are obtained. The magnitude response of a filter using such coefficients is virtually identical to the response obtained using the floating-point coefficients of Table 16.1. If the coefficients are

TABLE 16.1 Coefficients for 21-tap Lowpass Filter Using a von Hann Window

n	$h[n]$
0, 20	0.000
1, 19	−0.000823149720361
2, 18	−0.002233281959082
3, 17	0.005508892585759
4, 16	0.017431813641454
5, 17	−0.000000000000050
6, 16	−0.049534952531101
7, 15	−0.049511869643024
8, 14	0.084615800641299
9, 13	0.295322344140975
10	0.40

TABLE 16.2   Truncated 16-bit Coefficients for 21-tap Lowpass Filter

n	Sign	Hex value	Decimal value
0, 20	+	0000	0.0
1, 19	−	0035	−0.000808715820312
2, 18	−	0092	−0.002227783203125
3, 17	+	0169	0.005508422851562
4, 16	+	0476	0.017425537109375
5, 15	+	0000	0.0
6, 14	−	0cae	−0.049530029296875
7, 13	−	0cac	−0.049499511718750
8, 12	+	15a9	0.084609985351562
9, 11	+	4b9a	0.295318603515625
10	+	6666	0.399993896484375

TABLE 16.3   Truncated 10-bit Coefficients for 21-tap Lowpass Filter

n	Sign	Hex value	Decimal value
0, 20	+	000	0.0
1, 19	−	000	0.0
2, 18	−	008	−0.001953125
3, 17	+	014	0.0048828125
4, 16	+	044	0.0166015625
5, 15	+	000	0.0
6, 14	−	0c8	−0.048828125
7, 13	−	0c8	−0.048828125
8, 12	+	158	0.083984375
9, 11	+	4b8	0.294921875
10	+	664	0.3994140625

further truncated to 14- or 12-bit magnitudes, slight degradations in stop-band attenuation can be observed.

The degradations in filter response are really quite significant for the 10-bit coefficients listed in Table 16.3. As shown in Fig. 16.4, the fourth sidelobe is narrowed, and the fifth sidelobe peaks at −50.7 dB—a value significantly worse than the −68.2 dB of the baseline case. The filter response for 8- and 6-bit coefficients are shown in Figs. 16.5 and 16.6, respectively.

16.3   Quantization Noise

The finite digital word lengths used to represent numeric values within a digital filter limit the precision of other quantities besides the filter coefficients. Each sample of the input and output, as well as all intermediate results of mathematical operations, must be represented with finite precision. As we saw in the previous section, the effects of coefficient quantization are straightforward and easy to characterize. The effects of signal quantization are somewhat different.

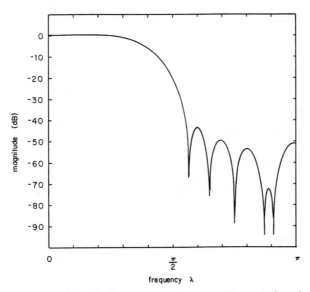

Figure 16.4 Magnitude response for a von Hann-windowed 21-tap lowpass filter with coefficients quantized to 10 bits plus sign.

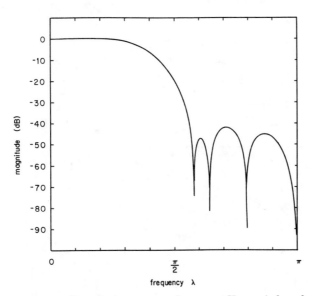

Figure 16.5 Magnitude response for a von Hann-windowed 21-tap lowpass filter with coefficients quantized to 8 bits plus sign.

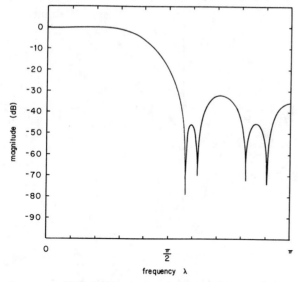

Figure 16.6 Magnitude response for a von Hann-windowed 21-tap lowpass filter with coefficients quantized to 6 bits plus sign.

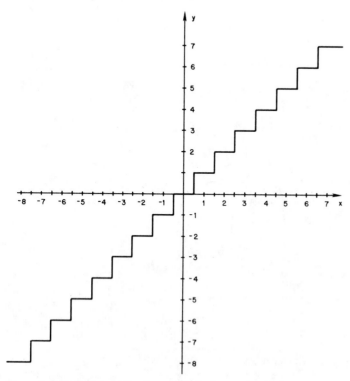

Figure 16.7 Typical transfer characteristic for a rounding quantizer.

Typically, an *analog-to-digital converter* (ADC) is used to sample and quantize an analog signal that can be thought of as a continuous amplitude function of continuous time. The ADC can be viewed as a sampler and quantizer in cascade. Sampling was discussed in Chap. 7, and in this section we examine the operation of quantization. The transfer characteristic of a typical quantizer is shown in Fig. 16.7. This particular quantizer *rounds* the analog value to the nearest "legal" quantized value. The resulting sequence of quantized signal values $y[n]$ can be viewed as the sampled continuous-time signal $x[n]$ plus an error sequence $e[n]$ whose values are equal to the errors introduced by the quantizer:

$$y[n] = x[n] + e[n]$$

A typical discrete-time signal along with the corresponding quantized sequence and error sequence are shown in Fig. 16.8. Because the quantizer rounds to the nearest quantizer level, the magnitude of the error will never exceed $Q/2$, where Q is the increment between two consecutive legal quantizer output levels, that is,

$$\frac{-Q}{2} \le e(t) \le \frac{Q}{2} \qquad \text{for all } t$$

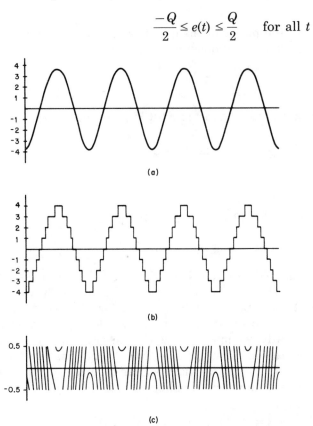

Figure 16.8 (*a*) Discrete-time continuous amplitude signal, (*b*) corresponding quantized signal, and (*c*) error sequence.

The error is usually assumed to be uniformly distributed between $-Q/2$ and $Q/2$ and consequently to have a mean and variance of 0 and $Q^2/12$, respectively. For most practical applications, this assumption is reasonable. The quantization interval Q can be related to the number of bits in the digital word. Assume a word length of $L+1$ bits with 1 bit used for the sign and L bits for the magnitude. For the fixed-point format of Fig. 16.2, the relationship between Q and L is then given by $Q = 2^{-L}$.

It is often useful to characterize the quantization noise by means of a *signal-to-noise ratio* (SNR). In order to accomplish this characterization, the following additional assumptions are usually made:

1. The error sequence is assumed to be a sample sequence of a stationary random proces; that is, the statistical properties of the error sequence do not change over time.

2. The error is a white-noise process; or equivalently, the error signal is uncorrelated.

3. The error sequence $e[n]$ is uncorrelated with the sequence of unquantized samples $x[n]$.

Based on these assumptions, the power of the quantization noise is equal to the error variance that was given previously as

$$\sigma_e^2 = \frac{Q^2}{12} = \frac{2^{-2L}}{12}$$

If we let σ_x^2 denote the signal power, then the SNR is given by

$$\frac{\sigma_x^2}{\sigma_e^2} = \frac{\sigma_x^2}{2^{-2L}/12} = (12 \cdot 2^{2L})\sigma_x^2$$

Expressed in decibels, this SNR is

$$10 \log\left(\frac{\sigma_x^2}{\sigma_e^2}\right) = 10 \log 12 + 20L \log 2 + 10 \log \sigma_x^2$$

$$= 10.792 + 6.021L + 10 \log \sigma_x^2 \qquad (16.4)$$

The major insight to be gained from (16.4) is that the SNR improves by 6.02 dB for each bit added to the digital word format. We are not yet in a position to compute an SNR using Eq. (16.4), because the term σ_x^2 needs some further examination. How do we go about obtaining a value for σ_x^2? Whatever the value of σ_x^2 may be originally, we must realize that in practical systems, the input signal is subjected to some amplification prior to digitization. For a constant amplifier gain of A, the unquantized signal becomes $Ax[n]$, the signal power becomes $A^2\sigma_x^2$, and the corresponding SNR is given by

$$\text{SNR} = 10 \log\left(\frac{A^2\sigma_x^2}{\sigma_e^2}\right) = 10.792 + 6.021L + 10 \log(A^2\sigma_x^2) \qquad (16.5)$$

A general rule of thumb often used in practical DSP applications is to set A so that $A\sigma_x$ is equal to 25 percent of the ADC full-scale value. Since we have been treating full scale as being normalized to unity, this indicates a value of A such that

$$A\sigma_x = 0.25 \quad \text{or} \quad A = \frac{1}{4\sigma_x}$$

Substituting this value of A into (16.5) yields

$$\text{SNR} = 10.79 + 6.02L + 10\log\left(\frac{1}{16}\right)$$

$$= 6.02L - 1.249 \text{ dB}$$

Using a value of $A = 1/(4\sigma_x)$ means that the ADC will introduce clipping any time the unquantized input signal exceeds $4\sigma_x$. Increasing A improves the SNR but decreases the *dynamic range*, that is, the range of signal values that can be accommodated without clipping. Thus, for a fixed word length, we can improve the SNR at the expense of degraded dynamic range. Conversely, by decreasing A, we could improve dynamic range at the expense of degraded SNR. The only way to simultaneously improve both dynamic range and quantization SNR is to increase the number of bits in the digital word length.

Global Definitions

```
/**************************************/
/*                                    */
/*  Appendix A -- Global Definitions  */
/*                                    */
/*  globDefs.h                        */
/*                                    */
/*  global definitions                */
/*                                    */
/**************************************/

#include <stdio.h>
#include <math.h>
#include <time.h>

#define EOL 10
#define STOP_CHAR 38
#define SPACE 32
#define TRUE 1
#define FALSE 0
#define PI 3.14159265
#define TWO_PI 6.2831853
#define TEN (double) 10.0
#define MAX_COLUMNS 20
#define MAX_ROWS 20

/*  structure definition for single precision complex */
/* struct complex
    {
    float Re;
    float Im;
    }; */
```

```
/*  structure definition for double precision complex */
struct complex
    {
    double Re;
    double Im;
    };

typedef int logical;
typedef double real;
```

Prototypes for C Functions

```
/**************************************************/
/*                                                */
/*  Appendix B -- Prototypes for C Functions      */
/*                                                */
/**************************************************/

int LaguerreMethod(  int order,
                     struct complex coef[],
                     struct complex *zz,
                     real epsilon,
                     real epsilon2,
                     int maxIterations);

void unwrapPhase( int ix, real *phase);

void butterworthFreqResponse( int order,
                             real frequency,
                             real *magnitude,
                             real *phase);

void butterworthImpulseResponse(  int order,
                                 real deltaT,
                                 int npts,
                                 real yval[]);

void chebyshevFreqResponse(  int order,
                            float ripple,
                            char normalizationType,
                            float frequency,
                            float *magnitude,
                            float *phase);
```

```
void chebyshevImpulseResponse(    int order,
                                  float ripple,
                                  char normalizationType,
                                  float deltaT,
                                  int npts,
                                  float yval[]);


void cauerOrderEstim(real omegaPass,
                     real omegaStop,
                     real maxPassLoss,
                     real maxStopLoss,
                     int *order,
                     real *actualMinStopLoss);

void cauerCoeffs(real omegaPass,
                 real omegaStop,
                 real maxPassLoss,
                 int order,
                 real aa[],
                 real bb[],
                 real cc[],
                 int *numSecs,
                 real *hZero,
                 real *pZero);

void cauerFreqResponse(    int order,
                           real aa[],
                           real bb[],
                           real cc[],
                           real hZero,
                           real pZero,
                           real frequency,
                           real *magnitude,
                           real *phase);

void cauerRescale(    int order,
                      real aa[],
                      real bb[],
                      real cc[],
                      real *hZero,
                      real *pZero,
                      real alpha);

void besselCoefficients(   int order,
                           char typeOfNormalization,
                           real coef[]);
```

```
void besselFreqResponse(  int order,
                          real coef[],
                          real frequency,
                          real *magnitude,
                          real *phase);

void besselGroupDelay(    int order,
                          real coef[],
                          real frequency,
                          real delta,
                          real *groupDelay);

void dft(     struct complex x[],
              struct complex xx[],
              int nn);

void dft2(    struct complex x[],
              struct complex xx[],
              int nn);

void fft(     struct complex x[],
              struct complex xx[],
              int nn);

void cgdFirResponse(  int firType,
                      int numbTaps,
                      real hh[],
                      logical dbScale,
                      int numberOfPoints,
                      real hD[]);

void normalizeResponse(   logical dbScale,
                          int numberOfPoints,
                          real hh[]);

void idealLowpass(    int numbTaps,
                      real omegaU,
                      real coefficient[]);

void idealHighpass(   int numbTaps,
                      real omegaL,
                      real coefficient[]);

void idealBandpass(   int numbTaps,
                      real omegaL,
                      real omegaU,
                      real coefficient[]);
```

```
void idealBandstop(  int numbTaps,
                     real omegaL,
                     real omegaU,
                     real coefficient[]);

real contRectangularResponse( real freq,
                              real tau,
                              logical dbScale);

real discRectangularResponse( real freq,
                              int M,
                              logical normAmp);

real contTriangularResponse(  real freq,
                              real tau,
                              logical dbScale);

real discTriangularResponse(  real freq,
                              int M,
                              logical normAmp);

void triangularWindow( int N, real window[]);

void makeLagWindow(  int N,
                     real window[],
                     int center,
                     real outWindow[]);

void makeDataWindow( int N,
                     real window[],
                     real outWindow[]);

void hannWindow( int nn, real window[]);
void hammingWindow( int nn, real window[]);

int fsDesign(    int nn,
                 int firType,
                 real aa[],
                 real h[]);

findSbPeak(  int bandConfig[],
             int numPts,
             real hh[]);

real goldenSearch(   int firType,
                     int numbTaps,
                     real hD[],
                     real gsTol,
```

```
                        int numFreqPts,
                        int bandConfig[],
                        real *fmin);

void setTrans(    int bandConfig[],
                  real x,
                  real hD[]);

real goldenSearch2(    real rhoMin,
                       real rhoMax,
                       int firType,
                       int numbTaps,
                       real hD[],
                       real gsTol,
                       int numFreqPts,
                       real origins[],
                       real slopes[],
                       int bandConfig[],
                       real *fmin);



void setTransition(    real origins[],
                       real slopes[],
                       int bandConfig[],
                       real x,
                       real Hd[]);

void optimize2(    real yBase,
                   int firType,
                   int numbTaps,
                   real hD[],
                   real gsTol,
                   int numFreqPts,
                   int bandConfig[],
                   real tweakFactor,
                   real rectComps[]);

void dumpRectComps(    real origins[],
                       real slopes[],
                       int numTransSamps,
                       real x);

real gridFreq(    real gridParam[], int gI);

real desLpfResp(    real freqP, real freq);

real weightLp(    real kk, real freqP, real freq);
```

```
void remezError( real gridParam[],
                 int gridMax,
                 int r,
                 real kk,
                 real freqP,
                 int iFF[],
                 real ee[]);


real computeRemezA(  real gridParam[],
                     int gridMax,
                     int r,
                     real kk,
                     real freqP,
                     int iFF[],
                     int initFlag,
                     real contFreq);

void remezSearch(real ee[],
                 real absDelta,
                 int gP,
                 int iFF[],
                 int gridMax,
                 int r,
                 real gridParam[]);

int remezStop(  int iFF[],  int r);

int remezStop2(  real ee[], int iFF[], int r);

void remezFinish(real extFreq[],
                 int nn,
                 int r,
                 real freqP,
                 real kk,
                 real aa[],
                 real h[]);

void remez(  int nn,
             int r,
             int gridDensity,
             real kk,
             real freqP,
             real freqS,
             real extFreq[],
             real h[]);
```

```
iirResponse( struct complex a[],
             int bigN,
             struct complex b[],
             int bigM,
             int numberOfPoints,
             logical dbScale,
             real magnitude[],
             real phase[]);

void impulseInvar(  struct complex pole[],
                    int numPoles,
                    struct complex zero[],
                    int numZeros,
                    real hZero,
                    real bigT,
                    struct complex a[],
                    struct complex b[]);

void stepInvar(  struct complex pole[],
                 int numPoles,
                 struct complex zero[],
                 int numZeros,
                 real hZero,
                 real bigT,
                 struct complex a[],
                 struct complex b[]);

void bilinear(  struct complex pole[],
                int numPoles,
                struct complex zero[],
                int numZeros,
                real hZero,
                real bigT,
                struct complex a[],
                struct complex b[]);


struct complex cmplx(  real A, real B);
struct complex cAdd( struct complex A, struct complex B);
struct complex cSub( struct complex A, struct complex B);
real cMag(struct complex A);
real cAbs(struct complex A);
double cdAbs(struct complex A);
real arg(struct complex A);
struct complex cSqrt( struct complex A);
struct complex cMult(  struct complex A, struct complex B);
struct complex sMult( real a, struct complex B);
struct complex cDiv( struct complex numer, struct complex denom);
```

```
real sincSqrd( real x);
real sinc( real x);
real acosh( real x);
void pause( logical enabled);
int bitRev( int L, int N);
int log2( int N );
real ipow(  real x, int k);
```

Functions for Complex Arithmetic

```
/********************************************************/
/*                                                      */
/*  Appendix C -- Functions for Complex Arithmetic      */
/*                                                      */
/********************************************************/
#include "globDefs.h"
#include "protos.h"


/****************************************/
/*                                      */
/*      cmplx()                         */
/*                                      */
/*  merges two real into one complex    */
/*                                      */
/****************************************/
struct complex cmplx(  real A, real B)
{
struct complex result;

result.Re = A;
result.Im = B;
return( result);
}


/****************************************/
/*                                      */
/*  cAdd()                              */
/*                                      */
/****************************************/
struct complex cAdd(
                    struct complex A,
                    struct complex B)
{
struct complex result;
```

```
result.Re = A.Re + B.Re;
result.Im = A.Im + B.Im;
return( result);
}

/***************************************/
/*                                     */
/*   cSub()                            */
/*                                     */
/***************************************/
struct complex cSub(
                    struct complex A,
                    struct complex B)
{
struct complex result;

result.Re = A.Re - B.Re;
result.Im = A.Im - B.Im;
return( result);
}

/***************************************/
/*                                     */
/*   cMag()                            */
/*                                     */
/***************************************/
real cMag(struct complex A)
{
real result;
result = sqrt(A.Re*A.Re + A.Im*A.Im);
return( result);
}

/***************************************/
/*                                     */
/*   cAbs()                            */
/*                                     */
/***************************************/
real cAbs(struct complex A)
{
real result;
result = sqrt(A.Re*A.Re + A.Im*A.Im);
return( result);
}
```

```
/*****************************************/
/*                                       */
/*   cdAbs()                             */
/*                                       */
/*****************************************/
double cdAbs(struct complex A)
{
double result;
result = sqrt(A.Re*A.Re + A.Im*A.Im);
return( result);
}


/*****************************************/
/*                                       */
/*   arg()                               */
/*                                       */
/*****************************************/
real arg(struct complex A)
{
real result;

if( (A.Re == 0.0)  && (A.Im == 0.0) )
    {
    result = 0.0;
    }
else
    {
    result = atan2( A.Im, A.Re );
    }
return( result);
}


/*****************************************/
/*                                       */
/*   cSqrt()                             */
/*                                       */
/*****************************************/
struct complex cSqrt( struct complex A)
{
struct complex result;
double r, theta;

r = sqrt(cdAbs(A));
theta = arg(A)/2.0;
result.Re = r * cos(theta);
result.Im = r * sin(theta);
return( result);
}
```

```
/****************************************/
/*                                      */
/*   cMult()                            */
/*                                      */
/****************************************/
struct complex cMult(
                        struct complex A,
                        struct complex B)
{
struct complex result;

result.Re = A.Re*B.Re - A.Im*B.Im;
result.Im = A.Re*B.Im + A.Im*B.Re;
return( result);
}
/****************************************/
/*                                      */
/*   sMult()                            */
/*                                      */
/****************************************/
struct complex sMult(
                        real a,
                        struct complex B)
{
struct complex result;

result.Re = a*B.Re;
result.Im = a*B.Im;
return( result);
}


/****************************************/
/*                                      */
/*   cDiv()                             */
/*                                      */
/****************************************/
struct complex cDiv(
                        struct complex numer,
                        struct complex denom)
{
real bottom,real_top,imag_top;
struct complex result;

bottom = denom.Re*denom.Re + denom.Im*denom.Im;
real_top = numer.Re*denom.Re + numer.Im*denom.Im;
imag_top = numer.Im*denom.Re - numer.Re*denom.Im;
result.Re = real_top/bottom;
result.Im = imag_top/bottom;
return( result);
}
```

Miscellaneous Support Functions

```
/*****************************************************/
/*                                                   */
/*   Appendix D                                      */
/*                                                   */
/*   Miscellaneous Support Functions                 */
/*                                                   */
/*****************************************************/
#include <stdlib.h>
#include <math.h>
#include <ctype.h>
#include "globDefs.h"
#include "protos.h"


/***********************************/
/*                                 */
/*   sincSqrd()                    */
/*                                 */
/***********************************/


real sincSqrd( real x)
{
real result;
if( x==0.0)
    {
    result = 1.0;
    }
else
    {
    result = sin(x)/x;
    result = result * result;
```

```
    }
return(result);
}
/**********************************/
/*                              */
/*   sinc()                     */
/*                              */
/**********************************/

real sinc( real x)
{
real result;
if( x==0.0)
    {
    result = 1.0;
    }
else
    {
    result = sin(x)/x;
    }
return(result);
}


/**********************************/
/*                              */
/*   acosh()                    */
/*                              */
/**********************************/

real acosh( real x)
{
real result;
result = log(x+sqrt(x*x-1.0));
return(result);
}
/**********************************/
/*                              */
/*   pause()                    */
/*                              */
/**********************************/

void pause( logical enabled)
{
char inputString[20];
if(enabled) {
    printf("enter anything to continue\n");
    gets(inputString);
```

```
    }
return;
}


/**********************************/
/*                              */
/*   bitRev()                   */
/*                              */
/**********************************/

int bitRev(  int L, int N)
{
int work, work2, i, bit;

work2 = 0;
work = N;
for(i=0; i<L; i++) {
    bit = work%2;
    work2 = 2 * work2 + bit;
    work /=2;
    }
return(work2);
}


/**********************************/
/*                              */
/*   log2()                     */
/*                              */
/**********************************/

int log2(  int N )
{
int work, result;

result = 0;
work = N;
for(;;) {
    if(work == 0) break;
    work /=2;
    result ++;
    }
return(result-1);
}
```

```
/**********************************/
/*                                */
/*    ipow()                      */
/*                                */
/**********************************/

real ipow(   real x,
             int k)
{
real result;
int n;
if(k==0)
    {result = 1.0;}
else
    {result = x;
    for( n=2; n<=k; n++)
        { result = result * x;}
    }
return(result);
}
```

Bibliography

Abramowitz, M., and I. A. Stegun: *Handbook of Mathematical Functions*, National Bureau of Standards, Appl. Math Series 55, 1966.

Antoniou, A.: *Digital Filters: Analysis and Design*, McGraw-Hill, New York, 1979.

Antoniou, A.: "Accelerated Procedure for the Design of Equiripple Non-recursive Digital Filters," *Proceedings IEE, PART G*, vol. 129, pp. 1–10.

Bartlett, M. S.: "Periodogram Analysis and Continuous Spectra," *Biometrika*, vol. 37, pp. 1–16, 1950.

Blackman, R. B., and J. W. Tukey: *The Measurement of Power Spectra*, Dover, New York, 1958.

Boyer, C. B.: *A History of Mathematics*, Wiley, New York, 1968.

Brigham, E. O.: *The Fast Fourier Transform*, Prentice-Hall, Englewood Cliffs, N.J., 1974.

Burrus, C. S., and T. W. Parks: *DFT/FFT and Convolution Algorithms*, Wiley-Interscience, New York, 1984.

Cadzow, J. A.: *Discrete-Time Systems*, Prentice-Hall, Englewood Cliffs, N.J., 1973.

Chen, C-T.: *Linear System Theory and Design*, Holt, Rinehart and Winston, New York, 1984.

Cheyney, E. W.: *Introduction to Approximation Theory*, McGraw-Hill, New York, 1966.

Dolph, C. L.: "A Current Distribution for Broadside Arrays Which Optimizes the Relationship Between Beam Width and Side-Lobe Level," *Proc. IRE*, vol. 35, pp. 335–348, June 1946.

Dym, H., and H. P. McKean: *Fourier Series and Integrals*, Academic, New York, 1972.

Hamming, R. W.: *Numerical Methods for Engineers and Scientists*, McGraw-Hill, New York, 1962.

Hamming, R. W.: *Digital Filters*, 2d ed., Prentice-Hall, Englewood Cliffs, N.J., 1983.

Harris, F. J.: "On the Use of Windows for Harmonic Analysis with the Discrete Fourier Transform, "*Proc. IEEE*, vol. 66, pp. 51–83, January 1978.

Haykin, S.: *Communication Systems*, 2d ed., Wiley, New York, 1983.

Helms, H. D.: "Nonrecursive Digital Filters: Design Methods for Achieving Specifications on Frequency Response," *IEEE Trans. Audio and Electroacoust.*, vol. AU-16, pp. 336–342, September 1968.

Helms, H. D.: "Digital Filters with Equiripple or Minimax Responses," *IEEE Trans Audio Electroacoust.*, vol. AU-19, pp. 87–94, March 1971.

Herrmann, O.: "Design of Nonrecursive Digital Filters with Linear Phase," *Electronics Letters*, vol. 6, pp. 328–329, 1970.

Hofstetter, E. M., A. V. Oppenheim, and J. Siegel: "A New Technique for the Design of Non-Recursive Digital Filters," *Proc. Fifth Annual Princeton Conf. on Inform. Sci. and Syst.*, pp. 64–72, 1971.

Kanefsky, M.: *Communication Techniques for Digital and Analog Signals*, Harper & Row, New York, 1985.

Kay, S. M.: *Modern Spectral Estimators: Theory & Application*, Prentice-Hall, Englewood Cliffs, N.J., 1988.

Marple, S. L.: *Digital Spectral Analysis with Applications*, Prentice-Hall, Englewood Cliffs, N.J., 1987.

Nussbaumer, H. J.: *Fast Fourier Transform and Convolution Algorithms*, Springer-Verlag, New York, 1982.

Oppenheim, A. V., and R. W. Schafer: *Digital Signal Processing*, Prentice-Hall, Englewood Cliffs, N.J., 1975.

Oppenheim, A. V., and R. W. Schafer: *Discrete-Time Signal Processing*, Prentice-Hall, Englewood Cliffs, N.J., 1989.

Papoulis, A.: *The Fourier Integral and Its Applications*, McGraw-Hill, New York, 1962.

Parks, T. W., and C. S. Burrus: *Digital Filter Design*, Wiley-Interscience, New York, 1987.

Parks, T. W., and J. H. McClellan: "Chebyshev Approximation for Nonrecursive Digital Filters with Linear Phase," *IEEE Trans. Circuit Theory*, vol. CT-19, pp. 189–194, March 1972.

Parks, T. W., and J. H. McClellan: "A Computer Program for Designing Optimum FIR Linear Phase Digital Filters," *IEEE Trans. Audio Electroacoust.*, vol. AU-21, pp. 506–526, December 1973.

Peled, A., and B. Liu: *Digital Signal Processing*, Wiley, New York, 1976.

Press, W. H., et al.: *Numerical Recipes*, Cambridge University Press, Cambridge, 1986.

Priestley, M. B.: *Spectral Analysis and Time Series*, vol. 1: *Univariate Series*, Academic, London, 1981.

Rabiner, L. R., and B. Gold: *Theory and Application of Digital Signal Processing*, Prentice-Hall, Englewood Cliffs, N.J., 1975.

Roberts, A. A., and C. T. Mullis: *Digital Signal Processing*, Addison-Wesley, Reading, Mass., 1987.

Rorabaugh, B.: *Signal Processing Design Techniques*, TAB Professional and Reference Books, Blue Ridge Summit, Pa., 1986.

Schwartz, L.: *Théorie des distributions*, Herman & Cie, Paris, 1950.

Schwartz, R. J., and B. Friedland: *Linear Systems*, McGraw-Hill, New York, 1965.

Spiegel, M. R.: *Laplace Transforms*, Schaum's Outline Series, McGraw-Hill, New York, 1965.

Stanley, W. D.: *Digital Signal Processing*, Reston, Reston, Va., 1975.

Tufts, D. W., and J. T. Francis: "Designing Digital Low-pass Filters—Comparison of Some Methods and Criteria," *IEEE Trans. Audio Electroacoust.*, vol. AU-18, pp. 487–494, December 1970.

Tufts, D. W., D. W. Rorabacher, and M. E. Mosier: "Designing Simple, Effective Digital Filters," *IEEE Trans. Audio Electroacoust.*, vol. AU-18, pp. 142–158, 1970.

Van Valkenburg, M. E.: *Network Analysis*, Prentice-Hall, Englewood Cliffs, N.J., 1974.

Weaver, H. J.: *Theory of Discrete and Continuous Fourier Analysis*, Wiley, New York, 1989.

Williams, C. S.: *Designing Digital Filters*, Prentice-Hall, Englewood Cliffs, N.J., 1986.

Index

ABOUT THE AUTHOR

C. Britton Rorabaugh holds BSEE and MSEE degrees from Drexel University. His previous books include *Circuit Design and Analysis* and *Communications Formulas and Algorithms*, published by McGraw-Hill, and *Data Communications and LAN Handbook* and *Signal Processing Design Techniques*, published by TAB Professional and Reference Books.

DISK WARRANTY

This software is protected by both United States copyright law and international copyright treaty provision. You must treat this software just like a book, except that you may copy it into a computer to be used and you may make archival copies of the software for the sole purpose of backing up our software and protecting your investment from loss.

By saying, "just like a book," McGraw-Hill means, for example, that this software may be used by any number of people and may be freely moved from one computer location to another, so long as there is no possibility of its being used at one location or on one computer while it is being used at another. Just as a book cannot be read by two different people in two different places at the same time, neither can the software be used by two different people in two different places at the same time (unless, of course, McGraw-Hill's copyright is being violated).

LIMITED WARRANTY

McGraw-Hill warrants the physical diskette(s) enclosed herein to be free of defects in materials and workmanship for a period of sixty days from the purchase date. If McGraw-Hill receives written notification within the warranty period of defects in materials or workmanship, and such notification is determined by McGraw-Hill to be correct, McGraw-Hill will replace the defective diskette(s). Send requests to:

Customer Service
TAB/McGraw-Hill
13311 Monterey Ave.
Blue Ridge Summit, PA 17294-0850

The entire and exclusive liability and remedy for breach of this Limited Warranty shall be limited to replacement of defective diskette(s) and shall not include or extend to any claim for or right to cover any other damages, including but not limited to, loss of profit, data, or use of the software, or special, incidental, or consequential damages or other similar claims, even if McGraw-Hill has been specifically advised of the possibility of such damages. In no event will McGraw-Hill's liability for any damages to you or any other person ever exceed the lower of suggested list price or actual price paid for the license to use the software, regardless of any form of the claim.

McGRAW-HILL, INC. SPECIFICALLY DISCLAIMS ALL OTHER WARRANTIES, EXPRESS OR IMPLIED, INCLUDING BUT NOT LIMITED TO, ANY IMPLIED WARRANTY OF MERCHANTABILITY OR FITNESS FOR A PARTICULAR PURPOSE. Specifically, McGraw-Hill makes no representation or warranty that the software is fit for any particular purpose and any implied warranty of merchantability is limited to the sixty-day duration of the Limited Warranty covering the physical diskette(s) only (and not the software) and is otherwise expressly and specifically disclaimed.

This limited warranty gives you specific legal rights; you may have others which may vary from state to state. Some states do not allow the exclusion of incidental or consequential damages, or the limitation on how long an implied warranty lasts, so some of the above may not apply to you.